SLOW COOKED

Previous page:

Mussels (page 79)
Fruits of the forest
vanilla compote with
Poached meringues
(pages 233 and 234)

Clockwise from top right:

Sweet potato, spinach and
paneer curry (page 167)
Beetroot orzotto (page 104)
Chilli with dark chocolate
(page 91)

Clockwise from top left:

Pho (page 152)

Soy-braised pigs' cheeks (page 36)

Poached octopus (page 80)

Octopus, polenta and pepper salad (page 81)

Clockwise from top left:

Miss South's store cupboard (recipes from page 185)

Brixton baked beans (page 94)

Roast chicken (page 59)

Jerk chicken (page 66)

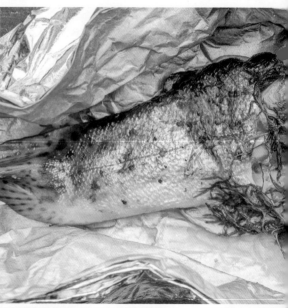

Clockwise from top left:

Macaroni cheese (page 107)

Whole baked trout (page 71)

Pulled pork (page 46)

Moroccan lamb breast (page 48)

Clockwise from top left:

Sticky-glazed balsamic beetroot (page 115)

Vermouth-brined turkey with Thanksgiving stuffing (page 55 and 127)

Dulce de leche coffee cake (page 210)

Cherry Bakewell pudding (page 244)

Clockwise from top left:

Buckwheat, cauliflower and tahini salad (page 105)
Beef rendang (page 159)
Cinnamon-spiced buns (page 216)
Baked apples (page 232)

Clockwise from top left:

Stout-soaked Christmas pudding (page 248)

Gooey red velvet pudding (page 241)

White bread (page 218)

Apple-glazed ribs (page 39)

Top:
Cream-cheese brownies (page 215)
Bottom:
Bunnychow (page 169)

SLOW COOKED

Over 200 recipes

Miss South's easy, thrifty and delicious recipes for slow cookers

EBURY
PRESS

1 3 5 7 9 10 8 6 4 2

Published in 2014 by Ebury Press, an imprint of Ebury Publishing

A Random House Group Company

Text © Miss South 2014

Photography by Mister North © Ebury Press 2014

The Random House Group Limited Reg. No. 954009

Addresses for companies within the Random House Group can be found at
www.randomhouse.co.uk

A CIP catalogue record for this book is available from the British Library

To buy books by your favourite authors and register for offers visit
www.randomhouse.co.uk

Design: Anti Limited

Photography: Mister North

Food stylist: Olia Hercules

Prop stylist: Jo Harris

Colour origination by Tag Response

Printed and bound in China by C&C Offset Printing Co., Ltd

ISBN 9780091958053

CONTENTS

INTRODUCTION

I was delighted to write this book. I have always loved slow-simmered stews, hearty soups and puddings, but found it hard to justify cooking them from scratch for one person, especially when I factored in rising energy prices and the commitment of time they took to keep an eye on the oven or baste things. If only there was a way I could have more delicious food in my life and less hard work. The answer arrived on my birthday in the shape of a slow cooker.

The simplicity of a slow cooker was the perfect addition to my home kitchen. I'd been cooking for the last twelve or so years as well as blogging at North/South Food along with my brother, Mister North, and I felt ready for a new challenge.

I opened the booklet that came with the slow cooker and got going. My kitchen smelled wonderful and there was something truly comforting about home-cooked food bubbling away in the corner while I got on with life. The food was nice. But nothing more than that. It filled me up and I loved the ability to batch cook something with ease, but none of the dishes wowed me yet.

Never one to do things by halves, I did some slow-cooker research and something leapt out at me: most people using slow cookers concentrated on the first part of the name and less on the second; many of the recipes seemed to be just heating ingredients up very slowly, rather than cooking them to create something delicious.

I thought about how the slow cooker actually works: the metal outer casing of the slow cooker contains a heating element that conducts heat through a ceramic or glass crock, trapping the warmth in with a lid. Unlike the dry heat of an oven or open heat source, the lid forms a seal around the food, using the steam created in cooking to form a vacuum. This moist environment cooks the food with heat from below and above simultaneously, combining braising, baking or poaching with steaming all at the same time. The moisture in the food and the added liquid of a recipe can't evaporate because of the tight seal on the lid. Food is more watery and the flavourings diluted by this extra liquid and this can result in the blandness that many people complain about in meals cooked in a slow cooker. Instead of fighting against the slow cooker's style, I needed to work with it.

The obvious place to start was with my ingredients. I needed to select the right type as my foundation of the dishes and build from there. I turned my attention to cuisines and cultures that used long slow cooking and noted the ingredients they used. Fortuitously, these ingredients also suited my own frugal budget: the cheaper cuts of meat that come from the parts of the animal that do the hard work (legs and shoulder cuts); starchy and root vegetables like the humble spud or the swede and pulses all feature in slow-cooked food from around the world, opening up a wealth of opportunity and variety. I halved the amount of liquid and doubled the amount of herbs and spices and learned to work with the steam to cook a wide selection of dishes beyond the usual brown stews that people associate with the slow cooker. Once I really started to cook, not just heat, with my slow cooker, it became an essential part of my kitchen.

I've chosen over two hundred of the recipes I feel will best help people get to grips with the slow cooker and build a relationship with it that will make it valued in the kitchen throughout the year. I've gone for dishes I wanted to cook and eat. Some of these are best for batch cooking, some will impress others with your new-found skills and others will mean you don't have to turn the oven on at all. The ragus and roasts are tastier and more tender than their traditional counterparts. The soups are simpler and the preserves and baked goods will wow everyone.

Most of the dishes you know and love will work in the slow cooker, but with a few adjustments. Pasta and rice require careful handling in a slow cooker or they become starchy and sticky and I find recipes beyond the lasagne, cannelloni and macaroni cheese listed in the book too difficult to get right, preferring the traditional methods instead. Use less alcohol in your recipes as it doesn't evaporate in the same way and may leave a stronger flavour than you are used to.

The good news is that this change in expectations opens up all kinds of fresh ideas to your repertoire as you find new ways to revisit ingredients you might think of as old fashioned, like suet or barley. It's introduced me to a different method of cooking a wide style of dishes, from curries to custards, and my main difficulty with the book was deciding which recipes to include because I had so much fun using my imagination and trying things out.

THINGS TO KNOW ABOUT SLOW COOKERS

One of the first things people ask is: can you really leave a slow cooker unattended all day while you're off living your life? Combining my experience, some common sense and the Fire Brigade's advice, yes, you can. I've repeatedly left mine switched on overnight while I sleep and during the day while off gallivanting and I've never seen any fires, puffs of smoke or reason to call a fireman.

Put your slow cooker on a sturdy surface like a table or countertop rather than a carpet or shelf, keep the cable away from taps or fire sources and make sure it doesn't have frayed wires or anything like that. Plugging it into a socket with a surge protector gives you even more peace of mind. If the slow cooker is between half and three-quarters full as it cooks, there will also be no chance of the food burning inside it.

The size and style of your slow cooker is the first thing you need to consider when starting out. Think about how you want the slow cooker to fit into your life. Do you want to be able to pop everything in before you leave the house in the morning or do you want it to turn itself on after you've left? Do you want to serve the food straight to the table or simply use the crock to batch-cook things for the freezer?

Small 1.5-litre slow cookers tend to be round and are excellent if you only ever plan to cook two portions of food at a time. They won't accommodate a whole chicken, joint of meat or loaf of bread. Most standard 3.5-litre cookers are oval and will fit these larger items, while cooking enough food for four people at a time. Larger 6.5-litre slow cookers are usually oval and tend to be deeper rather than much wider. This size is best for big joints of meat or cooking for bigger families.

Most slow cookers have crocks you can lift out from the base and set on a table with care, bearing in mind that the ceramic crock can be heavy with the food in it. It can also be cumbersome to hand wash in a sink if you don't have a dishwasher. If this is a problem for you, consider a slow cooker with the newer non-stick versions of the crock that are easier and lighter to handle.

More modern slow cookers also come with lots of useful features that make them useful for modern lives. Many have a warm function that automatically prevents the slow cooker from overcooking food, but keeps it at the right temperature to eat if you're running late from work or the household all eat at different times. Digital slow cookers allow you to start your slow cooker whenever you like, including when you're not there or overnight, although you can also use a standard timer plug to create this feature for yourself on a basic model.

All slow cookers are extremely economical to run. They cost about the same to run per day as a non-energy-saving light bulb. When I first got my slow cooker, despite energy rises that winter, my electric bill went down as I used my oven less often. Even using the six slow cookers I tested the recipes with, my bill only went up £30 on the previous year! (And with the warmth they create in the room, I didn't need the heat on as much either.)

It takes a little time to get to know your slow cooker. Each model will cook at a slightly different temperature to the next, usually reaching just above 100°C as the maximum heat after 8 hours. All slow cookers have a low and high setting. The main difference between the settings is that they take different times to reach the same temperature, with the low setting taking twice as long as the high setting. It's useful to test your slow cooker by pouring room temperature water into the crock, putting it on high and seeing how long it takes to reach 100°C. It will vary between 4–5 hours, but allows you to get a sense of whether your model cooks a little hotter or cooler. This will also reassure you that the slow cooker heats food hot enough to keep it very safe.

Don't lift the lid on the crock until food is cooked as this causes the temperature to drop (and it can take up to 20 minutes each time to recover). It will turn slow cooking into never-ending cooking if you can't leave that lid alone. Serving the food is similar to other forms of cooking: serve it hot, chill leftovers in a sealed container in the fridge and reheat until piping hot in the oven, microwave or on the hob. You can't reheat food in a slow cooker.

Many people recommend greasing the crock before cooking to stop things sticking, but I find it much easier to use a reusable baking liner available in cook shops (and my branch of a well-known pound shop!) Like indestructible greaseproof paper, it saves on washing up and allows you to lift cakes, breads, omelettes and desserts out easily. Aside from this, the only other extra equipment I have used is a hand blender and a good serving spoon. Slow cookers remove the need to have *exactly* the right-sized pan for things.

I don't adhere to a common rule of slow cookers and brown my ingredients before putting them in the crock. Usually, when making a stew you brown the meat, creating what is known as the Maillard reaction or a good seal on the meat or vegetables, enhancing their depth of flavour. It seems a shame and a waste of time to me to brown food in a pan, then put it in a slow cooker, leaving all the tasty bits stuck to the pan. I also found that sealing meat and vegetables increased the chances of overcooking them and creating the woolly texture people complain about in slow-cooker food. So missing out the browning stage not only makes life easier, but makes the food tastier too.

If you like caramelised onions to add depth to your food, it's much easier to do a big batch of them in the slow cooker, refrigerate or freeze them until needed, and add to dishes as you go, instead of trying to brown one onion early in the morning. However, I like my veg with a little bite and if you cut them evenly and put your root vegetables close to the base of the crock to cook more evenly, you can have them tender without being mushy or overcooked.

Don't be afraid of adding flavour to your slow-cooker meals. Savoury dishes need much more in the way of herbs and spices than their oven and stove counterparts. I get my best results with using a balance of whole and ground spices, dried and fresh herbs and fresh garlic and ginger rather than purées. I've never had the issues some complain of with pepper becoming bitter as it cooks, but this did happen with garlic purée, which is why I avoid it.

I prefer to spend my slow-cooker prep time on maximising the flavour, so where I can I toast whole spices before adding them. I often measure the spices out the night before and then spend 2 minutes the next morning toasting them in a dry pan. I'm really not a morning person, but even I can manage this after a cup of tea!

No matter how much anyone tells you that you need to at least halve the liquid of standard recipes and that you mustn't keep taking the lid off and stirring it all, it's hard to break those habits. Begin with the dishes that are straightforward such as cooking pulses from scratch, pot roast or poached chicken or the beef shin and build up, and then you won't find yourself relegating the slow cooker to the back of the cupboard after three tries. Although it does make a very handy bread bin in between uses...

FRUGAL COOKING = FUN COOKING

Everyone's shopping budget varies and so do people's tastes. I have a small weekly budget of under £20 so I know it can be alarming when you see the cost of buying things to add flavour to your food, but with a few simple tips, much of the pain can be taken out of it. You can keep costs down and still enjoy your food.

Firstly, and so common sense it seems almost too obvious to say, think about what you like and need. There's not much point buying chillies if you don't like spicy food. Think about what you like to cook and eat or would like to try and prioritise from there.

Secondly, do some research about the different types of ingredients and how to use and store them. I am a fully fledged anchovy addict. I love their savoury flavour and use them in everything I can. I often buy anchovy paste instead of tinned because it's more intensely flavoured, a third of the price and goes much further in the volume I use it. Knowing that you can keep fresh ginger and spices in the freezer to prolong their life also helps you make the most of the seemingly vast choices out there.

Shop wisely for your ingredients. It may be more time consuming, but in my long experience of shopping on a budget, there is no one shop that ticks all the boxes.

Supermarkets can be great for staples like pearl barley or soup mix that would cost more in a health food shop. However, the health food shop may allow you to buy herbs and spices by the weight you desire. My local deli is expensive for spices, but sells litre bottles of vinegar for the same price as a 250ml one elsewhere. It's knowing your prices and taking time to compare that gets the best results.

Don't be afraid to go down a shelf or a brand in the supermarkets to get those well-priced staples or buy things like dried peas that are versatile, but not as fashionable these days. Wander through the 'world foods' section and often you'll save on spices and items like coconut milk especially. Venture into your local Polski Sklep or Asian-run grocery store if you have one and you'll find all kinds of fantastic ingredients in bigger packets for smaller prices.

I'm lucky to have Brixton market on my doorstep, but I've made sure that everything I've used for the book can be bought in the major supermarkets too. The difference is that you may find them cheaper if you look further afield — try your local grocer or look online. Every so often I save up and do an online shop when I need tins and heavy items so I can make the most of the minimum order and the delivery charge. Sometimes I go to a Chinese supermarket a bus journey away and stock up on things I know I will find useful.

My recipes include frugal ingredients and I've made sure to give you lots of ideas for how to use certain items again and again to make the most of your store cupboard and allow cooking to become easier and more enjoyable, no matter how little time you have for it. My cooking is all about creating foundations on which to build. I poach a chicken and use the meat and the bones to make soups. Ragus make the basis of a whole lasagne or other dishes to fill the freezer. I rely on a big bag of dried chillies to save stopping off too often to buy fresh ones. Instead of using wine in my cooking, I use vermouth because, being fortified, it keeps indefinitely and is much cheaper than the equivalent volume of white wine. (It also seems more expensive than it is and it's nice not to feel frugal all the time.) I also take advantage of seasonal offers, getting duck or goose fat around Christmastime, for example, knowing these fats last well in the fridge.

The perk of building your store cupboard slowly is that it allows you to try things out and find your own cooking style. I've offered a wide variety of flavours and tastes throughout the book and ended up trying new things I wouldn't usually have in the house. I've then made those items earn their spot in my small cupboard and used them multiple times, creating new favourites. Hopefully this will give you the reassurance to do the same and create slow-cooking favourites.

TESTING NOTES

Every recipe in the book was tested before being included here. Some were tested several times to refine them, others were just right first go. Some were tested by other people as well as me and their feedback noted.

I tested at home, using a variety of brands from Morphy Richards, Lakeland and Russell Hobbs. The majority of the recipes were tested in a 3.5-litre oval crock without preheating. You should check your manufacturer's instructions to see if this step is required for your slow cooker.

None of the slow cookers used for testing were digital. I tested the food with a probe thermometer and occasionally used a timer plug at the wall. Trying to work out how to programme it was the trickiest bit of the whole book.

I hand-washed all my crocks as I don't have a dishwasher. I also have limited patience with standing over the sink, so I soaked mine with hot water and soda crystals to make it easier. I didn't use non-stick cooking spray on my crocks, as many people advise, as I don't like the taste of it in my food.

I only used the low and high settings on the slow cookers as all models have these. I didn't use the warm or auto functions, so you will need to get to know how your slow cooker works on these settings, if you have them.

RECIPE NOTES

- All spoon measures are level unless otherwise stated. Some amounts of herbs and spices may seem larger than expected. Trust me, no typos here, just dishes with lots of flavour

- All milk is full-fat or semi-skimmed

- Yoghurt is unsweetened and plain, usually between 2–4% fat

- All eggs are large as that's what my local shop stocks

- All butter is salted. I don't use margarine, so no recipes were tested with it

- All sugar is white and granulated unless otherwise stated. I don't seek out caster sugar, even for baking, as I find that granulated works perfectly well

- Parsley can be either curly or flat-leaved unless one type is specified in the recipe

- Breadcrumbs are always fresh and not golden

MEAT

Slow cookers really come into their own with meat. They take those cheaper cuts and turn them into something really tender and tasty. This is the time to braise and casserole cuts you might not usually have the chance to eat, like pigs' cheeks or oxtail. Don't be afraid, these cuts become soft and tender when slow cooked and you don't need to add extra oil or fats to cook them, you can just rely on their natural flavours.

Cuts of meat can have a variety of names so, if you can, check your chuck steak and your brisket with a butcher to help you become more confident cooking with new cuts. Building a relationship with a local butcher can be very beneficial, but not always possible. Several of the big supermarkets have good butchery counters and you can buy the exact amounts you need for a dish there, which can be very useful compared to pre-packed portions which could be more expensive.

I always try to cook meat from room temperature rather than fridge cold. It means the slow cooker doesn't have to work as hard and spends more time making the meat tender. Simply take the meat out of the fridge about an hour before cooking if you can. This is especially important as I very rarely sear or brown meat before I add it to the slow cooker. I don't find the extra time and washing up makes the dish taste different enough to make it worth my while. If you have one of the new non-stick crocks that can be heated on the hob as well as in the slow cooker, it's definitely worth searing your meat as all the flavour is kept in the crock. Using a frying pan leaves it behind and defeats the purpose. If I do specify browning or searing the meat, it's because it's really important to that recipe.

Nearly every recipe in this chapter can be cooked in advance and reheated on the hob or in the microwave as needed, allowing all those lovely slow-cooked flavours to mingle together and taste even better. You won't know what you did without your slow cooker when it comes to cooking meat!

SLOW-BRAISED BEEF SHIN

Beef shin is one of those cuts of meat that has become unfashionable and unloved in the era of frying steak and chicken breast. Usually bought with a circle of bone in each slice, it needs a very low slow cooking to turn it into the rich, sticky dish it deserves to be. What looks like quite a small piece of meat, unfurls into soft strands that pull apart and double the amount of meat you were expecting. Cooked into a glossy gravy, it makes a stunning stew or the basis of the best cottage pie you've ever eaten.

This is a versatile dish, just made for the slow cooker, and is a great way to get the hang of how to cook meat with less liquid than you would in the oven, as it shows how the meat steams and braises all at once.

SERVES 4

2 tablespoons plain flour

½ teaspoon salt

½ teaspoon black pepper

¼ teaspoon ground mace

1 teaspoon mustard powder

650g beef shin, preferably bone in

2 carrots, diced

2 stalks of celery, diced

1 large onion, diced

2 star anise

1 teaspoon Worcestershire sauce

1 teaspoon Marmite

250ml beer, preferably a dark ale or stout

Mix the flour with the salt, pepper, mace and mustard powder and toss the uncut pieces of the beef shin in it (they should look like steaks rather than cubes). It cooks best this way, rather than trying to chop it smaller.

Set the floured meat in the slow cooker and add the diced vegetables. Add the star anise, Worcestershire sauce, Marmite and pour the beer over it all. Don't be tempted to add more beer for more flavour as it will dilute the gravy and the rich intensity of it all.

Put the lid on the slow cooker and braise the beef shin on low for 8–9 hours. The meat will have melted into a thick, sticky tangle with the vegetables collapsing into it all.

Use the braised beef shin as a stew or bake it into a lovely pie in the oven. It is stunning in a lasagne or made into a cottage pie with some mashed potato piled on top, textured with the back of a fork and put under a hot grill until crispy on the edges.

BRACIOLE

This is basically the more glamorous Italian name for what your granny probably would have called beef olives. Braising steak is beaten out thinly and stuffed with breadcrumbs and capers before being slow cooked in a tomato sauce. It's simple and delicious and makes a lovely alternative to a pot roast or stew. I also like to take any life frustrations out on the meat with a rolling pin, making this therapy you can eat at the end!

SERVES 4

600g braising steak, in 2 large pieces rather than cubed

50g breadcrumbs

1 heaped tablespoon capers

10 black olives, pitted and chopped

½ lemon, zested (if waxed, give it a vigorous scrub under the hot tap first)

2 cloves of garlic, chopped

20g Parmesan

1 teaspoon vegetable or olive oil

1 onion, finely diced

1 x 400g tin chopped tomatoes

50ml tomato juice or water

1 teaspoon dried oregano

½ teaspoon sugar

salt and pepper

Start by putting your braising steak between two sheets of greaseproof paper or reusable baking liner and then hitting it hard with a rolling pin to flatten it out. This makes it easier to roll up and makes a small amount of meat go much further. You should aim to double the area of the beef, but don't forget to protect with the paper first or it will tear.

Mix up the stuffing by putting the breadcrumbs, capers, olives, lemon zest and garlic in a bowl with the Parmesan. Add the oil and stir through so it sticks together slightly.

Spoon half of it onto each piece of flattened-out beef, spreading it evenly, and roll it up, tucking the sides in to make a parcel. Tie it with string or hold it together with toothpicks, making sure the stuffing can't escape. Place the parcels in the slow-cooker crock.

Mix the onion through the chopped tomatoes, along with the tomato juice or water and the dried oregano and sugar. Season it well. Pour the tomato mixture over the beef and add a little more water or tomato juice if more than the very tip of the meat is sticking out.

Put the lid on the slow cooker and cook the braciole on low for 7–8 hours. The meat will become soft and tender, but hold its shape beautifully, allowing you to lift the parcels out of the tomato sauce with a slotted spoon. Remove all the toothpicks or string and then cut the braciole into slices and serve over pasta or gnocchi with the sauce over the top.

SCOUSE

You know a stew is good when a whole city becomes famed for it. Originally known as Lobscouse by the Danish sailors who brought it to Britain, this dish became scouse and the people of Liverpool who ate it became Scousers. And it's no wonder they loved it so much. It's simple and delicious and warming enough to deal with any breeze off the Mersey.

Scouse is usually half beef and half breast of lamb if you can get it. However, there are as many version of scouse as there are grannies in Liverpool. I've used beef and lamb neck as the mix of meats is what makes it unique. As long as you buy the best meat you can afford and serve it with pickled red cabbage on the side, you can't go far wrong!

SERVES 4 WITH LEFTOVERS

1kg potatoes

350g stewing steak, cubed

250g lamb neck or lamb breast, cubed

1 large onion, diced

2 carrots, diced

2 teaspoons Worcestershire sauce

750ml hot beef stock or water

salt and pepper

This is a very simple dish to make. I find potatoes don't lose their shape as easily in the slow cooker, so I've adapted the recipe slightly by cutting most of the potatoes very small. This way they will collapse into the gravy and thicken it. Without their thickening trick, the scouse is a bit watery.

Peel two-thirds of the potatoes and cut them into 1cm cubes. Put in the slow-cooker crock with the chunks of stewing steak and lamb neck. Add the onion and carrot and use your hands to toss it all through evenly.

Season well and add the Worcestershire sauce. Add the remaining third of the potatoes — I leave the skins on and cut them into 4cm chunks. Pour the stock or water over it all. I usually use Bovril to make my beef stock as it seems meatier to me than stock cubes and a little goes a long way (add 3½ teaspoons Bovril to 750ml boiling water).

Put the lid on the slow cooker and cook the scouse on low for 8–10 hours. You will end up with a thickened gravy from the small pieces of potato along with meat so tender it falls apart and helps thicken the dish further. This mix of textures is what makes scouse unlike other stews.

Serve with pickled cabbage and some of the Pickled Beetroot from page 194. I can also imagine a pickled onion or two being bliss with this.

STOVIES

This is a very simple dish that's absolutely packed with flavour. It reminds me of Guide camps when I was little, when a bunch of tweens and teens would be let loose with a can of corned beef and a campfire to make their own dinner. The dish was equal parts foolproof and delicious, but I much prefer the slow-cooker version. Not only does making it at home mean I get to sleep in my own bed rather than in a tent, but the slow cooking makes the dish much more velvety and creates a lovely gravy round it. Everyone asks for seconds, even my friend Claire who ate the original wood-smoked version.

SERVES 4-6 AS IT
IS A PROPER RIB-
STICKING DISH

25g beef dripping
   or 1 tablespoon
   vegetable oil
700g potatoes
1 x 340g tin corned
   beef, chopped
1 large onion, cut in
   half moons
4 sprigs of fresh thyme
   or 1 teaspoon dried
   thyme
2 teaspoons
   Worcestershire sauce
300ml water
black pepper

Start by cutting the dripping in half. Cube it and scatter half of it over the bottom of the crock. If you don't have any dripping, brush the crock with the vegetable oil instead.

Peel the potatoes and slice them thinly. Put two layers into the bottom of the crock, then add half the corned beef and half the onion. Add 2 sprigs of fresh thyme or ½ teaspoon dried thyme and season with black pepper. Drizzle half the Worcestershire sauce over it all.

Add another layer of sliced potatoes and the other half of the corned beef and onions. Add the rest of the fresh or dried thyme and the Worcestershire sauce. Layer the last of the potatoes on top of the corned beef and pour the water over it all.

Scatter the remaining dripping or brush another teaspoon of vegetable oil over the top of the potatoes and put the lid on the slow cooker. Cook the stovies on high for 7-8 hours. The corned beef should melt down to make a thick, rich gravy and the potatoes should be soft and tender and about to break down completely.

Serve in deep bowls. It makes a great one-pot meal, but I love some cabbage or spring greens on the side of it. Maybe a few peas as well. Plastic plate and fork optional.

GOULASH

When I first moved to London, I lived in a crowded shared house where we all passed like ships in the night, except on Monday nights. Monday night was goulash night. Originally taken from a Lindsey Bareham recipe in the *Evening Standard*, we took it in turns to make a huge pot of paprika-rich stew and then sit down together around the kitchen table. The amount of cheap red wine consumed with it tended to make Tuesday mornings hangover morning, but I still love goulash and make it quite often.

It works fabulously well in the slow cooker. If you can make it the day before and leave the flavours to infuse, it is even better. Don't skimp on the sour cream though.

SERVES 2 WITH
LEFTOVERS OR
4 WITHOUT

500g stewing steak or
  beef brisket, cubed

1 tablespoon plain flour

1 onion, chopped

2 cloves of garlic,
  finely diced

1 red pepper or 75g
  char-grilled red
  peppers from a jar

1 x 400g tin chopped
  tomatoes

2 tablespoons smoked
  paprika, preferably
  sweet

1 teaspoon caraway
  seeds

¼ teaspoon cayenne
  pepper

1 x 400g tin plum
  tomatoes

500ml hot beef stock
  or water

150ml sour cream, to
  serve

25g chopped fresh
  parsley, to serve

salt and pepper

Season the meat well and toss it in the plain flour. Put it in the slow-cooker crock with the onion and garlic.

Chop the red pepper into small pieces and combine in a bowl with the chopped tomatoes. Blitz them together with a hand blender until they form a smooth purée. Add the smoked paprika, caraway seeds and cayenne pepper and blend well together.

Pour the tomato and pepper purée into the slow-cooker crock and stir it all together well to coat the meat and the onions. Add in the plum tomatoes and pour the water or beef stock in. Make sure the meat is just covered — you may not need all the water.

Put the lid on the slow cooker and cook the goulash on low for 8–10 hours or until the meat is soft and tender and the sauce has thickened. Serve with a hefty dollop of sour cream and fresh parsley scattered over it with steamed rice or mashed potato on the side.

STIFADO

I associate this gorgeous Greek dish with my dad, who always brings sachets of stifado mix back from his Greek holidays and adds them to a little parcel of strange and wonderful items he sends me as a present. They are a bit like getting an orange in your Christmas stocking! I love making stifado from them, so imagine my excitement when I realised I could make the dish from scratch and have it more often than once a year. Full of tender beef, this stew is special with its use of spices and whole caramelised shallots.

SERVES 4 WITH LEFTOVERS

300g shallots, peeled and left whole

25ml olive oil

500g stewing steak

1 teaspoon fennel seeds

60ml vermouth

2 onions, diced

2 stalks of celery, diced

1 carrot, diced

3 cloves of garlic, diced

1 cinnamon stick or piece of cinnamon bark

4 cloves

½ nutmeg, grated

4 allspice berries

1 teaspoon dried oregano

1 large sprig of fresh rosemary

2 bay leaves

4 tablespoons tomato purée

1 x 400g tin chopped tomatoes

200ml water

60ml red wine vinegar

salt and pepper

Start by preparing your shallots. Peel them by pouring boiling water over them and leaving them to sit for 10 minutes. The skins will slip off, leaving the tip and root intact. Heat the olive oil in a frying or sauté pan on the hob and add the shallots. Cook them over a medium heat until golden and becoming slightly sticky on all sides. This should take about 5–7 minutes.

I quite often seal the meat for this dish since I have the pan out anyway. If you do this, give it about a minute and a half each side over a medium heat until browned. You might need to do it in two batches or the pan gets overcrowded and the meat steams instead of browning.

Put the shallots and the meat into the slow cooker, adding any leftover sticky browned bits from the pan and the remaining olive oil as well. Use the same pan to fry the fennel seeds until they smell aromatic. Take them off the heat and crush them using a pestle and mortar and then pour the vermouth over them to infuse. This will give the aniseed kick you'd usually get from ouzo if you were in Greece, where it doesn't cost £15 a bottle.

Add the diced onion, celery, carrot and garlic and toss in the cinnamon, cloves, nutmeg, allspice, oregano, rosemary and bay leaves. Season well.

Stir in the tomato purée and pour the chopped tomatoes over it all. Add the water, vinegar and the infused vermouth, including the seeds. It's OK if the meat isn't all covered with liquid — you want quite a thick sauce here.

Put the lid on the slow cooker and cook the stifado on low for 8–9 hours. Serve with orzo for an approximation of Greek *hilopites*, a type of egg pasta, or some rosemary roast potatoes.

CARBONNADE

Imagine how happy life would be if you could combine a beef and ale stew with a sandwich? Well, the good news is that those crafty Belgians have already done it with carbonnade. Tender chunks of beef are cooked in one of their excellent beers and lots of tangy wholegrain mustard, before being topped with slices of mustard-smothered bread then baked. All with a name that sounds much more stylish than a stew sandwich.

I've made an Irish reworked version before with Guinness and Veda bread, which worked really well. Provided you don't use a light lager or sliced white, you can tailor this deep, dark stew to what you have at home too. I'm sure I've just insulted many Belgians with my suggestion of stout, so I'll try to redeem myself with the instruction that you should use the best beer or ale you can afford. Many supermarkets run offers on Chimay and Leffe Brune, which are both perfect here, but as long as it's dark and good enough to drink, it will be great!

SERVES 4–6 WITH LEFTOVERS

500g stewing steak or beef brisket, cubed

1 teaspoon mustard powder

1 teaspoon sea salt

1 teaspoon black pepper

3 tablespoons plain flour

2 onions (preferably Caramelised Onions, see page 122)

1 carrot, diced

2 large flat mushrooms, sliced

1 heaped teaspoon brown sugar

1 tablespoon balsamic vinegar

1 bay leaf

3 sprigs of fresh thyme or 1 teaspoon dried thyme

350ml ale or stout

4 tablespoons wholegrain mustard

1 tablespoon room-temperature butter

1 demi baguette

chopped fresh parsley, to serve

Put the cubed meat into the slow cooker and add the mustard powder, salt, pepper and the flour. Toss well with your hands to evenly coat the meat. Add in the caramelised onions and the carrot and mushroom.

Season with the sugar, vinegar, bay leaf and thyme and pour the beer over it all. The meat should be at least two-thirds submerged. Stir half the wholegrain mustard through it all. Put the lid on the slow cooker and cook the stew on low for 6 hours.

After 6 hours, beat the butter and the remaining wholegrain mustard together. Cut the demi baguette into 4cm rounds, discarding the small end slices. Spread the mustard and butter on one side of the bread and put the rounds under the grill until the edges start to crisp up and the butter and mustard mixture darkens.

Lift the lid off the crock and carefully set the buttery, mustard-coated bread on top of the simmering stew, butter side up, pressing the rounds down a bit so the gravy soaks into the base of them.

Replace the lid and cook for another 2 hours. Serve this one-pot dish in bowls scattered with fresh parsley.

OXTAIL WITH DARK CHOCOLATE AND GUINNESS

Few things are better for being slow cooked than oxtail. This knobbly-looking cut becomes meltingly soft and sticky after hours of low heat. A little goes a long way because the meat is rich and packed with flavour from being cooked on the bone. A smidgen of dark chocolate melted through before serving makes this something really special indeed. I only remember oxtail being served as soup when I was a kid, but this is so much better.

Don't be shy about trying a new cut of meat. I also just like an excuse for more Guinness in my life, if I'm honest. Few other things go so incredibly well with chocolate.

SERVES 4

750g oxtail

2 tablespoons plain flour

2 onions, diced

4 cloves of garlic, chopped

1 x 400g tin chopped tomatoes

½ teaspoon ground cloves

½ teaspoon ground allspice

1 tablespoon tomato purée

500ml Guinness or other stout

2 star anise

100ml cold water (if needed)

4 squares of dark chocolate, approximately 25g

salt and pepper

If you can, get the butcher to cut the oxtail chunks in half as pieces will fit better in the slow cooker, but if you can only get it in whole chunks, don't worry. You might just need a little bit more liquid to cover it completely.

Season the flour with salt and pepper and toss the oxtail in it. Put the meat into the slow cooker along with the onion, garlic and chopped tomatoes. Scatter the clove and the allspice over it all and stir well to combine. Dollop in the tomato purée.

Pour the Guinness over it all (if you prefer not to use alcohol here, you could substitute it with beef stock). Bob the star anise into the stew and if any oxtail is poking too far out of the Guinness, add the cold water.

Put the lid on the slow cooker and cook the oxtail on low for 12 hours. It will be soft and tender and falling off the bone by this stage. Oxtail is quite a fatty cut of meat and this will have made the most wonderful gravy.

Remove the star anise and as many of the bones as you can with a spoon to make it easier to eat, then chop the squares of chocolate in half and stir them through to create a slightly bittersweet note that just brings the whole dish together.

Serve with steamed rice or mashed potato to soak up as much of the malty, meaty gravy as you can.

PERFECT MINCE

As a child, you could pick anything you wanted for your birthday tea in our house. My brother Mister North memorably asked for a mint Viennetta once. I, without fail, asked for mince and potatoes.

Hands down my favourite meal as a child, I still adore a plate of this ultimate comfort food, bonding with a friend's future husband when I discovered he served his with suet dumplings on the side too (see below). But like Proust and his madeleine, I had never been able to get my mince to taste like those birthday teas until I got my slow cooker, but now it's utterly foolproof. There may not be birthday cake afterwards, but it's my idea of perfection all the same.

Cooking mince in the slow cooker without pan frying it first will give quite a different and looser texture as it falls apart rather than forms little nuggets of meat. I really like this smooth finish to the meat, but if you prefer it more rugged, you could seal the meat in a pan for about 5 minutes first.

SERVES 2–4 WITH ENOUGH FOR SECONDS OR TO MAKE COTTAGE PIE

500g beef mince

2 tablespoons plain flour

200ml hot beef stock

1 teaspoon Worcestershire sauce

1 teaspoon tomato purée

½ teaspoon soy sauce

drop or 2 of gravy browning

salt and pepper

Put the mince into the slow-cooker crock, sprinkle the flour over it and stir well to evenly coat all the meat. Season.

Make sure your beef stock is heated. I tend to use Bovril here made with boiling water (1 teaspoon Bovril to 200ml boiling water), but if you are using fresh, warm it through. Add the Worcestershire sauce, tomato purée, soy and gravy browning and mix it all to combine.

Pour this stock mixture over the mince and stir it well. Put the lid on the slow cooker and cook on low for 8 hours. The mince will thicken and create a rich gravy. It may look like it has separated slightly, but all it needs is a good stir and it's ready to serve.

Note: If the idea appeals to you, simply make some suet dumplings by mixing 100g self-raising flour with 50g beef suet, a pinch of salt, pepper and mustard powder and 60ml cold water to make a thick, stiff dough. Bring together and roll into eight dumplings. Add them to the mince (or a stew) at least an hour before the end of cooking and enjoy!

TONGUE AND CHEEK PUDDING

I used to be wary of offal. Put off by the very nature of it, I'd also had it overcooked a few times and disliked the grainy texture it develops that way. The only offal I really loved when I was a kid was tongue and then, when I became vegetarian, I was squeamish about all the wobbly bits of the animal. When I started eating meat again, I was convinced I wouldn't like offal and so never learned to cook it.

Slightly unsure of what to write about when we started blogging, I decided to start trying offal again because even if I didn't like it, it would be something to write about. My tastes, and a lot of cooking in Britain, have come on in the last 20 years and much of the offal I tried was delicious.

Mister North has never been afraid of offal and helped encourage me by telling me all kinds of things were black pudding and now I'm obsessed. Sadly, offal is often too delicate for the slow cooker, but Mister North created this dish, which works perfectly and reintroduced me to tongue.

I am lucky to have a farmers' market near me on a Sunday and in amongst the stalls, there are a couple of butchers that stock an unusual selection of meats that are perfect for experimenting. I've ordered both pork and veal tongues there for a few pounds. A whole ox tongue is too big here. If you can't get either tongue or cheeks, then simply use the same amounts of steak and kidney instead.

SERVES 6

2 pigs' tongues

4 pigs' cheeks

100ml red wine

200g black pudding

1 heaped teaspoon paprika

1 onion, finely chopped

400ml hot chicken stock

2 teaspoons Worcestershire sauce

2 bay leaves

1 heaped teaspoon cornflour (optional, for thickening)

100g suet

200g self-raising flour

75–150ml cold water

salt and pepper

Wipe the tongues down and brown them on each side in a frying pan over a medium heat. I usually do them one at a time. Set them into the slow cooker. Seal the pigs' cheeks in the same pan and add to the slow cooker. Deglaze the pan with the red wine and pour over the tongue and cheeks.

Slice open the skin of the black pudding and crumble the contents over the meat. Add the paprika and onion and season well. Pour in the chicken stock so that the tongues are nearly submerged. Add the Worcestershire sauce and the bay leaves.

Put the lid on the slow cooker and cook the meat on low for 8–9 hours. I usually do mine overnight so that I awake to a lovely smell in the morning. Lift the meat out of the gravy that has formed and set aside to cool.

The black pudding should have melted into the stock to create a thick gravy, but if it seems too liquid, mix the cornflour with a tiny amount of water, mix it into the sauce and cook for another hour in the slow cooker or simmer over a medium heat in a large saucepan for about 10 minutes.

Turn your attention to the cooled meats. Pull the cheeks apart with two forks into strands of tender pork. Peel the skin off the tongues gently and slice or shred the meat inside. This is much easier when the tongue is cooked rather than before cooking. Mix the meats together. Taste and see if the mixture needs any more seasoning. Keep the meat separate from the gravy and set both aside.

Prepare your pudding basin by greasing and flouring it well so it is ready for the pastry. I use a 1.2-litre lidded plastic basin as it saves getting creative with tin foil. Make the suet pastry by mixing the suet and the flour together in a large bowl. Season well. I sometimes add a pinch of mustard powder too. Add up to 150ml of the water as you bring the pastry together. It should be firm, but slightly sticky. If it is too dry, add the remaining water. Keep the pastry rough with lumps of suet visible.

Don't knead the dough, but roll out two-thirds of it on a floured surface until it is 5mm thick. Lift this carefully over the pudding basin and allow it to flop into it. Don't push it down, but leave about 2cm hanging over the edge of the basin. Patch any holes or cracks carefully. Roll the remaining pastry out in a circle and leave aside.

Start filling the pudding by adding a layer of the meat about 5cm deep, then a layer of the gravy about 2cm deep. Repeat until the basin is almost full and then pour any of the remaining gravy over the top.

Wet the edges of the suet pastry with a little water and put the lid on top, crimping the edges together with your finger and thumb to seal it. Trim off the excess and place the lid on the bowl well. There should be enough of a gap in the basin to allow the pudding room to expand.

Set the basin into the slow cooker and pour boiling water into the crock until it comes about half way up the sides. Put the lid on the slow cooker and steam the pudding on high for 4 hours.

Carefully lift the pudding out and turn it out on a serving plate. It will slide out easily and sit up proudly for about 30 seconds before the suet pastry slumps down and cracks open, exposing a river of rich gravy. This is the sign of a seriously successful steamed pudding.

Serve with heaps of steamed Savoy cabbage on the side.

RAG PUDDING

Closely related to those clootie and apple dumplings (see page 243) we used to eat for Halloween, this is the Lancastrian version, made with meat instead of fruit. Brought into my life by my brother Mister North's connection with the county he lived in for most of a decade, it's a brilliant way to make the leftovers of the Perfect Mince on page 23 go a long way. Rolled into a long shape, this dish is what happens when you combine a sausage roll with a suet dumpling and put it in its Sunday best.

This is a simple recipe to make, but it's a good idea to prepare the slow cooker and cloth in advance as suet pastry is quite fragile and needs to handled carefully.

**SERVES 4
GENEROUSLY**

100g suet

100g self-raising flour

75ml cold water

150g cooked beef mince (see page 21)

salt and pepper

Put a small dish or ramekins in the slow-cooker crock. I used three of the sort you get from posh ready-made desserts. Soak a cloth in warm water, then wring out the excess. Lay it out flat. Liberally flour the whole cloth, which will prevent the pudding from sticking. Then flour it again to be sure.

Put the suet, flour and salt and pepper in a large bowl, and add the water. Bring it all together with your hands and combine. It will feel slightly rough, but do not knead the dough.

Turn it out onto a floured surface and roll into a rectangle until about 5mm thick. Put the mince in the middle, making sure you leave a little space at the ends. Roll up the pastry as tightly as you can to make a suet sausage and set onto the floured cloth.

Roll the cloth up tightly to hold the shape, tie two lengths of string round the body of it and secure each end with string. It will look like a big Christmas cracker. Fold the ends of the cloth over the top and place the whole pudding parcel on top of your ramekins. It's fine if the pudding bends a bit at the ends to get it in there. Pour boiling water into the slow cooker without getting the cloth wet. It should come no more than two-thirds up the way of the ramekins.

Put the lid on the slow cooker and steam the pudding on high for 6–7 hours. Some people boil their rag puddings directly in water, but I found that it made the dough heavy and wet. Steaming in the slow cooker, however, created a melt-in-the-mouth pudding.

Lift the pudding out using the string and unwrap it. Serve it sliced with Mushy Peas (see page 100) and lashings of Easy Tomato Ketchup (see page 188).

MEAT RAGU

You might know this as the humble Bolognese sauce, but I think it's much more versatile than simply dolloping it onto spaghetti. Few dishes have their authenticity examined as much as this one, but the one thing it really needs is slow cooking.

I have adapted my recipe via famed Italian cook Marcella Hazan's rules and my dad's influence to make this rich, tasty version. There is no garlic in mine as it dominates, but lots of parsley stalks. Marcella's suggestion of using milk to neutralise the acidity of the tomatoes is fabulous. Because my dad never used it, there's no pancetta in my ragu.

It is a dish that needs slow cooking and would always have it in Italy, so while the ingredients aren't that different to the ones used to make the quick midweek version, they are so much more than the sum of their parts. I make a big batch and use the leftovers in cannelloni, lasagne or with creamy slow-cooked polenta instead of pasta. I never tire of this ragu.

SERVES 2-4 WITH LEFTOVERS

- 1 tablespoon olive oil
- 2 stalks of celery, finely diced
- 2 carrots, peeled and finely diced
- 1 large onion, finely diced
- ½ bunch of fresh parsley stalks, finely chopped
- 500g beef mince (or 250g pork and 250g beef mince)
- 50ml milk
- ¼ teaspoon fresh nutmeg or ground mace
- 2 x 400g tins chopped tomatoes
- 1 heaped tablespoon tomato purée
- 75ml wine (red or white)
- 1 bay leaf
- salt and pepper

Start the dish by warming the olive oil in the crock for about 10 minutes. Add the celery, carrot, onion and parsley stalks, which should all be diced and chopped to the same size for ease of cooking. The parsley stalks are more robust than the leaves so better for slow cooking, but impart the same flavour.

Coat the vegetables well in the oil and then add the mince. If you can, use the mixture of the meats. It makes a wonderfully light yet rich ragu that's hard to beat, but if you only use beef on its own it will stilll be delicious.

Stir the mince well and combine with the vegetables. It won't brown in the slow cooker, which gives a softer quality to the ragu than you might be used to if you brown the meat in a pan. Add the milk and stir well. It will start to absorb into the meat almost immediately and it lends a creaminess to the meat and stops the tomatoes from being slightly acidic.

Season the mixture well with salt and black pepper. Add the nutmeg or mace. You want enough of it to flavour the ragu, but not too much that it defines the taste of the whole dish.

Add the chopped tomatoes, tomato purée and the wine. Stir well to make sure everything is evenly distributed and add the bay leaf. Put the lid on and cook the ragu on low for 8-9 hours at least. It won't harm it to have an hour or two more if you have the chance. In fact, for even slower cooking, the ragu is best allowed to cool, left overnight in the fridge and eaten the next day when the flavours have intensified. However, it's still the best ragu you've ever had when served straight away.

CREAMY CANNELLONI

These cannelloni use the Meat Ragu on page 25. I add some red chilli flakes then top the pasta tubes with a creamy white sauce (velouté) to keep the whole dish moist. The pasta cooks comparatively quickly for the slow cooker, making this a meal I can avail myself of any time. I succumb to the cannelloni temptation quite often, not just because it's delicious, but because it allows me to have fun with a piping bag to fill the tubes.

SERVES 2-4
DEPENDING ON
GREED

50g butter

50g plain flour

250ml milk

500ml hot chicken
  stock

50g Parmesan, grated
  (optional)

250g Meat Ragu
  (see page 25)

½ teaspoon red chilli
  flakes or chilli powder

125g cannelloni tubes
  or lasagne sheets

salt and pepper

I begin by making the white sauce so the roux that thickens it has time to cook down on the stove and make the sauce smooth and creamy. (I often use stock because it's cheaper than milk and less likely to overcook in the slow cooker.)

Melt the butter in a saucepan over a medium heat. When it bubbles, add the plain flour and stir well. It will come together into a paste. Lower the heat and cook for about 3-4 minutes. Stir frequently and don't let it colour too much.

Add half the milk, whisking constantly. It might look lumpy, but keep whisking and you'll see the milk vanishing into the roux. Repeat with the rest of the milk, then start adding the stock. Keep whisking until it all comes together and then allow the white sauce to simmer for 8-10 minutes. It will thicken nicely. Add the Parmesan and stir well.

Prepare the meat ragu by adding the red chilli flakes and seasoning again if needed. If you aren't using pre-bought cannelloni tubes, but lasagne sheets instead, you'll need to blanch them in boiling water now in order to be able to roll them. Cook them for 2 minutes, two at a time, and lift them out with tongs. Lay on a clean tea towel until needed.

Filling the pasta becomes ridiculously good fun with the use of a piping bag. If you have a reusable one, that's great, or you can use the disposable ones or a good strong freezer bag with the corner cut off diagonally. All the ragu should fit in the bag at once and it's easier to pipe if the bag is nice and plump. Twist the top tight and you're ready.

Simply fill each cannelloni tube until about 5mm remains at each end, placing them into the slow cooker as you go. If you are making your own with the lasagne sheets, fold them round so the join is at the bottom and overlaps to make a seam. Fill and stack the same way as the tubes. Don't tuck extra cannelloni in at the sides of the crock or they will burn, but you can stack them up to three layers deep.

Pour the white sauce over the cannelloni, making sure they are evenly coated then cook on low for 3 hours. The sauce will soak into the pasta slightly. Serve with extra Parmesan.

LASAGNE

No matter what I do, I never have the right dish for a lasagne. It's like Goldilocks, but with pasta instead of porridge. The dish is too big or too small or too deep or not deep enough. The result being that I rarely make lasagne, which is a real shame because a good lasagne is a truly marvellous thing. I like mine the Northern Irish way with chips on the side, but I'm going to be grown-up here and say serve this with a green salad.

I usually make this lasagne when I've done a big batch of either of the meat ragu recipes in this chapter. Slow cooking them twice makes them melt-in-the-mouth tender and the lasagne very simple to make. If you don't have any, simply fry 400g beef mince until brown along with an onion. Add ½ teaspoon dried oregano and 400g chopped tomatoes, simmer for 20 minutes and use in place of the ragu here.

SERVES 4–6
DEPENDING ON YOUR
CHOICE OF SIDE DISH

9 dried or fresh lasagne
  sheets
50g butter
50g plain flour
500ml milk
50g Parmesan, grated
500g Meat or Sausage
  Ragu (see page 25
  or 30)
200g mozzarella, grated

If you are using dried lasagne sheets, put a large pan of water on to boil on the stove. Boil each sheet for about 60–90 seconds to soften them. Lift out with tongs and place each one in a single layer side by side on a clean tea towel. Trim the corners of six of them into a rounded shape with kitchen scissors when the sheets are cool enough to handle.

Make the white sauce (béchamel) by melting the butter in a saucepan over a medium heat. Stir the plain flour into it to make a roux. Cook it for about 2 minutes, stirring constantly to soften it. Add the milk in increments, whisking constantly to make a smooth white sauce. Melt the grated Parmesan into it and turn off the heat.

Line the slow-cooker crock with some reusable baking liner and start making the lasagne by layering about half the ragu into it. Put three sheets of lasagne on top of it, using the rounded ones at the edges.

Pour half the white sauce on top of the lasagne sheets and arrange a second layer of the pasta on top of it. Cover these with the rest of the ragu and arrange the third layer of lasagne on top of that. Finish with white sauce.

Put the lid on the slow cooker and cook the lasagne on low for 3 hours. The white sauce on top will look like it is drying out slightly, but don't worry. It is just baking beautifully. About 90 minutes before you are ready to eat, scatter the mozzarella over the top of the lasagne and replace the lid.

Cook for another hour and then turn off the heat and allow it all to sit for 30 minutes. This makes it easier to cut and serve and the lasagne tastes better when not served radioactively hot. Eat in slices with salad and/or chips and a cheeky glass of red wine.

BEEF MEATBALLS

Meatballs are such a favourite of mine that they deserve several recipes in this book. These are a classic Italian-style beef meatball, perfect for cooking in a tomato sauce to make that Italian-American classic, spaghetti and meatballs, or putting into a wrap or sub for a seriously special lunch. I also use them for the Bunnychow on page 169 and if I know I'm using them for that, I omit the Parmesan and oregano. These are really versatile, but I could honestly just eat a huge plateful as they are because they are so light and tasty.

**SERVES 2-4
(THEY FREEZE WELL
UNCOOKED)**

2 slices of bread (white or brown) or 80g breadcrumbs (not golden)

75ml milk

500g beef mince, not too lean, chilled

1 medium onion, finely diced

2 cloves of garlic, finely diced

1 teaspoon dried oregano

50g Parmesan, grated (optional)

1 teaspoon tomato purée

1 x 400g tin chopped tomatoes

1 x 400g tin plum tomatoes

½ teaspoon sugar

50ml white wine or vermouth

50ml water

salt and pepper

Remove the crusts from the bread and then soak the bread in the milk for about 10 minutes. This works best with stale bread. If using breadcrumbs, soak them too. Make sure you don't use 'golden' breadcrumbs, which are very oily. Either use packaged white ones or make your own from stale bread and freeze until needed.

Squeeze out any excess moisture from the bread and place it into a large bowl together with the chilled minced beef, the chopped onion and garlic, dried oregano, Parmesan, if using, and salt and pepper. Add the tomato purée. Mix well with your hands to combine everything, but don't overmix.

Add the beaten egg half at a time, mixing it all in well with your hands to break down the meat.

Wet your hands slightly and then pinch off small portions of the meat mix and roll into balls about the size of an unshelled walnut. Put each one on a plate as you go. If the meat gets sticky, pop it back in the fridge for 5 minutes and then start rolling again once chilled.

Chill the meatballs for at least 30 minutes before cooking. Set them into the slow cooker in one layer. It doesn't matter if they are touching slightly. Mix the two cans of tomatoes together, breaking the plum tomatoes up slightly. Season well and add the sugar to stop any acidity. Add the wine or vermouth and the water so that the meatballs are submerged.

Put the lid on the slow cooker and cook the meatballs on low for 7-8 hours. The sauce will thicken and all the flavours will combine. Serve warm, but not piping hot, over pasta or gnocchi.

MEATLOAF

A staple way to feed a family inexpensively in America, the humble meatloaf hasn't had its heyday in the UK yet and I just don't know why. It's easy, economical and utterly delicious. Plus, it reminds me of my very first job working in a fifties-style American diner, where it was called 'Meat Loaf Me in St Louis' on the menu and sounded hilarious ordered in a Belfast accent. Serve it here with mashed potatoes and green beans and the Tomato Ketchup on page 188. Puns optional.

SERVES 4–6

350g pork mince, chilled

150g breadcrumbs

1 tablespoon fresh thyme or 1 teaspoon dried

1 teaspoon mustard powder

1 teaspoon Worcestershire sauce

2 medium onions, finely chopped

2 stalks of celery, finely chopped

75g chorizo, finely chopped

1 egg, beaten

3 tablespoons milk

touch of cornflour (optional)

This is so very easy to make. Add the mince, breadcrumbs and the thyme, mustard powder and Worcestershire sauce to the chopped vegetables and chorizo and mix well with your hands. Break the mince up and then add the beaten egg. Keep mixing with your hands, adding the milk a tablespoon at a time until it is smooth.

Pack the meatloaf mix into a lightly oiled loaf tin and cover the top of the mixture with foil to prevent any moisture getting into it. I used two of those foil takeaway containers, one inside the other. They don't have the deep lip of most loaf tins, so fit better in the crock.

Set it into the slow-cooker crock and then pour boiling water halfway up the side of the loaf tin. Cook the meatloaf on high for 5–6 hours or 7–8 hours on low.

Carefully lift out the meatloaf in its tin when you are ready. There will be quite a lot of gravy in the tin, which you don't want to spill. Pour it off and thicken with a touch of cornflour mixed with cold water if you prefer.

Tip the meatloaf out of its tin and serve in slices. It's best warm rather than piping hot. I am inordinately fond of it cold in a sandwich with lots of ketchup.

SAUSAGE RAGU

Despite sounding like a student kitchen special, this dish is utterly delicious and a really good way to make those premium packets of sausages go further among more people. Inspired by traditional Italian dishes, I strip the skins off the high-meat-content sausages and crumble them into a rich tomatoey sauce, which slow cooks down to become something simply stunning. It works well on pasta or makes the Lasagne on page 27 even more amazing. This is a brilliant way to perk up your sausages…

SERVES 4 WITH LEFTOVERS FOR A SNEAKY BAKED POTATO LUNCH

450g premium sausages or sausage meat

2 teaspoons fennel seeds

4 cloves of garlic, chopped

1 teaspoon sugar

1 x 400g tin chopped tomatoes

100ml red wine (optional)

2 tablespoons balsamic vinegar

4 tablespoons tomato purée

chopped fresh flat-leaf parsley, to serve

salt and pepper

I like to use an Italian-style sausage for this or a rich, garlicky Toulouse-style one, which suit the style of the dish much better than a British banger. These Continental sausages are often on offer in the supermarkets and have a coarser ground meat that works well here.

If you are using sausages, put a nick in each skin and rip it back, pushing the meat out of the casing. Put the sausages into a hot frying pan on the hob and seal on each side on a medium heat for 2–3 minutes in total. If you are using sausage meat, simply put handfuls of it into the pan and do the same.

Put the sealed sausage meat into the slow-cooker crock and then, using the same pan, lightly toast the fennel seeds in the remaining fat from the sausages. After about 60–90 seconds they will smell very aromatic. Remove from the heat immediately and add to the slow-cooker crock.

Add the chopped garlic, salt and pepper and the sugar. Pour the tomatoes, red wine and 1 tablespoon of the vinegar over it all and add the tomato purée. If it all looks too thick, add 200ml water.

Put the lid on the slow cooker and cook the ragu on low for 10–12 hours. The longer the better for this one. You want the tomatoes to reduce down and become almost jammy and thick.

When you are ready to serve, add the remaining tablespoon of balsamic vinegar and stir through. Scatter with chopped parsley if you are using over pasta or a baked potato.

LEMON AND OLIVE MEATBALLS

I adore meatballs and these are based on a perfect version my friend Carolyne once made me for my birthday. Not only do I love eating meatballs, I find the act of making them incredibly relaxing. There's something very satisfying about getting your hands in there, mixing everything through, and then rolling and shaping them so that you end up with a plump plateful in front of you, ready to be devoured.

Two little tips will make your meatballs perfect every time. Firstly, make sure your meat is well chilled before shaping or you'll repeat the meat slush puppie I made the time I skipped this step. Secondly, use breadcrumbs to keep the texture light and make your meat go further. They also hold the shape better when the meatballs are cooked. You may become slightly obsessed with making them like I am, but luckily they freeze well...

SERVES 2-4

1 teaspoon oil

10g butter

1 medium onion, finely diced

2 slices of bread or 80g breadcrumbs (not golden)

75ml milk

500g pork mince, chilled

1 large egg

50g Parmesan, grated (optional)

½ lemon, zested (if waxed, give it a vigorous scrub under the hot tap first) or ¼ Preserved Lemon, chopped (see page 186)

75g black olives, pitted and chopped

200–250ml hot chicken stock

1 lemon, juiced

salt and pepper

Heat the oil and butter in a small pan and sweat the chopped onion in it for about 10 minutes. Allow to cool slightly (or if you have a batch of the Caramelised Onions from page 122, use these instead to skip this step).

Remove the crusts from the bread and then soak the bread in the milk for about 10 minutes. This works best with stale bread. If using breadcrumbs, soak them too. Make sure you don't use 'golden' breadcrumbs, which are very oily. Either use packaged white ones or make your own from stale bread and freeze until needed.

Squeeze out any excess moisture from the bread and place it into a large bowl together with the chilled minced pork, the softened onion, the egg, Parmesan, lemon zest, chopped olives and salt and pepper. Mix well to combine everything, but don't overmix.

Wet your hands slightly and then pinch off small portions of the meat mix and roll into balls about the size of an unshelled walnut. Put each one on a plate as you go. If the meat gets sticky, pop it back in the fridge for 5 minutes and then start rolling again.

Chill the meatballs for at least 30 minutes before cooking. I usually drop them into the slow cooker straight from the fridge, half cover with chicken stock and cook them on low for 6-7 hours.

Drizzle the lemon juice over the meatballs before serving to lift them from 'good' to Carolyne's 'queen of the meatballs' territory. Serve them with flatbreads or pasta.

SAUERKRAUT-SMOTHERED PORK CHOPS

People do tend to snigger about sauerkraut in the UK, associating it with jokes about the Germans. I can only assume they have never actually eaten sauerkraut because it's not to be joked about. It's to be devoured with indecent haste, in fact. It's tangy and salty and crunchy and utterly moreish and it loves being slow cooked.

You can buy large jars of it for next to nothing in the Polish section of any large supermarket these days and it's great value. Try it on top of hot dogs and the Caramelised Onions on page 122 as well as smothering it on these pork chops to tenderise the meat and add masses of flavour to the dish.

Not only is this a one-pot meal, it's practically a one-line recipe in its simplicity.

SERVES 4

2 onions, sliced

1 parsnip, cut into chunks

1 cooking apple, cored and cut into chunks

150ml water

4 spare rib chops

200g sauerkraut

salt and pepper

Layer the onion, parsnip and apple on the base of the slow-cooker crock and add the water. Season the pork chops, bearing in mind sauerkraut is quite salty, and place them on top of the fruit and vegetables.

Cover the chops with the sauerkraut, making sure the meat is completely covered, and then put the lid on the slow cooker. Cook it all on low for 8–9 hours.

The onion and apple and parsnip will make a sweetly delicious almost-gravy and the pork will be the most tender chops you have ever tasted. I serve the meal just as it is and it's best on a cold winter night.

CHOUCROUTE GARNIE

The older I get, the more I realise I am a Northern European through and through. My heart lies with the solid animal fats, like duck or goose and butter, rather than the olive oil of the Mediterranean. I love sturdy food like sausages and I've never met a cabbage I didn't like. I particularly love sauerkraut (or the French *choucroute*) and this dish is all about its savoury, salty charms. Studded with sausages and soft pork belly, it's the perfect porky one-pot meal.

Take advantage of the growing Polish grocery sections in the supermarket or take this as your cue to venture to your local Polski Sklep, or Polish shop, for the first time. You'll be goggle eyed at the selection of cured and smoked sausages.

Despite what it seems from the long recipe list, this is a very simple dish to make. Do try to use the sausages specified. The kabanos are small, thin, dried sausages and the kielbasa is a large, soft smoked sausage, almost like a large frankfurter. If you can't get either, use some bacon or ham and some frankfurters instead. As long as the dish involves lots of pork with your cabbage, it's still authentic.

SERVES 6 GENEROUSLY OR 4 WITH LEFTOVERS

600g sauerkraut

400g potatoes

1 large onion, diced

2 bay leaves

4 allspice berries

2 whole cloves

1 teaspoon caraway seeds

1 teaspoon juniper berries (optional)

200g pork belly

2 kabanos sausages

4 frankfurters or 100g smoked kielbasa sausage

250ml water

100ml vermouth

salt and pepper

Remove your sauerkraut from the jar, rinse lightly and leave to drain while you peel the potatoes and chop them into 3cm cubes. Put half the potatoes and the onion into the crock and add about half the sauerkraut. Tuck 1 bay leaf in along with 2 allspice berries and 1 clove. Scatter over half the caraway seeds and juniper berries.

Your pork belly will probably come as two slices. Cut each slice into four pieces and put half of them into the crock with 1 chopped kabanos. Chop the frankfurters or kielbasa into 1cm-thick slices and add half. Season well, bearing in mind that the meat and sauerkraut can be quite salty.

Cover it all with the remaining sauerkraut, onion and potato. Add the other half of the herbs and spices. Put the rest of the meat on top and pour the water and vermouth over it. Choucroute garnie usually uses sweet white wine, so add some if you have any instead of the vermouth. Season with more black pepper.

Put the lid on the slow cooker and cook it all on low for 8–9 hours. The sauerkraut will soften and the pork belly will become super tender, while the water creates a lovely porky broth.

Serve on plates with a dollop of mustard on the side and maybe a beer to add true Northern European charm.

APPLE AND GINGER POACHED HAM

Most people only seem to eat this kind of poached ham joint at Christmas, getting their piggy fix at lunch throughout the year with sliced versions from packets or the deli counter. I find that kind of sliced ham incredibly expensive for what you get (which is often extra water) and so I do ham or gammon joints all year round.

Poaching the ham in the slow cooker keeps it succulent and tender and easy to slice. Excellent in a sandwich or salad or as part of a meal, you get a lot more oink for your money. It's delicious simply poached with vegetables, like with the Pease Pudding on page 99, but I like to add a little sweet and spice with this apple and ginger version.

SERVES 4–6

6cm piece of fresh ginger

3 allspice berries

1 teaspoon black peppercorns

1 teaspoon ground ginger

1 bacon, ham or gammon joint, approximately 750g

500ml apple juice

500ml water

This is the simplest dish to make. Peel and grate the ginger, reserving any juice from it when you do. Put it in the slow-cooker crock with the allspice and black peppercorns.

Rub the ground ginger on the meat and place it on top of the ginger and allspice. Pour in the apple juice and just enough water to cover the meat. Put the lid on the slow cooker and poach on low for 3–4 hours.

Lift the meat out of the slow cooker carefully and eat either hot or cold. I don't find that bacon or gammon joints are salty enough to need soaking before cooking, but they are salty enough not to need any extra seasoning from me.

The ham will last safely for up 3 days in the fridge if you have more willpower than me and don't just eat ham sandwiches for every single meal after you've cooked this.

SWEET-AND-SOUR PINEAPPLE PORK

Growing up in Northern Ireland, sweet-and-sour pork was something that was usually deep-fried and served dipped into a sauce more orange than many people's politics. It wasn't until I moved to Brighton as a student that I realised there were further variations on the theme. My flatmate Carrie made a mean sweet-and-sour pork from scratch and we often ate it for dinner together after a long day in the library. I wish we'd had a slow cooker then. It would have saved a lot of sprinting across a large campus!

SERVES 4

450g pork loin steaks
  or pork shoulder
  steaks

1 x 227g tin pineapple
  chunks, juice
  reserved

2 tablespoons clear
  honey

2 tablespoons tomato
  purée

3 tablespoons
  tamarind syrup
  (see page 166)

3 tablespoons sweet
  chilli sauce

1 teaspoon soy sauce

1 onion, diced

1 carrot, diced

1 yellow or orange
  pepper, diced

100ml water

salt and pepper

Cut the pork steaks into quarters and set them into the slow-cooker crock. Drain the pineapple chunks and put the juice into a bowl. Add the pineapple to the pork.

Mix the honey, tomato purée, tamarind syrup and sweet chilli sauce in with the pineapple juice and the soy sauce to make a lovely glossy orange sauce. Pour this all over the meat and season well.

Add in the chopped vegetables and up to 100ml of water if the pork steaks are less than two-thirds covered in sauce. Don't add more as you want the sauce to be quite thick. Put the lid on the slow cooker and cook the pork on low for 8 hours.

The enzymes in the pineapple along with the long slow cooking help make the meat incredibly tender as well as adding the sweetness needed. All this dish needs to make people very happy is a big dish of steamed rice on the side and no essay deadline looming.

SOY-BRAISED PIGS' CHEEKS

I love pigs' cheeks because they are delicious, inexpensive and comic-sounding. But my soft spot for them comes from them being the thing that took my slow cooker from something I used to something I really love. Since my first batch of pigs' cheeks, the slow cooker hasn't been put in the cupboard once.

You might not get the cheeks in every supermarket so, if you see them, snap them up and freeze them if you can. I think freezing them helps tenderise the meat even more. Plus you'll want to make this again and again. And then again.

SERVES 2
COMFORTABLY

350g pigs' cheeks, cut into thirds

2 onions, cut into eighths

4 cloves of garlic, finely chopped

1 teaspoon brown sugar

3 tablespoons soy sauce

½ teaspoon gravy browning

150ml water

pepper

Arrange your meat, onion and garlic evenly in the crock. Try to get the onion pieces to sit side by side with the meat like they're sitting on the London Underground and don't dare make eye contact. This allows you to use less water and intensify the soy sauce flavour.

Sprinkle the sugar and pepper over them. Put the soy sauce, gravy browning and water in a jug and pour gently over the meat and onion. I use whatever soy I have in the cupboard, usually whatever was best value in the Chinese supermarket, so any version will work.

Cook on low for 6–7 hours. The cheeks become very tender, but hold their shape more than most meat does in the slow cooker, so you might be tempted to leave them longer. Don't worry if you do, you really can't overcook these lovely nuggets of meat.

Serve with brown rice and wilted greens for a simple, but stunning meal.

STEAMED PORK BELLY

Ever wondered how Chinese restaurants get their pork belly to taste so rich, but yet be so light at the same time? I knew vaguely that they steamed it and pressed it and all kinds of things that sounded like they would keep me over a hot stove for a long time. Then I got the slow cooker and thought that would help.

Slightly worryingly, it made it so simple and straightforward to make this bowl of steamed pork belly that I'm tempted to make it every single time I see a bit of belly pork at the butcher's, meaning that my diet could be about 50 per cent pig. It's one of the best things I've ever cooked and it's well worth the small preparation stage.

SERVES 4, BUT WITH FIGHTING OVER THE LAST SLICE...

500g boneless pork belly in one piece

2 cloves of garlic, thinly sliced

2 teaspoons Thai fish sauce

2 teaspoons dark soy sauce

You'll need to start the pork belly the night before you want to eat it. Try and get a piece that is all one section. It should be boneless. Bring a pot of water to the boil and put the pork belly into it. Boil for about 5 minutes. This tenderises the pork. Take it off the heat and out of the water, leaving the water in the pan.

Put the pork belly skin side down in a frying pan over a medium heat. This crisps the skin while rendering the fat so the skin isn't greasy. Cook the skin for about 5 minutes until golden and blistered. It may spatter, so it might need to be covered to protect your cooker.

Remove the pork belly from the frying pan and return it to the pan of water you cooked it in to start with. Leave it to soak for about 15 minutes before putting it in the fridge overnight. I put mine on a plate with a heavy weight on top to flatten it out again as it curls a bit during the cooking.

Next day, remove the pork from the fridge and cut into slices about the thickness of a pound coin. Layer these slices into a 1lb disposable foil loaf tin with the skin on the base of the tin.

Scatter the sliced garlic, Thai fish sauce and soy sauce over the top of the sliced pork and then cover the top of the loaf tin with some foil. Place the covered loaf tin into the slow-cooker crock and pour boiling water into the crock so it comes about halfway up the side of the loaf tin.

Put the lid on the slow cooker and steam the pork on high for 6 hours or low for 8–9 hours. Carefully remove the loaf tin and unwrap the foil. Your pork will now be meltingly tender slivers of soft, juicy meat.

Serve the pork with steamed rice and leafy greens, such as cabbage, pak choi or spinach, all drizzled with the amazing porky soy juice from the meat that is packed with flavour.

STICKY PORK BELLY

Pork belly has become much easier to get in supermarkets and butchers over the last few years. Slow cooking turns it into something amazing, rendering its natural fat content down to make it smooth, silky soft and very flavoursome. The Chinese have been working wonders with this cut of meat for centuries and I've taken inspiration here from our family friend Tony who is a dab hand at the Chinese style of lacquering meat to make it sticky and yet tender at the same time. This is well worth the slight effort.

Chinese five-spice powder has the distinctive taste of star anise, fennel seeds, Sichuan pepper, cinnamon and cloves for a warming, spicy flavour. It is available ready ground from many supermarkets, but if you can't get it, simply use equal amounts of star anise, fennel, cloves and cinnamon with a pinch of chilli flakes and make your own powder.

SERVES 4 WITH LARGE APPETITES

600g pork belly

3 tablespoons clear honey

2 tablespoons Thai fish sauce

2 tablespoons Chinese five-spice powder

1 tablespoon soy sauce

1 tablespoon sweet chilli sauce

It's best to have your pork belly in slices for this dish and I prefer mine without the ribs in as it makes it easier to eat. Start preparing the pork belly by blanching it in a pan of boiling water for about 60–90 seconds. This helps break down the fat and makes the meat more tender. Place the blanched meat into the slow-cooker crock and allow it to cool down slightly.

Mix the honey, Thai fish sauce, five-spice, soy and sweet chilli sauces together until they form a thick paste. Pour it all over the pork belly slices and toss them well so that the sticky paste coats the slices evenly on each side. Marinate the pork overnight if you can for maximum flavour.

Put the lid on the slow cooker and cook the pork belly on low for 7–8 hours. The pork will become super soft and the slices will look like they are collapsing and losing their shape as the fat has mingled with the marinade to make a sticky glaze.

Carefully lift the pork out and shred it with two forks. Serve with boiled rice and some wilted greens.

APPLE-GLAZED RIBS

Pork ribs are a really underrated cut of meat and often available very cheaply. They are a great crowd pleaser, especially if you are feeding small children for whom it is more socially acceptable to have a sticky face and hands. These glazed ribs are easier than getting the barbecue out (especially if, like me, you can't even get a firelighter started) so you can serve them all year round.

I've used the Apple Butter from page 197 here with all its sweet and spiced charms, but you could substitute the same amount of stewed apple or apple sauce with an extra tablespoon of honey if you don't have any left.

SERVES 4 AS A MAIN MEAL OR 6 AS A STARTER

75ml Apple Butter (see page 197)

1 tablespoon honey

1 teaspoon Worcestershire sauce

1 teaspoon smoked paprika

1 teaspoon Chinese five-spice powder

1kg pork ribs, cut individually

salt and pepper

Mix the apple butter, honey, Worcestershire sauce and spices together in a large bowl. Season the ribs well and then toss them in the apple glaze so they are well coated.

Tip directly into the slow-cooker crock and cook the ribs on low for 7–8 hours. The bits touching the edge of the crock will become crispy and the glaze coats them beautifully. The meat will be so tender it will drop off the bone with no effort. The only challenge is making sure you have quite enough kitchen roll handy...

DUBLIN CODDLE

This dish is so closely associated with the fair city of Dublin, I'm sure it's mentioned in the works of James Joyce, but unfortunately I've never got further than page 116 of *Ulysses* on my repeated attempts to tackle it. I have, however, eaten and enjoyed coddle on many occasions because what could better than a steaming bowl of sausages, bacon and onions? It has restorative powers if you've had a few pints of the black stuff the night before too…

Controversy rages, apparently, as to whether one browns the sausages for coddle or simply simmers them as they are. Personally, while I like my own pale Irish complexion, I don't care for it in a sausage. They look and taste better for me when they have a little colour about them. However, I don't fry the bacon as it creates a better stock left as it is.

SERVES 4–6 WITH
CABBAGE AND
CRUSTY BREAD
ON THE SIDE

4–6 sausages

150g bacon, cubed

500g potatoes

2 onions, sliced

1 carrot, cubed

3 sprigs of fresh thyme

600ml water

**chopped fresh parsley,
  to serve**

salt and pepper

Seal the sausages in a hot pan on the hob. You don't need to cook them, just add some nice caramelised go-faster stripes to each side. Add them to the slow-cooker crock along with the bacon. I use thick cubes of bacon-like lardons or pancetta if I can.

Peel the potatoes and cut into small 3cm cubes. Add to the slow cooker along with the onion and carrot (carrot isn't traditional in coddle, but I like the splash of colour). Scatter in the fresh thyme and season well.

Pour the water over it all, put the lid on the slow cooker and cook the coddle on low for 7–8 hours. Sprinkle it with some fresh parsley when cooked and serve with heaps of steamed cabbage and some bread to soak up the lovely bacon-rich stock.

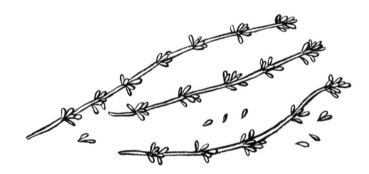

A KIND OF CASSOULET

One of France's most famous dishes, cassoulet is all about the pig and the pulses combined with garlic and tomatoes and then crowned with their beloved confit duck. Made on the stove, it's a long and complicated thing, but with a slow cooker, it's très facile. After all, if you've already made the Confit Duck on page 56, so all you're doing is throwing some beans, sausages and pork belly together in the morning and leaving it to stew in its own juices until dinner time. You won't believe something this good can be this simple.

If you don't have any confit duck, don't worry. You could pop another sausage or two in there instead. However, you do need to use a really good garlicky Toulouse sausage here with lovely coarse ground meat and plenty of herbs. I particularly like the ones from the orange-branded supermarket, which are frequently on offer and are so garlicky they need to be double bagged to protect other passengers when you bring them home on the bus. I make them go further by skinning them and crumbling them into the beans.

SERVES 4–6
(IN THE MANNER
IN WHICH ONE
EATS WHILE ON
HOLIDAY)

6 Toulouse sausages

200g dried haricot
  beans

1 onion, diced

1 carrot, diced

4 cloves of garlic

2 bay leaves

100g smoked bacon or
  pancetta, cubed

250g pork belly, cubed

1 x 400g tin plum
  tomatoes

2 Confit Duck legs
  (see page 56)

500ml water

1 tablespoon duck fat

200g breadcrumbs

salt and pepper

Slit the sausages and squeeze the meat out into the slow-cooker crock. Add the beans, onion, carrot, garlic cubes and bay leaves. Tuck the bacon and pork belly into it all, placing them evenly. Season well.

Break the plum tomatoes up a bit with your hands and dollop them over it all. Nestle the duck legs into the whole thing and carefully pour the water over everything. The beans and the pork belly should be completely submerged, but it's fine if the duck is above the water.

Put the lid on the slow cooker and cook the cassoulet on low for 8–9 hours until the beans are plump. Put the duck fat in a frying pan on the hob over a medium heat and fry the breadcrumbs until golden and crisp. Scatter half of them over the cassoulet about 30 minutes before you are ready to eat. Stir them in. Replace the lid and allow them to soak up some of the sauce.

Serve the cassoulet in bowls, sharing the duck legs among you when the meat simply slides off the bone after its second slow cooking. Sprinkle the remaining breadcrumbs over the top for some crunch. Eat the cassoulet with some green salad on the side, preferably with some bitter leaves or chicory in it.

FEIJOADA

Feijoada is a Portuguese-Brazilian dish that combines pork, pulses and my beloved black pudding and it was introduced to me by my brother Mister North. Traditionally designed to use the knobbly, bobbly bits of the pig and add flavour to cheaper pulses, feijoada is a wholesome hearty dish that is a must for anyone who loves pork. It's rich and delicious and, best of all, easy to make.

I've suggested cuts of meat that are easy to get but Feijoada can also be made with salt pork if you have it. Pigs' ears, snouts or tails add flavour if you can get them and make use of bits we often throw away now.

As you can see from the ingredients list, this is a pretty epic dish. It's not difficult to make, but it does have a few steps so it's one for when you're around the house at a weekend rather than going out to work all day. It will all fit in a 3.5-litre slow cooker, but it's easier in a 6.5-litre one.

SERVES 4 WITH LEFTOVERS OR 6 WITH BIG APPETITES

2 pigs' trotters

½ teaspoon sea salt

1 litre mineral water

2 red onions, diced

4 cloves of garlic, diced

200g dried black beans (f you can't get these, use tinned kidney beans)

5 spring onions, sliced

½ bunch of fresh coriander

75g chorizo, chopped into 2cm chunks

200g black pudding

200g beef brisket, cubed

250g pork belly, in slices

100g bacon or pancetta

1 bay leaf

60ml vermouth

salt and pepper

Start by scrubbing the pigs' trotters and putting them into a pan of cold water on the hob. Bring them to the boil and cook for 10 minutes over a medium heat to remove any impurities. Drain them and rinse any froth off them. Put them into the slow cooker. Add the sea salt and about 500ml of the mineral water. Put the lid on and simmer the trotters for 4–6 hours to create a glossy, fatty stock. Remove the now soft trotters from the stock and pour the stock into a bowl. Reserve any meat from the trotters and discard the skin and sinew.

Add the onion and garlic to the slow cooker with the dried black beans. Lay the beans out like a carpet on the base of the crock.

Add the spring onion and the chopped stalks of the fresh coriander and scatter over the beans. Add the chorizo to the crock. Skin the black pudding and crumble over the beans. Set the cubed brisket and pork belly on top of it and scatter with the bacon or pancetta.

Pour the reserved pork stock over it all and add enough of the remaining mineral water to make sure the meat is at least half covered. You may not need it all. It's important to use mineral water as black beans refuse to cook if there is any limescale in the water at all. Add the bay leaf and the vermouth.

Put the lid on the slow cooker and cook the feijoada on low for 8–9 hours. About an hour before you are ready to serve, lift the pork belly and brisket out with a slotted spoon and reserve. Take a heaped cupful of beans out and purée them with a blender or a potato masher and stir back through the rest of the beans to thicken them up. The black pudding should have melted into the beans to create a thick, dark gravy and the puréed beans enhance that.

Add the meat back in and cook it all for another hour or two. You can't really overcook this dish. Serve with boiled rice and wilted greens and a splash or two of hot sauce to cut through the richness of the dish. Any leftovers keep and reheat well and the flavours intensify beautifully. Scatter with fresh coriander leaves before eating for flavour and colour.

PORK IN MILK

This is, admittedly, a rather underwhelming name for a really outstanding dish. A pork shoulder bathed in full-fat milk, lemon and garlic, it makes the most tender meat you can imagine. I was first introduced to this by my friend Jeanie one Christmas and it is one of the best things I've ever eaten. It was among the first recipes I adapted to the slow cooker. Quite difficult and time consuming to cook on the hob without burning the milk, it works perfectly here.

You'll end up with lots of lovely tasty gravy here, probably more than you can eat with the pork, but it freezes beautifully once thickened up. It is important you use Caramelised Onions in the dish (from page 122) as raw ones will curdle the milk.

SERVES 2-4 WITH
LEFTOVERS

1kg piece of pork
    shoulder or hand of
    pork
½ teaspoon mustard
    powder
½ bulb of garlic, cloves
    peeled but whole
150g Caramelised
    Onions (see page 122)
6 sprigs of fresh thyme
    or 1 heaped teaspoon
    dried thyme
2 pieces of lemon peel
900ml full-fat milk
1 bay leaf
2 tablespoons
    cornflour
2 tablespoons cold
    water
salt and pepper

Season the pork with the salt and pepper and mustard powder. Put it directly on the meat if you are using the shoulder of pork and onto the skin if using a hand of pork.

Put the peeled whole garlic and the caramelised onions into the slow-cooker crock to make a bed for the pork. Put half the thyme here and 1 piece of lemon peel. Place the pork on top of it all.

Pour the milk over the pork slowly so the seasonings don't wash off completely. You want the meat to be almost fully covered, so don't be surprised if you need slightly more or less milk than stated due to the shape of the meat used. Float the bay leaf and second piece of the lemon peel in the milk.

Cook the pork on low for 8–10 hours. The combination of the slow cooking and the lactic acid in the milk make the pork unbelievably tender. I turned mine halfway through the cooking to cover the meat totally as a little bit was poking out, but this was more fussiness on my part.

When the pork is cooked, gently lift it out of the milk. It will be meltingly tender and probably likely to fall apart if you aren't careful. Remove the skin if you are using the hand of pork. Set on a plate to serve and allow to rest while you make the gravy.

Pour the cooked milk mixture through a sieve into a saucepan, leaving the aromatics behind. Lift the onions and a couple of the cloves of garlic out of the sieve and add to the milk. Heat it all gently.

Mix the cornflour and water together and stir it into the milk mixture. Keep stirring as it all thickens into a glossy, smooth gravy. Serve on the side of the sliced pork. I love this dish with sautéed rosemary potatoes and a green salad. It also makes lovely cold cuts.

PORK SHANK

A pork shank is a really inexpensive cut of meat that takes beautifully to slow cooking. I like to go a little bit Gallic with mine and cook it with garlicky lentils for a really easy meal that is equally good in summer or winter. I keep the bones from the shanks and use them to add to the stock when making Pho on page 152, making this frugal piece of meat go even further.

You may not find this cut in every supermarket. I tend to get mine at the one where they do all the butchery themselves at the counter and then wrap them in little blue trays. Do use the Puy lentils if you can. A little more expensive than green lentils, they hold their shape without becoming mushy in the slow cooker.

SERVES 2 WITH
LEFTOVERS OR
4 WITHOUT

2 onions, finely diced

4 cloves of garlic,
    finely diced

200g Puy lentils
    (uncooked weight)

1 teaspoon dried
    oregano

300ml hot chicken
    stock

100ml boiling water,
    if necessary

1 pork shank,
    approximately 1kg

salt and pepper

Add your onion and garlic to the slow cooker along with the lentils and oregano. Pour the hot chicken stock over them all and add up to 100ml boiling water if the lentils aren't fully covered.

Season the skin of the pork shank well with salt and pepper and place the shank on top of the lentils. The bottom of it will be covered.

Put the lid on the slow cooker and cook the whole thing on low for 8 hours. By the end the meat will be falling away from the bone and the lentils will be winking at you like little green jewels.

Remove the skin from the shank and serve the juicy meat with a generous spoonful of the lentils in deep bowls, along with any of the velvety soft sauce the lentils have made.

PULLED PORK

Few things work better in a slow cooker than pulled pork. At its most basic, it is a hunk of pork slow cooked until the strands of the meat can be pulled apart with two forks. It's also a fantastic way to make a joint of meat go a long way by adding masses of flavour and creating amazing leftovers.

Flavour combinations depend on your imagination. I've done various versions: glazed with orange, rubbed with cumin and coriander or basted with barbecue flavours, but this slightly Italian-inspired one my mum makes is my favourite. Mainly because it tastes sensational, but partly because it also makes a great pizza topping…

SERVES 6 WITH PHENOMENAL LEFTOVERS

200g Caramelised Onions (see page 122)

4 cloves of garlic

4 tablespoons tomato purée

2 tablespoons water

1.5kg pork shoulder

½ bunch of fresh parsley, chopped

1 x 400g tin chopped tomatoes

1 star anise

salt and pepper

If you don't have any caramelised onions, simply substitute them for 2 sliced raw onions. Either way, put the onions and the garlic cloves on the base of the slow-cooker crock to impart flavour to the meat.

Mix the tomato purée with the water to form a thick paste. Rub this over the pork. Season well. Place in the slow cooker on top of the onions and garlic. Scatter with chopped parsley and add the chopped tomatoes. Pop in the star anise.

Cook on low for 8–10 hours with the lid on. The meat will be falling apart with tenderness so when you lift it out of the crock, you'll have to be very gentle. Set on a plate until needed. You'll have a lot of sauce left behind as the juices from the meat will have combined with the tomatoes.

Pour this into a saucepan and reduce over a medium heat until it is about half the volume it was. Taste and season again if needed. Remove the star anise.

Shred the pork with two forks until you have soft tendrils of tender meat. Combine with the tomato-rich sauce and you are ready to serve. The only issue is what serving choice to make as it's one of the most versatile dishes I know!

I've served this over linguine for a hearty pasta dish, on mini soda-bread pizza bases with a scattering of mozzarella and some chilli flakes, or added to small wraps with shredded cabbage and fresh coriander to make tacos.

I've also made quesadillas by putting some grated cheese on top of my taco, adding a second wrap to make a sandwich and then dry-frying for about 2 minutes each side in a pan. I've combined the pork with leftover rice to make a stuffing for tomatoes and added it to the creamy Cuban-Style Black Beans on page 88. I've even eaten it straight from the fridge as I was passing.

DR PEPPER® PORK

When she lived in London, my friend Sara told me about proper Kansas City-barbecue style, the great perk of growing up between St Louis and Kansas City. We hunted for something similar in London but failed to find the authentic mix of molasses and tomato. Sara moved home soon after, although I'm not sure the two things were connected.

I've attempted making proper barbecue pork outside over wood smoke a couple of times, but it's just so time consuming I've given up on that and turned my attention to using the slow cooker instead and I'm very pleased with the results. I think I can probably lure Sara back when she sees this recipe.

SERVES 6 WITH LEFTOVERS

2 tablespoons black treacle or pomegranate molasses

1 tablespoon tomato purée

1 tablespoon Dijon mustard

1 tablespoon clear honey

1 teaspoon smoked paprika

½ teaspoon ground allspice

¼ teaspoon ground cloves

¼ teaspoon ground mace

¼ teaspoon sea salt

¼ teaspoon white pepper

1.5kg piece of pork shoulder or leg

3 onions, sliced into quite thick half moons

250ml Dr Pepper® (not diet)

2 tablespoons tomato ketchup

This is so simple to make. Make a marinade by combining the treacle, tomato purée, mustard, honey and the ground spices, salt and pepper together and rub it all over the pork.

Make a carpet of the onion over the base of the slow-cooker crock. Set the pork on top of it and then pour the Dr Pepper into the crock without washing the rub off the pork.

Put the lid on the slow cooker and cook the pork on low for 9–10 hours. Carefully lift the pork out and set on a plate. Allow to cool slightly while you make the sauce.

Purée the onions into the sauce with a hand blender and add the ketchup (for homemade ketchup, see page 188), stirring it all through so it is smooth and thick. Taste it to see if it needs more seasoning. Add it as needed. You will have about 600ml sauce.

Using two forks, pull sections of the pork away from the main piece of meat and then use the forks to fluff up the meat so it becomes small strands of pork. This is a way to show how tender the meat is and to make the meat go further as it makes a small portion look huge.

Add enough sauce to the pulled pork to keep it moist and tasty. Serve in rolls with some crunchy coleslaw for a traditional Midwest feel. The pork will keep well in the fridge for up to 5 days and is endlessly versatile.

MOROCCAN LAMB BREAST

I love lamb. It was a favourite of my dad's when we were kids and as a result we often had it at special family meals, so I associate it with good times. You're probably thinking it can be quite an expensive meat on a budget, but this is where lamb breast comes in. It's very good value, but can be greasy if not cooked carefully.

The slow cooker is perfect for doing it well, allowing it to stay tender, but not to cook in its own fat. Served as a rolled joint, it makes a lovely Sunday lunch. Don't forget to make your own good times!

SERVES 4

2 teaspoons smoked paprika

1 teaspoon ground ginger

½ teaspoon ground cinnamon

¼ teaspoon ground mace

¼ teaspoon ground cloves

¼ teaspoon sea salt

¼ teaspoon black pepper

1 tablespoon vegetable oil

1 rolled lamb breast joint, approximately 750g-1kg

2 onions, quartered

1 carrot, cut in batons

½ swede, cut in chunks

150ml water

Mix all the spices together along with the salt and pepper and combine with the oil to form a loose paste. Rub this all over the lamb breast joint. Marinate in the fridge overnight.

When you are ready to cook, place the lamb, skin side down, in a cold frying pan and set over a medium heat. This renders off any excess fat. Seal the lamb on each side for about one and a half minutes, or until browned. Remove from the heat and set aside.

Make a carpet of the vegetables on the base of the slow-cooker crock as you are going to use them as a vegetable trivet that you set the meat on. This will allow the meat to steam and roast without it being too fatty. Place the sealed lamb on the vegetables.

Add the water to the vegetables and put the lid on the slow cooker. Cook the lamb on low for 7–8 hours. The lamb will shrink slightly as the fat renders out into the vegetables and a lot of liquid will gather in the slow-cooker crock.

When the lamb is cooked, it will look soft and tender. Take it out of the crock and set aside to rest for 5–10 minutes. Using a hand blender, purée the vegetables in the slow-cooker crock into a thick glossy sauce.

Serve this sweet, spiced onion sauce with the sliced lamb. It makes a lovely variation on a roast dinner.

GARLIC, ANCHOVY AND MINT LAMB SHOULDER

This is probably the first ever dish I associated with a slow cooker. Years ago when I had not long moved to London, my boss at the time used to make it when we worked on a Sunday. She would rub the lamb with mint sauce, adding garlic and anchovy and popping it all in her slow cooker. I was rewarded for a day's work with commission and an invite to pop round the corner to her house to join her family for dinner.

The vinegar in the mint sauce marinates the meat as it slow cooks, making this the most tender lamb you'll ever try. The only difficult bit for you is getting it out of the crock as it tends to just fall apart as you lift it. The tricky bit for me was watching her eat the leftovers in a roll on a Monday lunchtime and trying not to go green with envy.

A 1kg piece of lamb shoulder will fit nicely into a 3.5-litre slow cooker and will probably be sold in a supermarket as a half shoulder. A larger whole shoulder will fit snugly into a 6.5-litre slow cooker and will, of course, serve more people. Simply double the amount of garlic, anchovy and mint sauce.

SERVES 4–6 WITH LEFTOVERS

1kg piece of lamb shoulder

4 anchovies, each cut into thirds

6 cloves of garlic, halved

150ml mint sauce

salt and pepper

Prepare your meat by taking a small, sharp knife and poking small slits into it, each about 2–3cm deep. You'll need about twelve of them. Wrap your anchovy pieces around the garlic. Stuff each one into the slits in the meat so they are obscured.

Rub the mint sauce all over the surface of the meat and place the lamb into the slow-cooker crock. Season well with salt and pepper. The anchovies are salty, but their flavour mellows into the meat to become neither salty nor fishy, but just incredibly savoury.

Put the lid on the slow cooker and cook the lamb on low for 8–9 hours. The meat will be transformed into something truly amazing. Serve with roast potatoes and green beans with mint sauce on the side.

LANCASHIRE HOTPOT

This is the dish that Mister North most enjoys making in his slow cooker. He lived in Lancashire for many years before venturing just across the Pennines to West Yorkshire, but his heart still lies with a dish that allows for more black pudding in his life. (He is a bona fide black pud obsessive, having even made his own!)

If you can get mutton for this dish, then do use it. Halal butchers often sell it and the older, more flavoursome meat works beautifully in the hotpot. If not, some lamb does the trick nicely.

SERVES 4 WITH LEFTOVERS

500g lamb or mutton shoulder, cut into 5cm cubes

1 tablespoon plain flour

500g potatoes

50g butter, melted

200g black pudding

1 large onion, diced

2 carrots, diced

1 bay leaf

2 teaspoons Worcestershire sauce

250ml water

salt and pepper

Coat your meat with the flour mixed with some salt and pepper. Set aside while you slice your potatoes as thinly as possible. If you have a mandolin, life will be easier. If not, use a knife to make them just a few millimetres thick.

Brush the bottom and the edges of the slow-cooker crock with about half the butter and then layer some potatoes into the base. I usually do two layers here and then I put in half the skinned and crumbled black pudding with some of the onion.

Add another layer or two of spuds and then half the lamb and carrots. Repeat another layer of potatoes, then the rest of black pudding and onion. Next up is more potato and then the remaining lamb and carrots. Add the bay leaf. Finish off with a final layer of potatoes.

Mix the Worcestershire sauce with the water and pour it all over the hotpot. Brush the top layer of potatoes with the remaining butter and put the lid on the slow cooker. Cook the hotpot on low for 8–9 hours.

The potatoes on the bottom will crisp up and caramelise, while the lamb steams and the black pudding melts it all together, making each layer extraordinarily good. Serve with red cabbage and a healthy appetite.

IRISH STEW

I grew up on Irish stew and I love it, but few other dishes have been so maligned and thus reinterpreted by people as this simple stew. Traditionally served more like a soup thickened with the potatoes than the casserole-type stew we think of now, people expect a rich gravy. I like mine served in deep bowls with lots of the lovely stock being poured over the top and supped with a spoon. Usually the stew pot was covered with greaseproof paper under the lid to stop the stock evaporating, but the slow cooker doesn't need that with its tendency to make food a bit more watery than the oven. This dish takes the potential flaw of the slow cooker and serves it up as a real warming treat.

The Marmite may not be traditional here, but as we're using lamb rather than the more mature hogget or mutton that's had time to develop more flavour, it gives a lovely oomph. You need lamb on the bone for this dish to create the stock. Lamb neck is perfect, but there isn't a huge amount of meat on it. I buy a small amount of neck and then bulk it out with frozen lamb chops.

SERVES 2 WITH
HEAPS OF
LEFTOVERS OR 4
HUNGRY PEOPLE

500g lamb chops or
 lamb neck

1 large onion, sliced
 into half moons

2 carrots, chopped
 small

500g potatoes,
 chopped into
 2cm cubes

3 sprigs of fresh thyme

1 teaspoon Marmite

750ml water

chopped fresh parsley,
 to serve

salt and pepper

Layer about half the lamb chops into the bottom of the slow cooker, cutting them in half if needs be so that they cover the crock evenly. Season the meat with salt and pepper. Lay half the chopped onion, carrot and potato on top. Add the thyme. Season again.

Put the rest of the lamb on top in another layer and season once more. Spread the Marmite over the meat and add the remaining potato, onion and carrot. Season a bit more. This dish needs serious seasoning to stop it being flat in flavour.

Pour the water over it all and put the lid on the slow cooker. Cook the stew on high for 7–8 hours. The lamb will become meltingly tender in the rich bone broth and the potatoes will start to collapse round the edges.

Stir it all up and allow the potatoes to break up slightly so that they thicken the stock into something more like gravy. Serve in deep bowls and scatter with chopped parsley. Slurp up the broth with a spoon among friends.

POULTRY

The first thing I really got to grips with cooking in the slow cooker was a whole chicken and it remains a firm favourite of mine. Chicken, turkey and duck all work brilliantly in the slow cooker, especially if you cook the meat on the bone. Cuts like chicken breast don't handle the long cooking well, becoming woolly and tasteless, so take the chance to try thighs, legs and drumsticks, which are much cheaper anyway.

A whole chicken is a great way to get to know how hot or cold your slow cooker is and how evenly it cooks. Pot roast it very simply and find your slow-cooking feet as you go. You can enjoy the leftovers and make stock from it in the slow cooker, making it even more frugal and easy.

I usually only brown the skin on poultry if I'm planning to eat it, like on a whole roast bird or chicken wings. It's definitely not necessary if you are removing the skin. Less washing up and more time eating!

One thing to bear in mind is that poultry cooks much more quickly than meat in the slow cooker, so if there is any danger of you not being ready to eat it at the end of the cooking time, leave your portions whole rather than cutting them into small chunks to give yourself a bit of wiggle room. Don't add too much liquid either and your poultry will be perfection.

VERMOUTH-BRINED TURKEY

If you want to know how to cook turkey, ask an American. This native bird is practically a religion in the US and they keep them moist by brining the bird before cooking. This simple step involves marinating the turkey in a salt and sugar solution that adds both flavour and moisture by plumping up the meat through osmosis. It's best to do this for about 24 hours and then slow cook the turkey crown or breast for amazingly juicy meat. This is a stress-free Christmas meal and gives you the best leftovers possible.

SERVES 4–6 WITH LEFTOVERS

30g sugar

75g table salt

2 star anise

2 allspice berries

4 whole cloves

1 tablespoon black peppercorns

2 bay leaves

4 sprigs of fresh rosemary

3 litres cold water

250ml vermouth

60ml white wine or cider vinegar

turkey crown or rolled breast joint, up to 3kg

25g butter and a drizzle of oil (optional)

You'll need to start this recipe at least 36 hours before you need it, but don't panic, there's very little actual work involved. The meat needs to brine for 24 hours in a sealed container in a cool place, so make sure any frozen meat is properly defrosted before you start the brining.

Start by making the brine. Add the sugar, salt, spices and fresh herbs to a large pan and pour in the cold water. Bring to the boil so the sugar and salt dissolve and the flavours infuse. Add the vermouth and the vinegar. Turn the heat off and allow the brine to cool down.

Put the turkey into the pan or container you are using and then pour the cooled brine over it. It should be completely submerged. Allow to infuse for up to 24 hours, turning once to make sure it is evenly covered. Remove from the brine after 24 hours and set onto kitchen roll to absorb any excess liquid. You can dispose of the brine at this stage. I often reserve the herbs to use in the cooking.

If you are using a turkey crown, I like to brown the skin before slow cooking it to make it look attractive at the table. Heat the butter and a drizzle of oil in a pan and seal the crown for about 2–3 minutes on all sides. If you are using a rolled breast joint, this isn't necessary as it usually comes in a net to hold the shape, which you can just leave on for ease of handling.

To cook the turkey joint, place in the slow-cooker crock, breast down if using the crown, and add the reserved rosemary and bay leaves. Cook the joint on low for 8–10 hours or 6 hours on high. You will end up with beautifully moist turkey meat and clear, flavoursome juices that make the perfect gravy.

To serve the turkey, remove from the slow cooker, carve and serve with your Christmas dinner trimmings of choice.

CONFIT DUCK

Have you ever wanted to be one of those people who can just effortlessly throw a stylish meal together from the contents of your fridge, rather than trying to identify the ends of things in the vegetable drawer? Here's your chance.

Confit is a style of cooking that uses slow cooking in fat to preserve meat or other ingredients. I've done it with peppers and tomatoes, but its spirit animal is definitely duck. The bird's own fat renders it soft and silky and tender and allows it to be stored in the fridge indefinitely until needed to whip up a fabulous meal like a cassoulet (see page 43), warm salad or something with white beans.

You'll often find jars or cans of duck fat reduced in price around Christmas and Easter and it keeps very well in the fridge. Its longevity makes it much better value than you think.

SERVES 2

2 duck legs

2 tablespoons sea salt, crushed

3 cloves of garlic, left whole

1 teaspoon black peppercorns

3 sprigs of fresh thyme

500ml duck fat

Place the duck legs on a plate and sprinkle the sea salt over the skin of the duck. Cover the plate with cling film. Leave in the fridge overnight to cure. Some moisture will come out of the meat, but this is normal. It is similar in action to brining the turkey on page 55.

Next day, brush the salt off the duck but don't rinse it. Place the duck legs in the crock, skin side up, and add the garlic, peppercorns and thyme. Dollop the duck fat over the meat and put the lid on the slow cooker.

Cook the duck legs on low for 6 hours. The solid duck fat will become liquid and cover the meat completely. The meat will become so incredibly tender, but remain firm enough to lift out of the fat easily.

Sterilise a wide glass jar like a Kilner jar (see page 185) and put the duck legs into it on their side. Cover them with at least 2.5cm of the duck fat to form a seal, which means the duck will stay fresh indefinitely. I strain the fat to keep it fresher. Don't include the garlic or the herbs in the jar. The duck will keep for at least 6 months in the fridge.

Strain the rest of the duck fat and pour it back into the jar it came from. You can reuse for more confit or the best roast potatoes around.

When you are ready to serve the confit duck, take it out from under the layer of duck fat and crisp up the skin in a hot pan for 3–4 minutes. You can eat the duck hot or cold.

DUCK LEGS WITH DICED ROOT VEGETABLES

Duck legs are one of those things that seem too expensive to buy full price, but often crop up in the reduced section of the supermarket and suddenly become excellent value because there is so much more meat on them than a chicken leg. Don't be put off by the fact duck is quite a fatty meat because this dish uses the fat to great effect and flavour. It's the kind of dish that takes no effort, but feels special enough to serve to people when they come round for dinner. This recipe is a firm favourite in my house!

SERVES 2-4

- 2-4 duck legs (one per person)
- 1 onion, finely diced
- 2 carrots, finely diced
- 2 stalks of celery, finely diced
- 2 medium potatoes, finely diced
- 2 sweet potatoes, finely diced
- ½ swede or celeriac, finely diced
- 1 teaspoon fresh or dried thyme
- 150ml water
- salt and pepper

It's important to seal the duck before you add it to the slow cooker. Season the skin with salt and pepper, add the duck, skin side down, to a cold frying pan and bring the temperature up until the skin starts to sizzle. Using the cold pan renders the fat and keeps the skin crisp. Cook the duck for about a minute and a half on either side. Lift the duck out of the pan, reserve the fat and set both aside until needed.

Add the vegetables to the slow-cooker crock, mixing them well with your hands to combine them evenly. Add the thyme and a little more salt and pepper. Pour the rendered duck fat over them all and stir to coat them well. Pour the water over the vegetables.

Place the duck legs on top of the vegetables, skin side up, and put the lid on the slow cooker. Cook the duck and vegetables on low for 7-8 hours.

The delicious, silky duck fat will render out of the duck and into the vegetables, which become soft and flavoursome while the meat becomes beautifully tender. All you need to do is serve both together and ponder whether you're having a glass of red wine with it. It's just that simple!

CHICKEN

There are few more frugal ways to eat than cooking a whole chicken and the slow cooker is the perfect way to do this with a minimum of effort and the most tender meat possible. Whether you roast your chicken or poach it in the slow cooker, you'll also be able to cook the leftover carcass again to create a stunning chicken stock. Using the slow cooker allows you to use every ounce of the chicken and prepare home-cooked meals that taste incredibly luxurious.

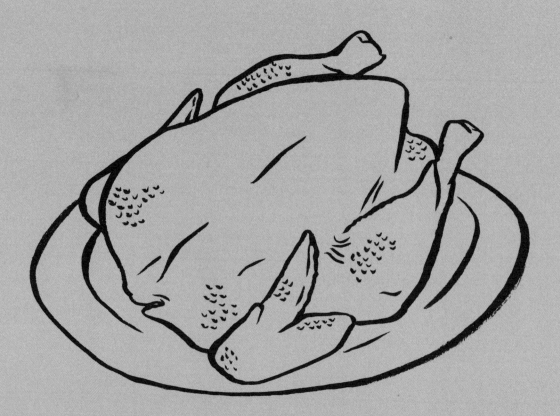

ROAST CHICKEN

Who doesn't love a roast chicken? It's the perfect Sunday lunch or economical way to feed several people over a week and few things work better in the slow cooker. You can pop your chook in the crock to slow cook while you go out for a walk before lunch or when you don't want to heat the kitchen up, but fancy cold chicken leftovers. It also creates wonderful roasting juices that make the best gravy I've ever made. All without rummaging in the cupboard for the right-sized roasting dish…

SERVES 4

**1 whole chicken,
  approximately
  1.5–1.7kg in weight**
1 lemon
25g butter
salt and pepper

Note: There are endless possibilities to flavour this dish aside from the basic lemon and salt and pepper. You could add fresh sage or tarragon to the cavity. You could rub the skin with paprika or garlic. Whatever you do, don't skip the lemon. A preserved one like on page 186 works beautifully. Just use slightly less salt when seasoning the skin.

Remove your chicken from any packaging about an hour before you want to cook it. A chicken will always roast best from room temperature, but it's also advisable to take it out of the packaging and allow the skin to dry off slightly. I often pat mine down with some kitchen paper and then leave unwrapped. This will let the skin crisp up better, especially since it won't get just as burnished in the slow cooker as the oven.

When you are ready to cook the chicken, cut the lemon in half and put both halves inside the cavity. Rub the butter over the skin, not forgetting the tip of the legs and the wings. Sprinkle the bird generously with salt and pepper.

Place breast down in the slow-cooker crock and season the base of the bird too. Put the lid on the slow cooker and cook on high for 5 hours. I like to turn the chicken after 4 hours if I can, to evenly colour the skin.

The chicken is cooked when the juices run clear at the thickest part of the leg when pierced with a skewer. If you are unsure, cook for a further 30–45 minutes, especially if the chicken wasn't room temperature to begin with. Carefully lift the chicken out and place on a plate to rest.

While the chicken is resting, pour the wonderful juices the chicken has created into a saucepan via a measuring jug to make Chicken Gravy (see page 61).

If you are serving the chicken as cold cuts rather than a roast, reserve the juices and add to the stock you make from the bones. They will become jellied as they set in the fridge. Don't worry about this. It's a sign of the very best stock possible.

Carve the chicken and serve with the gravy for the easiest chicken dinner you'll ever make.

POACHED CHICKEN

Poaching a chicken is so simple in the slow cooker and creates incredibly moist chicken that keeps well without drying out. It also creates a wonderful golden chicken stock as it cooks that you can use for soups or a risotto. I cook mine overnight, strip the meat off the bones and then put them back in the slow cooker with some carrot and celery and make a second batch of equally good stock. I can get a week's worth of meals out of a poached chicken this way, making it incredibly frugal and delicious.

SERVES 4

1 whole chicken,
  approximately
  1.5–1.7kg in weight
1.25 litres cold water
2 carrots, peeled
2 stalks of celery
salt and pepper

When I said this was simple, I really meant it. Allow your chicken to come to room temperature before poaching. I take mine out of the fridge about an hour beforehand.

Check to see if the chicken fits in your slow-cooker crock. I quite often have to cut mine in half with poultry shears and put the two halves on top of each other. Fit them snugly into the crock and then cover the chicken with about 500ml of the cold water. The bird should be as well submerged as possible, so you may need a bit more water depending on its size.

Add the salt and pepper. Put the lid on and cook on low for 7–8 hours. The stock will be golden and glorious and the chicken so tender, it is almost falling apart. Remove it from the crock very carefully so it doesn't collapse.

Reserve the first batch of stock. Remove the meat from the chicken carcass and then put the stripped bones back into the crock. Cover them all with the remaining cold water, about 750ml, add the carrot and celery and cook for another 8 hours on low.

Keep the chicken and the stock in the fridge until needed.

CHICKEN STOCK

The best thing about buying a whole chicken is that you can then make chicken stock. However, it can be a temperamental beast when made on the hob: it mustn't boil, you need to top the water up to prevent it burning and you need to keep skimming it to keep it clear. It's quite a labour of love. In the slow cooker though, it's ridiculously easy.

MAKES 1.2 LITRES

1 chicken carcass

any remaining chicken thigh bones you've frozen

1 carrot

2 stalks of celery

1.2 litres cold water

salt and white pepper

Use either raw or cooked chicken bones for this. Strip any cooked meat from the chicken. Put the bones into the slow-cooker crock along with any remaining skin or joints. Add the carrot and celery. Cover it all with the cold water.

Season well with salt and white pepper (as instructed by my friend Carolyne who makes extraordinarily good chicken soup and knows that it tastes even better when the stock remains clear and black-speck free). Put the lid on and cook it on low for 8 hours. Allow to cool and store in the fridge or freezer until needed. (The stock will become jellied as it cools.)

SIMPLE CHICKEN GRAVY

I love gravy. I learned everything I know about this beautiful brown elixir from my mum. I have made this gravy from the juices of slow-cooked chicken, a brined turkey and batches of pulled pork and it has worked every time. This is a thickened gravy rather than a jus. It is happiest being poured over a roast dinner or, since you can only take the girl out of Belfast, served over a portion of rice and chips for a home-made version of our post-pub meal of a gravy half-and-half.

SERVES 2–4

400ml meat juices

90ml vermouth or Marsala

½ teaspoon Worcestershire sauce

1 tablespoon cornflour

1 tablespoon cold water

splash of gravy browning (optional)

dash of malt vinegar

salt and pepper

Pour the meat juices into a saucepan and reduce them over a high heat by a quarter so that you have about 300ml remaining. Add the vermouth or Marsala and the Worcestershire sauce.

Mix the cornflour with the cold water and then add this mixture to the meat juices and stir as it thickens into a gravy. Taste and check for seasoning. Add salt and pepper to taste and the gravy browning, if using.

Add the merest dash of malt vinegar to lift it all and serve.

BRIXTON CHICKEN WINGS

My adopted home of Brixton, in South London, has strong influences from both the Caribbean and Portugal as shown by my next-door neighbours who are Jamaican and Portuguese. This cultural melting pot means that spicy peri peri chicken is a way of life round here. I've combined it with the butter-basted beauty of the Buffalo wing so popular in America and created Brixton chicken wings. Serve with the Mushy Peas on page 100 or some corn on the cob.

ALLOW 4 CHICKEN WINGS PER PERSON WITH SIDES

16 chicken wings

1 tablespoon smoked paprika

1 teaspoon brown sugar

1 teaspoon hot sauce

¼ teaspoon cayenne pepper (optional)

1 fresh red chilli

100g butter

1 Scotch bonnet pepper

salt and pepper

Try and get nice plump chicken wings for this dish if you can. Snip the very boniest tips off them with poultry shears or a very sharp knife so they are easier to eat. Seal the chicken wings in a hot pan on the hob for 2–3 minutes each side to brown them. This makes them tastier and they look much more alluring too. You'll need to brown the wings only a few at a time or they will steam and the skin will remain stubbornly pale. Set each batch aside to cool down.

Mix the smoked paprika, sugar, hot sauce, cayenne pepper, red chilli and the butter together to make a deep-red paste. Omit the cayenne if you like your chilli a little milder. I like to use a Caribbean-style hot sauce or something like Tabasco, but you could also use sweet chilli sauce if little mouths are eating the wings.

Using gloved hands, rub this chilli paprika butter into the wings and layer them into the slow cooker, skin side up. You can do this several layers deep if you are cooking for lots of people. Season well with salt and pepper.

Pour about 100ml of water into the slow-cooker crock to help steam the wings to make them very tender as they cook. Put the whole Scotch bonnet chilli into the crock to infuse the chicken with its lovely fruity flavour without adding its fierce heat.

Put the lid on the slow cooker and cook the wings on high for 4 hours or low for 6 hours. Serve with the buttery juices drizzled over them and a little extra hot sauce if liked. Eat with your hands and a whole roll of kitchen roll close by.

CHICKEN MOLE

Mole (pronounced 'mol-ay') is a slow-cooked Mexican sauce thickened with nuts and flavoured with dark chocolate and dried fruit. It has a real depth from the bitter chocolate, hints of chilli and the sweetness of the fruit. My dad, who spent some time visiting Mexico, introduced me to the dish. I haven't used as many kinds of chillies as he did because they are hard to get here, but if you've ever wondered if the whole chocolate and chilli thing works, try this dish and be completely converted. It is worth the long ingredient list.

SERVES 2–4 WITH LEFTOVERS

- 2 onions, finely diced
- 4 cloves of garlic, finely diced
- 50g prunes or raisins (I used the Stewed Earl Grey Prunes on page 229)
- 50g unsweetened cocoa powder or dark chocolate, grated
- 1 tablespoon smoked paprika
- 2 teaspoons ground cumin
- 2 teaspoons ground cinnamon
- ½ teaspoon ground cloves
- 1 teaspoon coriander seeds
- 3 dried red chillies
- 6 chicken thighs or drumsticks
- 2 tablespoons breadcrumbs
- 1 x 400g tin chopped tomatoes
- 400ml water
- 2 tablespoons peanut butter
- 1 star anise
- chopped fresh coriander, to serve (optional)
- salt and pepper

This is another very easy recipe. Put the onion, garlic, prunes, cocoa powder or grated chocolate, paprika, cumin, cinnamon, cloves, coriander seeds and the dried chillies into the bowl of a hand blender or use a mortar and pestle to blend to a paste.

Remove the skin from the chicken and if you are using thighs, cut a couple of slashes in them to allow the marinade to infuse even better. Coat the chicken in the paste you have just made and marinate overnight in the fridge.

When you are ready to cook, place the chicken in the slow-cooker crock and scatter the breadcrumbs over it. Pour the chopped tomatoes and water over the meat and dollop the peanut butter into it. You won't taste the peanut flavour when you cook the mole, but using peanut butter thickens the sauce. Drop in the star anise.

Cover with the lid and cook for 7–8 hours on low. The sauce will combine and thicken, with all the flavours combining to create something incredibly dark, rich and deep. Serve with rice and a sprinkling of fresh coriander, if you have it.

SPICED CHICKEN WITH GREEN FIGS

The idea for this gorgeous chicken dish came from my mum and in the absence of being able to nip round easily and demand she makes it for me, I've adopted it and practised making it many times. It has become a huge favourite of mine.

The Green Figs in Syrup from page 193 keep this dish moist and flavoursome. If you don't have any, use 3 tablespoons of the Fig and Pomegranate Relish from page 192 or the same amount of dried figs and 100ml more water.

SERVES 4

50g chorizo, finely chopped

4-6 chicken thighs, skin on and bone in

2 tablespoons pomegranate molasses

1 teaspoon paprika

½ teaspoon ground cinnamon

¼ teaspoon nutmeg or ground mace

¼ teaspoon ground allspice

1 cardamom pod, seeds crushed

1 medium onion, sliced

2 cloves of garlic, sliced

2-3 Green Figs in Syrup, halved (see page 193)

175ml water

This is one of the few dishes where I precook anything before putting it in the slow cooker, but the extra step is so worth it for the flavour.

Warm the chorizo gently in a pan over a medium heat. When the beautiful red oil starts to come out into the pan, add the chicken, skin side down, and brown it for about 2 minutes in the oil. Once the skin is golden, take it out of the pan and put into the slow-cooker crock.

Drizzle the pomegranate molasses over the browned chicken and then scatter all the spices over the chicken, tossing it gently to coat it all. Add in the onion, garlic and the halved figs and pour in the water.

Cook on low for 7–8 hours. The chicken will become incredibly moist and tender and the figs, chorizo and spices add huge amounts of sweet-and-sour flavours. I serve this with bulgur wheat or couscous with the intense sauce over it all.

GARLICKY TAHINI CHICKEN

This recipe is inspired by the garlic chicken recipe in Nigella Lawson's *How to Eat*. I have a soft spot for it because it was the first thing I ever cooked for a dinner party and because it introduced me to the amazing effect long cooking can have on garlic, turning it from a brisk shout to a breathy whisper of flavour. Don't be put off by the amount of garlic in this recipe, it mellows beautifully. It must be fresh garlic rather than purée to achieve this smooth effect.

SERVES 2–4

12 cloves of garlic, peeled

4–6 chicken thighs, on the bone

4 tablespoons tahini

2 tablespoons water

3 tablespoons cider vinegar or lemon juice

salt and pepper

Pop the peeled garlic into a pan of boiling water and boil for about 10–15 minutes, until they are very soft and starting to shed their skins.

While the garlic is cooking, remove the skin from the chicken and slash the flesh of each one twice to allow the marinade to infuse better. Season with salt and pepper.

Once the garlic is softened and popping out of its skin, drain it and squeeze each clove from the now fragile papery skin into the bowl of a hand blender, or use a pestle and mortar. Add the tahini. If you can only get the thicker, stiff tahini from the health food section of the supermarket, thin it with the water until it is liquid enough to drop from a spoon. Add the vinegar or lemon juice and then blend until the marinade is smooth and combined.

Pour the marinade over the chicken thighs, tossing them in it so they are well coated. Cover the chicken and marinate overnight in the fridge or for up to 24 hours.

When you are ready to cook, place the chicken in the slow-cooker crock and pour the remaining marinade over the chicken, spreading it out evenly so none of the meat is exposed. Cook on low for 6–7 hours.

The marinade will baste the chicken with the oil from the tahini and it will become tender enough to fall off the bone. Serve the chicken hot on a tortilla with some crunchy shredded white cabbage and discover the dinner party-friendly take on a chicken kebab with garlic sauce.

JERK CHICKEN

Living in Brixton, jerk chicken has become a staple of my culinary life. The word 'jerk' refers to the seasoning on the meat and to the style of cooking. Allspice is essential to both. It's rubbed into the meat to marinate it and the wood of the allspice tree is used on the drum to create lots of smoke that infuses the meat with a wonderful flavour.

This jerk chicken is very easy to make, but the Scotch bonnet peppers are essential to add their unique fruity flavour and lip-tingling heat. Many major supermarkets stock them and they freeze brilliantly, so keep some in the freezer ready to make this time and time again.

The slow cooker can't add smoke, but something amazing happens when you slow cook the jerk rub – you end up with juicy chicken with a wonderful, almost charred outer skin, that brings a splash of summer at any time of the year.

SERVES 4 WITH LEFTOVERS

- 4 spring onions, roughly chopped
- 4 cloves of garlic, roughly chopped
- 1 Scotch bonnet pepper
- 6 sprigs of fresh thyme or 1 tablespoon dried thyme
- 2 tablespoons ground allspice (honestly! It's not a typo)
- 1 teaspoon ground ginger
- ½ teaspoon ground cloves
- ½ teaspoon sea salt
- ¼ teaspoon ground mace
- ¼ teaspoon black pepper
- 2 limes, juiced
- 2 teaspoons brown sugar
- 1 tablespoon black treacle
- 1 teaspoon soy sauce
- 500g chicken thighs or drumsticks, skin on and bone in

Put the spring onion and garlic in a blender. Take the stalk off the Scotch bonnet and put it in whole. This fiery little pepper will make your hands or eyes tingle if you get the juice on your hands, so this is safest.

Add the rest of the herbs and spices. Squeeze the lime juice in and add the sugar, treacle and soy. Season well and blitz it all in the blender until it is a rough paste. It should be liquid enough to drop from a spoon. Add the juice of another lime or about a tablespoon of water if it's too dry. This is your jerk marinade.

Make two to three cuts in the skin of each chicken thigh. If your slow-cooker crock fits in the fridge, place them directly in the slow-cooker crock skin side up. Pour about two-thirds of the jerk marinade over them all and, using gloved hands or a spatula, toss them to coat well with the marinade. If your crock doesn't fit, use a freezer bag or Tupperware. Marinate the chicken overnight in the fridge. Reserve the remaining marinade.

Next day, add the remaining marinade to the chicken in the slow-cooker crock so that it covers the chicken skin well. This helps form a lovely crust on the meat that gives a barbecued effect. Put the lid on the slow cooker and cook the chicken on high for 8–9 hours. This will make the sugar and treacle caramelise on the skin and the meat become incredibly tender. Serve the jerk chicken with rice and some crunchy coleslaw.

CHICKEN LIVER PÂTÉ

I adore pâté. One of my favourite light meals is pâté on toast. The bread must be brown and the pâté must be chicken liver and spread generously. It reminds me of having tea at my uncle Tom and aunt Kathleen's house, where I used to spend evenings when visiting my granny. Kathleen would even make Melba toast sometimes, which made me feel ridiculously sophisticated. In those days, pâté on toast was served on proper china and followed by playing on the electric organ in their living room. These days, I tend to eat it curled up on the sofa, plate balanced on my knee, reading a good book.

This pâté is best made using frozen chicken livers, which have a looser texture than fresh ones and need to be baked in the slow cooker as a water bath to firm them up. It's so easy that it leaves lots of reading time handy.

SERVES 4–6 AND KEEPS WELL IN THE FRIDGE

350g frozen chicken livers

85g butter

2 shallots, finely chopped

2 rashers of streaky bacon, finely chopped

1 tablespoon red wine, port or brandy (optional)

75ml double cream

1 tablespoon chopped fresh parsley

salt and pepper

Trim the livers of anything that looks unappealing. Chop them finely and set aside. Frozen livers are quite wet and they will create lots of liquid as you chop. Reserve this.

Melt the butter in a frying pan on the hob, add the shallots and bacon and sweat them both over a medium heat. You want the shallots to become translucent, but not coloured. The bacon should just start to crisp around the edges.

At this stage, add the chopped chicken livers and any liquid from them. Cook them for about 1 minute until they just start to change colour. Add the alcohol if you are using it and allow it to bubble slightly.

Pour in the cream and season. Sprinkle over the parsley and cook it all for 1–2 minutes until the livers are almost completely cooked. Remove from the heat immediately.

Blend with a hand blender until it is smooth, but retains a little bit of texture. Pour the mixture into a shallow dish or ramekins. Cover with foil. Set the dish into the slow-cooker crock and pour boiling water into the crock so that it comes about halfway up the side of the pâté dish.

Cook the pâté on low for 3 hours to firm up the texture. Allow to cool for at least 20 minutes before eating. It will keep for about 3 days in the fridge. Keep it covered, but don't be surprised if the top of it oxidises and darkens slightly. This is natural and doesn't affect eating it. Mine rarely lasts long enough for that to be an issue.

FISH AND SEAFOOD

I love fish and seafood. It's a family joke that if you left an old boot in the sea for long enough, I would eat it. Yet not as many British and Irish people share my love as you'd expect for island dwellers. One of the reasons for this is that they are unsure how to cook fish, believing it to be difficult. They also dislike the smell of fish in the house, and the bones, and so the majority of fish eaten in the UK comes from the chippie or with a crumb coating.

You probably don't think of a slow cooker as the way to introduce people to fish or seafood, but it's a great fuss-free way to get to grips with cooking it, mainly because there is very little odour during or after cooking. Invaluable in a day and age when so many kitchens are part of the living room!

Fish and seafood doesn't need the long cooking that many cuts of meat benefit from, but several hours cooking will give you tender and tasty cuts of fish using the natural abilities of the slow cooker to steam and poach food. You can copy the 'just steam' fish dishes available to buy, but for less money and with more variety. Seafood can also be cooked easily due to the capacity of the crock and it's difficult to overcook either by a minute or two, which can often make all the difference with traditionally cooked fish.

WHOLE BAKED TROUT

Fish is a favourite meal for me when I'm eating alone. I am lucky enough to have an excellent fishmonger near me and I really enjoy picking out my fish of the week. There's such a wide choice I don't know what half of them are and constantly ask my fishmonger, Donna, questions. And then I buy a trout anyway because they are my absolute favourite fish. I've given the recipe here for trout, but I've also done mackerel, snapper, sea bream and sea bass the same way in the slow cooker. It's so easy you can definitely experiment!

Take one whole trout with the head and tail still on. This makes it easier to cook the fish well and allows you to see how fresh the fish is. Look for bright sparkly eyes, shiny glossy scales and a tail that doesn't look like it's starting to droop. It shouldn't smell fishy, at most it should smell of the sea. Ask the fishmonger to gut it if it's whole.

Fill the inside of the fish with any of the following, depending how you feel: fresh dill, tarragon, rosemary, sage or parsley and lemon for a Mediterranean feel; fresh lemongrass, sliced red chilli, fresh ginger and star anise for an Asian feel; or fresh sliced tomatoes, onions, garlic, lime, whole allspice berries and Scotch bonnet peppers for a Caribbean version.

Season the skin well and then place your stuffed fish on some tin foil and wrap it up like a present, allowing some room at the top for steam to collect. Make sure there are no gaps in your parcel to allow this to escape. Place the parcel of fish in the slow-cooker crock (you can layer them on top of each other if you have more than one fish) and pour 3–4cm boiling water into the base of the crock. The tail will bend to fit it into the crock so the skin might split slightly. Don't panic. This is fine.

Put the lid on and cook the fish on high for 2 hours. Take the fish out of the slow cooker and serve immediately with a side dish of your choice and a squirt of lemon juice to bring out the flavours of the fish. It will be perfectly moist and will come away from the bones easily.

KIPPERS

Unless you are my dad's cat Mitch, you'll no doubt prefer to cook kippers without the whole house smelling of fish. Well, the good news for humans is that you can in the slow cooker. Mitch has to sit right above the slow cooker now to get a waft of kipper.

Slow-cooker kippers are so simple they don't really need a recipe. Allow one kipper per person. Lay it on a rectangle of tin foil. Add a slice of unsalted butter, a goodly sprinkle of white pepper and some dill, if you have it. Make a neat little parcel with the foil, folding the sides and the top over, and place in the slow-cooker crock, making sure there are no gaps or holes. Add enough boiling water to create steam in the slow cooker, about 2–3cm for one or two kippers. Put the lid on and cook the kippers on low for 2 hours. Carefully remove the tin foil parcels from the slow cooker and open them onto a plate, making sure you don't spill the gloriously fish-infused butter. Pour it over the kippers and serve with scrambled egg.

OMELETTE ARNOLD BENNETT

I have never ordered one of these when I'm out for breakfast because I always get Arnold Bennett, the novelist, mixed up with Gordon Bennett, the expletive you can say in front of your granny, and risk culinary embarrassment. But one day, faced with a nice bit of smoked haddock, some spare egg whites and a slow cooker, I realised my moment had come. And oh my, it's the best omelette I've ever eaten. Light and fluffy and very luxurious, I make it all the time now. I add a few spring onions and sometimes sub the haddock for some blue cheese to keep it vegetarian. Slow cooking eggs is the way to go!

SERVES 2

3 eggs

150g smoked haddock, cut into small pieces

2 spring onions, finely sliced

25g Parmesan

3 egg whites

chopped fresh parsley, to serve

salt and pepper

Line the slow-cooker crock with a sheet of reusable baking liner and set aside.

Break the 3 whole eggs into a large bowl and beat until well combined. Add the haddock, spring onion and the Parmesan and season carefully with salt and pepper. Mix well so that everything is well coated with egg.

In a separate bowl, whisk the egg whites to soft peaks so they are light and fluffy. Fold them into the whole egg and fish mixture. Don't overmix as you want to keep the air in.

Pour the egg mix into the lined slow-cooker crock. Put the lid on the slow cooker and cook on high for 2 hours. The base of the omelette will become slightly crisped and golden. Lift it out of the slow cooker, peel away the liner and serve with some chopped parsley and a green salad.

Note: I don't mind that the top of the omelette is quite pale, but if you prefer it more bronzed, simply grill in the liner for 3–4 minutes before serving.

POACHED FISH

This is probably the easiest way to cook fish in the slow cooker because the liquid in a slow cooker takes a long time to heat and it's almost impossible to boil or overcook the fish. Both fresh and smoked fish work well with this method. I've given a recipe here for both steaks and fish fillets, which can be used as a guide for most types of fish.

I've never cooked something as delicate as flat fish in here, preferring more robust fish like salmon, coley and smoked haddock. Frozen fish doesn't work so well as it tends to shrink as it defrosts and cooks, so make this your opportunity to trying cooking fresh fish.

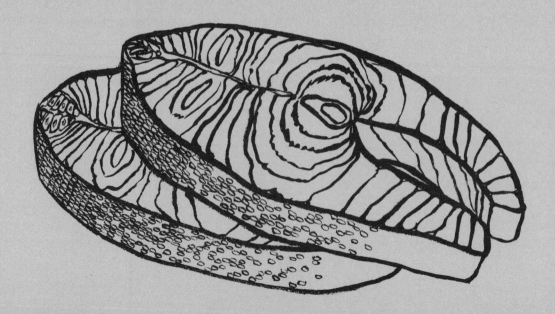

POACHED SMOKED HADDOCK FILLETS

Smoked haddock is a simple thing. Don't buy the sort that is luridly yellow in colour, but more muted in tone, cook it slowly and simply and it will reward you by being delicious. It's perfect in the slow cooker, especially as it keeps any fishy smells self contained.

Pour 2–3cm of milk into the slow-cooker crock. Don't use skimmed; full-fat or semi-skimmed is best. Add a generous knob of unsalted butter and a selection of the following herbs: dill, thyme, chives and rosemary. Season with white pepper. This amount of milk should cover up to 4 fillets of fish. Add a little more if you are cooking more.

Put the lid on the slow cooker and gently poach the haddock on low for 2 hours. Lift out of the milk carefully with a slotted spoon and serve with a freshly poached egg for a gorgeous breakfast or brunch.

POACHED SALMON STEAKS

I really like salmon because it can be served hot or cold and it's a versatile ingredient that features in many dishes from around the world. I used salmon steaks here as they cook well and they tend to be less expensive than salmon fillet.

Try to get salmon steaks that are at least 2–3cm thick (4cm is even better here, so don't be afraid to ask the fishmonger to cut them specially). A specialist fishmonger will be used to such requests and the supermarket fishmonger will be happy to have something different to do.

Fish is traditionally poached in a *court bouillon*, which is a stock made from carrot, celery, onion, black pepper and bay leaves. This adds more flavour than water alone and is very easy to make.

Chop a carrot, two stalks of celery and an onion into the slow-cooker crock. Add a teaspoon of black peppercorns and sea salt and a bay leaf. Set the salmon steaks on top of this all.

Add just enough cold water to cover the fish. You can do two layers of steaks with this amount of court bouillon and the cooking time will be the same for four steaks as one. Put the lid on the slow cooker and poach the fish on high for 2 hours. Turn the heat off and allow the fish to sit for 5 minutes.

Lift the steaks out of the *court bouillon* with a slotted spoon and serve warm as a part of a meal or allow to cool to make delicious salads or sandwiches. This is a perfect summer dish, when cold poached salmon just seems so right alongside summer sun and a small glass of Pimm's with lots of cucumber. You can skip the standing over a hot stove bit and go straight to the cold drink in a deckchair bit too...

SALMON, CAPER AND DILL LOAF

On Sunday afternoons at my granny's house, afternoon tea in front of the fire wasn't complete without a tinned salmon sandwich. Fresh salmon was a once a year event in those days, but tinned salmon was the taste of childhood. It was often accompanied by a slice or two of cucumber and a dollop of salad cream and I adored it.

So it seemed apt to find the basis of this recipe in a handwritten cookbook of my granny's. Designed to make a tin of salmon serve lots of people, it combines leftover mashed potato and breadcrumbs to lighten it. It makes a lovely lunch with some garden peas or is excellent for a picnic. I just have to serve mine with salad cream. Old habits die hard.

SERVES 4 WITH
LEFTOVERS

115g mashed potato

75g breadcrumbs

1 x 212g tin pink salmon, drained

1 tablespoon capers, drained

½ lemon, zested (if waxed, give it a vigorous scrub under the hot tap first)

1 tablespoon cider vinegar

50g fresh parsley and dill (optional), chopped

2 eggs, beaten

salt and pepper

I'm not entirely au fait with the concept of leftover mash as I tend to be able to eat all the mash I make, no matter how much there is, so I often use instant mash when a recipe calls for a small amount. Use whichever is easiest for you here.

Put the mashed potato in a large bowl along with the breadcrumbs and flake the salmon into it. Add the capers, lemon zest and cider vinegar and herbs, if using, and season well.

Beat the eggs into it all and mix until well combined. The mixture will come together without being sticky. Put it all into a greased loaf tin and cover with foil.

Place the covered loaf tin in the slow cooker and fill the crock with boiling water so the water comes about two-thirds of the way up the tin. Steam on low for 3–4 hours.

You will end up with something similar to a terrine in texture. Turn the loaf out onto a plate and serve in slices. As well as being an excellent vehicle for salad cream, this is lovely with a fried egg for breakfast.

STUFFED SALMON

See that sceptical look you have about being able to cook salmon in the slow cooker? Be prepared to replace it with a very impressed one because you can cook the perfect steamed salmon in there with almost no effort. This would make a fantastic centrepiece for Christmas or Easter or a family meal where you want to spend more time with your family than your kitchen.

You can scale this recipe up to a much bigger piece, although I don't recommend scaling it down. For each 100g more in weight, give it another 20 minutes cooking.

SERVES 2–4 WITH LEFTOVERS

vegetable oil

650g fresh salmon fillet

25g fresh dill

1 medium courgette (about 150g), grated

1 lemon, sliced

salt and pepper

Make sure your salmon fillet is cut into two roughly equal-sized pieces so you can make a salmon sandwich out of it.

Lay a large piece of foil out on the worktop. Brush it lightly with vegetable oil and place one piece of the salmon on it skin side down. Season it well with salt and pepper.

Mix the dill in with the grated courgette and then put the courgette on top of the salmon. Put the other piece of salmon on top of the courgette, flesh side up. Place the lemon slices on top of the salmon skin.

Wrap up this salmon sandwich up tightly in the foil and place it on top of some reusable baking liner in the slow-cooker crock.

Put the lid on the slow cooker and cook the salmon on low for 2 hours 45 minutes. Lift the salmon out, unwrap it and remove the lemon slices before serving.

Serve the salmon cold or at room temperature along with some green beans or a potato salad.

SOUSED MACKEREL

I cannot enthuse enough about mackerel. A truly beautiful fish with its gorgeous grey markings, it's one of the healthy oily fish we are encouraged to eat more of. Not only that, it's sustainable, not seasonal, usually local to British waters and inexpensive to buy. It's the perfect fish for me.

Sousing is a traditional way to serve fish in Britain. It's more or less poaching the fish in an acidic solution such as vinegar to preserve it in the fridge for up to a week, but isn't quite as intense as pickling it to last for months. It's a perfect method for mackerel or herring as the sharpness of the vinegar cuts through the rich oiliness of them. I like it for lunch on some rye crispbread as one mackerel fillet goes a long way, making it very economical as well as easy.

You need your mackerel filleted for this recipe. A fishmonger will be able to do this without any trouble, even those in the supermarket. You can also do it at home if you can only get mackerel whole. I've done it with help from some of the instruction videos you can access online. Either way, make sure your mackerel are very fresh. They should be shiny with bright eyes and no fishy smell.

SERVES 4–6
(DEPENDING ON
HOW YOU SERVE IT)

1 red onion

1 bay leaf

1 teaspoon black
   peppercorns

½ teaspoon sea salt

4 cloves

2 fresh mackerel,
   filleted

150ml wine or cider
   vinegar

150ml water

Slice your onion as thinly as possible and add half of it to the crock. Scatter the herbs and seasoning on top of it and lay the mackerel fillets on it all. Place the rest of the onion on top and pour the vinegar and water over it all. The fish should be completely submerged.

Put the lid on the slow cooker and cook the fish on high for 1 hour 30 minutes. Turn the heat off and remove the lid, allowing the fish to cool down in the vinegar liquor. This helps souse them beyond the initial cooking to add flavour.

After about an hour's cooling, remove the fish from the slow cooker and serve along with the onion as part of a salad or as a light starter with bread. You can also put them into a glass jar, cover with the vinegar and a bit more water and keep them for up to a week in the fridge. They'll get sharper in flavour the longer they sit, so I usually serve the last of them with something like avocado to balance it out.

MUSSELS

Mussels remain an inexpensive seafood since they are abundantly available in and around the British Isles. They are generally in season when there's an R in the month and since they are packed with flavour and much more filling than you'd imagine, they can make a great dinner with lots of crusty bread. The advantage to using the slow cooker is that cooking mussels in the shell takes up a lot of space and you never seem to have a pan big enough to make it worth your while. However, a crock makes it very easy indeed.

SERVES 2 AS A
MAIN MEAL OR 4
AS A STARTER

1kg fresh mussels in
the shell

200g cherry tomatoes

2 cloves of garlic,
finely sliced

1 anchovy, chopped

200ml beer
(something darker,
rather than a very
light lager, is best)

fresh flat-leaf parsley,
to serve

salt and pepper

Begin by cleaning your mussels, even if they have come in a net bag from a fishmonger's counter. Scrub them under cold running water, making sure they close when tapped or poked. If they don't, they are most likely dead and must be discarded, along with any broken ones. Pull the wiry beards out of the shells and then soak the mussels in cold water for 10–15 minutes to remove any grit or sand.

Halve the cherry tomatoes and add to the crock along with the finely sliced garlic and the anchovy. Put the cleaned mussels in and season carefully, bearing in mind the saltiness of the anchovy and the brininess of the mussels.

Pour the beer over it all. I used Guinness as I had some left from another recipe, but you could use anything with a bit of flavour. Bear in mind that the Belgians are equally famed for beer and mussels.

Put the lid on the slow cooker and cook the mussels on high for 1 hour. Serve the mussels in bowls with some of the lovely beer-infused liquor at the bottom and some fresh parsley on top. Some crusty bread is perfect or, if you've got the Belgian thing going, some skinny little *frites* are excellent.

Use the shell of the first mussel you eat to then extract the meat, pincer-like, from all the other mussels. This is much easier than using a fork. Don't forget to discard any mussels that haven't opened during cooking as they aren't safe to eat even if you can lever them open.

You'll also realise that the slow-cooker crock comes into its own as a great big dish for the empty shells as you go. The most mess-free mussels possible.

POACHED OCTOPUS

You may not immediately think of octopus as a budget ingredient, but I've often seen them marked down on the wet fish counter in supermarkets or frozen ones in the Chinese supermarkets and considering there is no waste on a cleaned one, they become very good value.

Octopus is much more robust than its cousin, the squid, so it needs longer cooking to make it tender and melt in the mouth. This makes it perfect for the slow cooker. Set aside any scepticism or squeamishness and you will be rewarded. You can also use baby octopi, just keep them whole and halve the cooking time.

This is such a simple summer dish to make with very little effort.

SERVES 4 AS PART OF A MAIN MEAL

1 onion, halved

1 lemon, halved

1 teaspoon salt

1 teaspoon black peppercorns

1 bay leaf

1 whole octopus or 8–10 baby ones (approximately 1kg), cleaned

500ml boiling water

Put the onion, lemon and seasonings in the slow-cooker crock and nestle your octopus on top of them. Pour the boiling water over them all. This 'scares' the octopus so its tentacles bunch up slightly and it looks a bit tense. Doing this actually helps it become more tender, so don't skip this stage.

Pour enough cold water into the crock to cover the octopus, put the lid on and cook on low for 5–6 hours. You don't want to boil the octopus, you want it to come to heat slowly and gently so this mix of water is essential.

Lift the octopus out with a slotted spoon. It will have shrunk slightly and darkened in colour, becoming more purple than when it was raw. This is normal. The water will be a fantastic pinky purple shade.

Allow the octopus to cool slightly; it is best not served piping hot. I cut it into 4cm chunks across the body and the tentacles into two pieces and toss it through a Tomato Sauce like on page 132 and serve with a pasta like tagliatelle and a little chopped chilli or I make Octopus, Polenta and Pepper Salad (see page 81).

OCTOPUS, POLENTA AND PEPPER SALAD

This is a simple recipe that uses many ingredients you have around the house and is substantial enough to have with a glass of something white and chilled while sitting in the sun if you have it as a summer lunch.

**SERVES 4 AS
A MAIN MEAL**

**50g romaine lettuce
(or kale in winter)**

**1 Poached Octopus
(see page 80)**

**1 char-grilled Romano
pepper from a jar or
Confit Peppers (see
page 134)**

**50g black olives,
pitted**

**3 tablespoons
mayonnaise**

1 teaspoon olive oil

**1 clove of garlic,
crushed**

**1 teaspoon smoked
paprika**

**150g Polenta Croutons
(see page 106)**

**chopped fresh parsley,
to serve**

I'm using croutons made from leftover polenta from page 106, but if you don't have any, simply use some boiled salad potatoes. Rick Stein boils them in the cooking water from the octopus for extra flavour. Simply decant it from the slow cooker to a saucepan and boil the potatoes as normal before draining well.

If you are using the kale, finely shred it and place in a serving bowl. Just rip the lettuce up. Chop the octopus in 3–4cm pieces, including the tentacles, and scatter over the greens. Cut the pepper into strips and halve the olives. Add to the bowl.

Mix the mayonnaise with the olive oil, the crushed garlic and the paprika. It should be loose enough to drizzle over the salad. If it isn't, add a drop or two of milk to it.

Toss the polenta croutons into the salad. Drizzle with the garlicky dressing, sprinkle with parsley and eat.

STUFFED SQUID

I really, really love squid. My last meal would quite definitely involve squid — exactly how, I am not sure because it is so versatile and I love it cooked in so many way so it might have to feature in every course.

Naturally shaped for stuffing, this is one of my favourite ways to serve squid since it combines my two great culinary loves of squid and stuffed food. Each time I make this, the stuffing varies slightly, but as long as it involves something green and leafy, like kale, and breadcrumbs, you can't go wrong.

SERVES 4

4 squid, cleaned

200g kale, shredded

4 anchovies, chopped

200g fresh breadcrumbs

1 tablespoon capers (optional)

pinch of mace

1 lemon, juiced and zested (if waxed, give it a vigorous scrub under the hot tap first)

300g cherry tomatoes

1 fresh red chilli, chopped, or 1 dried red chilli, whole

400g frozen and thawed or tinned spinach

100ml water or vegetable or fish stock

salt and pepper

This dish is best made with fresh whole squid rather than frozen or baby ones and it's a great way to bring out the lovely subtle flavour of the seafood. Make sure the squid is clean. Ask your fishmonger to do it or it's very easy to do yourself. Simply remove the eyes and pull everything out from the inside, including the plasticky quill and the ink sac. Try not to break this as it is genuinely ink and makes a real mess. Wash the squid out well and leave the sacs whole. Take the tentacles off and cut them finely.

Make the stuffing by mixing the kale and anchovies with the breadcrumbs and chopped squid tentacles, along with the capers, if using, and add some salt and pepper and the mace. Add the lemon juice and zest to help make the stuffing easier to handle.

Carefully stuff the squid with spoonfuls of the stuffing mix, taking care not to rip them. Lay them into the slow cooker as you fill each of them. Don't overfill them. You should be able to pinch the tops shut if need be.

Reserve any leftover stuffing. Tuck the cherry tomatoes in and around the filled squid. Scatter the chopped fresh chilli over it all or find a spot for the dried one. Cover it all with the spinach and season well.

Pour about 100ml water or stock into the slow-cooker crock. This creates just enough steam to cook the squid and keep the spinach moist. The tomatoes will give out liquid too, so don't be tempted to add more. Sprinkle any leftover stuffing over the top.

Put the lid on the slow cooker and cook the squid on high for 1 hour 30 minutes. The squid will become opaque and white and so tender you will have to be careful taking it out of the slow cooker.

Serve the squid with boiled potatoes along with some of the tomatoes and spinach on the side.

CHORIZO AND SQUID STEW

Lots of people don't like squid because when squid is badly cooked, it's awful. Its delicate texture becomes rubbery and stringy. Deep-frying at the wrong temperature ruins the joys of calamari and leaves people pulling equally rubbery faces of horror. All those people are now making those faces at the thought of slow-cooked squid and I'm here to tell them something that will change their lives. Squid needs cooking at a high temperature for 30 seconds or it needs low temperatures for 30 minutes. It's the in-between methods that ruin it. I'm doing it low and slow with chorizo and tomato and it will win over anyone.

This dish is best with fresh squid, but you can also use frozen baby squid or squid rings if that's easier. I've also made a version of it with a bag of defrosted seafood mix that was in the freezer for emergency meals and it was lovely.

SERVES 4

- 1 large squid or 4 small ones, cleaned
- 100g chorizo, cut into 1cm cubes
- 3 cloves of garlic, diced
- 1 onion, finely diced
- 600g potatoes
- 1 small bulb fennel
- 2 teaspoons smoked paprika
- 2 sprigs of fresh thyme or 1 teaspoon dried thyme
- 1 bay leaf
- 2 teaspoons fennel seeds
- 1 x 400g tin chopped tomatoes
- 2 tablespoons tomato purée
- 150ml water
- 50ml vermouth
- fresh flat-leaf parsley, to serve
- salt and white pepper

If you're using fresh squid, it needs to be cleaned, so ask your fishmonger to do it if you can. If not, it's very easy to do yourself. Simply remove the eyes and pull everything out from the inside, including the plasticky quill and the ink sac. Try not to break this as it is genuinely ink and makes a real mess. Wash the squid out well. If it is very large, take the tentacles off and reserve and cut it into thirds. If it's quite small or little baby ones, keep them whole with the tentacles on. Set aside until needed.

Put the chorizo in the slow cooker along with the diced garlic and onion. Leave the skins on, but chop the potatoes into 3–4cm cubes and add in with the chorizo and onion. Take the root off the fennel bulb and slice it as finely as you can before adding it into the crock.

Stir the paprika through, adding the thyme and bay leaf. Lightly bash the fennel seeds using a pestle and mortar to release the flavour and scatter them in. Pour the chopped tomatoes into it all along with the tomato purée. Pour in the water and vermouth and season well.

Put the lid on the slow cooker and cook on low for 8 hours or high for 5–6 hours until the tomatoes are reduced and the potatoes are tender. Taste and season again.

Add the squid and put the lid on the slow cooker, making sure it is on low, and cook the squid for 30 minutes. You could also add some fresh spinach at this stage if you like a bit of colour.

Serve the stew in bowls scattered with some flat-leaf parsley. The squid will reduce in size, but be beautifully tender and not at all rubbery. Seafood and chorizo is a beautiful combination that will make you feel like you're sitting on a Spanish beach relaxing.

PULSES AND GRAINS

If you've ever wanted to eat more pulses, then the slow cooker is your secret weapon. It allows you to cook dried pulses without soaking or boiling them first (except red kidney beans, which must still be soaked and boiled first to remove any toxins). This is fantastically useful because otherwise you need to plan your bean dishes several days in advance. It's also usually cheaper than buying tinned beans and allows you to experiment with a wide variety of pulses.

Beans are usually cooked from scratch without any salt as it toughens their skins, but the best thing about the slow cooker is that if you add your salt as standard, it stops the beans turning into mush and allows them to remain toothsome yet creamy. I've fallen in love with beans all over again thanks to the slow cooker.

Certain grains work very well in the slow cooker, but I find most pasta and rice dishes don't come into their own at all. Macaroni cheese, lasagne and cannelloni are the exceptions to that rule. Use your slow cooker to impress people with your own dried pulses, all while you get on with life!

BLACK BEAN AND SQUASH STEW WITH KALE AND BARLEY

This is one of my favourite autumn dishes. It looks and tastes amazing and is as close as I get to the whole superfood idea. Originally constructed out of what I had to hand one night, I realised it was the kind of dish nutritionists would urge you to try. Except they would probably only emphasise the healthiness of it whereas I'm all about the fact that it tastes delicious. Oh, and that it's super easy to make. That's my kind of superfood…

Before you panic, I'm not suggesting you cook the kale all day until it reminds you of school dinners. No, instead I'm going to suggest you give it a massage and add it in about 5 minutes before the end. Yup, I'm not joking about the massage. Instead of cooking the life out of kale, you can tenderise it by adding a little olive oil and rubbing it between your palms for a few minutes. It keeps it al dente, but removes the crunchy rabbit-food feel and gives you very soft hands.

Serves 4

200g dried black beans

100g pearl barley

1 medium butternut squash

1 medium onion, finely chopped

2 stalks of celery, finely chopped

3 cloves of garlic, finely chopped

3 sprigs of fresh thyme

1 teaspoon dried oregano

1 Parmesan rind (optional)

1 tablespoon cider or wine vinegar

600ml mineral water

200g kale

1 tablespoon olive oil

salt and pepper

Pop the beans and the barley in the slow cooker. Peel the squash and cut into 2–3cm cubes. I've used a butternut squash, but if you can get something like an onion or Crown Prince squash, you can use them the same way.

Add in the squash along with the onion, celery and garlic. Tuck in the thyme, the oregano and the Parmesan rind, if using (omit the Parmesan rind or use another Italian hard cheese instead to make this dish vegetarian). Sprinkle it all with the vinegar and pour the mineral water all over it. Black beans don't like hard water so this will stop them from becoming chalky.

Put the lid on the slow cooker and cook on low for 7–8 hours. The beans will be soft and the barley will plump up.

Remove the thick centre ribs from the kale and shred as finely as possible. Toss it in a bowl with the olive oil and massage it between your palms until it reduces in size by about half and is an impossibly deep green. This should take about 2 minutes.

Stir through the stew, season to taste and allow to sit for about 2 minutes before serving. I like some yoghurt heaped on top of this and a little chilli doesn't go amiss either.

CUBAN-STYLE BLACK BEANS

I am a big fan of the humble bean, but I think my favourite all-round bean is the beautiful black bean. As black as my beloved eyeliner, they make fantastic stews, soups, enchiladas and even cakes. Hard to find in tins outside areas with South American populations, you can cook up batches of plain ones in the slow cooker and freeze until needed or you can make this delicious Cuban-inspired *frijoles negros,* which everyone will love. Eat them as they are or turn them into a creamy soup.

Many of you will have cooked black beans before and found them to be unpleasantly chalky no matter how long you cook them for. You've checked the bag for the use-by-date and simmered them a bit more and yet they still aren't creamy and buttery and you've given up in a huff. The problem is that black beans are very sensitive to hard water, which makes them tough. Cook them in a good mineral water and they'll be beautifully soft. Works every time, even if you live in a soft water area.

SERVE 4 (AND THEY REHEAT BEAUTIFULLY)

- **200g dried black beans**
- **1 large onion, finely diced**
- **1 green pepper, finely diced**
- **3 spring onions, finely diced**
- **4 cloves of garlic, finely chopped**
- **1 teaspoon dried oregano**
- **1 bay leaf**
- **1 teaspoon cumin seeds**
- **2 teaspoons brown sugar**
- **3 tablespoons vinegar (any except balsamic)**
- **650ml mineral water**
- **salt and pepper**

Put the beans in the slow-cooker crock. Add the finely chopped vegetables and garlic. Scatter the herbs and spices in and stir well. Season well and add the sugar.

Pour the vinegar and the mineral water over the beans. Put the lid on the slow cooker and cook on low for 8–10 hours.

When you are ready to serve, stir the beans well. The vegetables should be almost dissolved into them and the beans should be soft and collapsing with a thick black bean liquor surrounding them. I give mine a little squish with a potato masher just to soften them further.

Add enough stock or water to make the beans into a soup or eat as they are. They are best with a dollop of sour cream and some chopped spring onion on top. I serve mine on tortillas or with rice. The Pulled Pork from page 46 works a treat here too.

Note: If you'd like to do plain beans for freezing, simply cook the dried beans in 350ml mineral water with a pinch of salt on low for 8 hours. Drain off any cooking liquor, allow to cool thoroughly and portion them in freezer bags.

HOPPIN' JOHN

I have no idea who John was because I associate this recipe with a friend of my parents from when I was a child. Cynthia was from New Orleans and I never quite worked out how she'd come to Belfast of all places in the 1970s. She had travelled the world, knew all kinds of things that even the *National Geographic* didn't and scared me a little with her serious demeanour, long liquorice paper cigarettes and her glamour. She also fascinated me and sparked much of the interest that led to me reading American Studies. This is the dish I recall her cooking.

Hoppin' John is eaten throughout the Southern states of the USA, especially on New Year's Eve, when the black-eyed peas (as they're called in the US) are thought to represent good luck. It is usually made with rice as well, but the recipe written down years ago for my parents by Cynthia only has beans. I serve it over rice to be more traditional.

SERVES 4
(REHEATS WELL)

200g dried black-eyed beans

400g bacon cubes, pancetta or ham hock

2 onions, chopped

4 cloves of garlic, chopped

650ml water

boiled rice, to serve

chopped spring onion, to serve

salt and pepper

Put the black-eyed beans in the slow-cooker crock along with the bacon, onion and garlic. Season well. The dish requires no other flavourings.

Pour the water over it all and put the lid on the slow cooker and cook on low for 8 hours. Roughly mash some of the beans together with a potato masher before you serve them.

Serve over fluffy white rice and topped with some chopped spring onions. Leftovers are apparently called Skippin' Jenny. The names are almost as good as the dish!

MOI MOI

I first discovered moi moi at MTK Restaurant in Brixton, which serves Nigerian and West African dishes. Moi moi is a kind of steamed bean loaf made from black-eyed beans and is particularly popular at West African parties. For something so simple to prepare, it's incredibly tasty and it makes a fantastic vegetarian main dish everyone will love.

Try to skin your black-eyed beans as best you can before you blend them. The best way to do this is to put the soaked beans in a bowl and use a hand blender to pulse them once or twice to crack the skins. Then put them into cold water and rub the beans between your palms so that the skins float to the top. Don't worry if you can't get every black eye off: I won't tell anyone.

SERVES 4-6

200g dried black-eyed beans

250ml cold water

2 tablespoons tomato purée

1 teaspoon mustard powder

1 onion, finely

2 cloves of garlic, finely diced

½ green pepper, finely diced

½ red pepper, finely diced

1 red chilli, finely diced

salt and pepper

Soak your black-eyed beans in cold water overnight. Drain and rinse them well and skin them using the method above. Add the skinned beans to a large bowl and start to blend them with a hand blender, adding in 250ml cold water to form a thick paste.

Once the paste is as smooth as possible, stir the tomato purée, mustard powder, onion, garlic, peppers and chilli through it. Season it generously. Pour the paste into a 1lb disposable foil loaf tin, leaving about 4cm to allow room for the moi moi to expand. Cover the top of the tin with foil.

Place the filled loaf tin in the slow-cooker crock and pour boiling water into the crock until it comes about halfway up the side of the tin. Put the lid on the slow cooker and steam the moi moi on high for 5–6 hours.

The moi moi will slip out of the tin easily when cooked and can be cut into slices. Traditionally it is served with hard-boiled eggs inside it, but boiled eggs don't work well in the slow cooker, so serve them on the side instead if you miss them. Don't forget to add some hot sauce to your plate of moi moi.

CHILLI WITH DARK CHOCOLATE

OK, it's confession time: I don't like kidney beans and since they are usually in chilli, I don't really eat chilli either. But on a trip to California, I had a Tex-Mex style one made with just white beans that was so good I've spent the last decade and a bit trying to recreate it. All smoky from the chillies used, slightly bitter from the chocolate and creamy from the beans, it was fantastic.

This is the closest I've got to it without using an array of expensive dried chillies such as chipotles, anchos etc. The secret ingredient is a touch of instant coffee, which doesn't add a mocha tint, but renders it smoky and reminiscent of cooking over a campfire. Don't be put off by the long recipe list, this vegetarian chilli is very easy and frugal to make.

SERVES 4-6

2 teaspoons cumin seeds

2 teaspoons coriander seeds

2 dried red chillies

2 whole cloves

½ star anise

100g dried black-eyed beans

100g dried haricot beans

1 bay leaf

2 teaspoons smoked paprika

¼ teaspoon cayenne pepper

1 teaspoon dried oregano

2 teaspoons Marmite

2 teaspoons soy sauce

1 heaped teaspoon instant coffee

1 teaspoon brown sugar

1 teaspoon cider vinegar

1 tablespoon tomato purée

1 x 400g tin chopped tomatoes

400ml water

4 squares dark chocolate (about 25g)

sour cream, to serve

salt and pepper

Now I've scared you with a long ingredients list, here is a very easy and short recipe: Toast the cumin seeds, coriander seeds, dried chillies, cloves and star anise in a dry frying pan over a medium heat for about 2 minutes until they smell very fragrant. Crush them lightly using a pestle and mortar and add to the slow-cooker crock.

Put the dried beans in and then add the rest of the herbs and spices. Dollop in the Marmite, soy, coffee, sugar and vinegar along with the tomato purée and the chopped tomatoes. Season it all well, bearing in mind that the Marmite is quite salty. Pour the water in and stir it all. If the beans aren't completely covered, add another 100ml. Put the lid on the slow cooker and cook the chilli on low for 8 hours.

About 15 minutes before you are ready to eat, break the chocolate into squares and stir through. Add a splash of water if the chilli looks a little dry. The beans should be coated in a thick sauce. Pop the lid back on and warm for another 15–20 minutes to allow the chocolate to melt in.

Serve spoonfuls of the chilli in bowls along with some sour cream, if you fancy it. Any leftovers make amazing nachos when spread over tortilla chips and covered with grated cheese.

This chilli will easily stretch to 6 servings with some steamed cornbread on the side (page 221).

WHITE CHILLI

Most chilli involves lashings of tomatoes to add colour and flavour, but this white version uses chicken and green chillies instead of kidney beans or tomatoes. I like to make this one in the summer while staying out of the sun to keep my Celtic skin going from white to red. The light flavour suits lighter, brighter days beautifully.

I make this chilli from scratch with unsoaked beans, so it's a simple one-pot easy meal. I have never tried it with tinned beans as the dried ones become so creamy and lovely.

SERVES 4
(REHEATS WELL)

100g dried haricot or cannellini beans

100g dried black-eyed beans

2 fresh green chillies

2 onions, diced

2 cloves of garlic, diced

2 stalks of celery, diced

4–6 chicken thighs

2 teaspoons cumin seeds

1 teaspoon coriander seeds

1 teaspoon dried oregano

¼ teaspoon ground cloves

¼ teaspoon cayenne pepper

330ml beer (I used a lager here as you don't want anything too dark)

150ml water

1 tablespoon cider vinegar

75g sliced pickled jalapeños, sliced

100g crumbly Lancashire cheese, to serve

25g fresh coriander, to serve

salt and white pepper

Put the dried beans in the slow-cooker crock and chop the green chillies, adding them in along with the seeds. Add the onion, garlic and celery. Skin and debone the chicken thighs and cut them into quarters. Add into the crock. Tie the bones together with some string and add them in as well.

Toast the cumin and coriander seeds in a dry frying pan until they smell aromatic. Remove from the heat immediately and give them a thump using a pestle and mortar or rolling pin to release the flavours. Toss them into the slow cooker along with the oregano, cloves and cayenne. Season well.

Pour the beer over it all. Make sure the beans are completely submerged by adding the water. Pour in the vinegar too. Put the lid on the slow cooker and cook the chilli on low for 8–9 hours.

Remove the chicken bones and stir well to break up the meat a bit.

Serve the chilli topped with sliced pickled jalapeños, grated cheese and fresh coriander. My local pound shop stocks a dazzling array of pickled and char-grilled veg in jars, so I've got quite into using them as a garnish on various things in between eating them straight out of the jar...

GUERNSEY BEAN JAR

I came across this slow-cooked bean dish from Guernsey when I turned up at my friend Alex's house for the inaugural meeting of our Twitter-based book group. I was expecting dips and chips to soak up the wine, but she had gone all out with the slow cooker since we were reading a Guernsey-based book and she felt we should have local flavours to accompany it.

The dish was so good I actually got Alex to write out the recipe long hand and this is my version of it. I'd just like to declare that I've never been to Guernsey, but I am aware of the hot debate on the island about putting carrots in a bean jar. Most people say no, but Alex does it and I trust her judgement on pretty much everything else, so I'm not doubting her now.

You can also make bean jar with pork instead of beef. A ham hock and a pigs' trotter make a lovely rich, thick version.

SERVES 4 AS A
MAIN MEAL WITH
LEFTOVERS

500g beef shin or brisket

100g dried haricot beans

100g dried butter beans

1 x 400g tin flageolet beans

2 onions, chopped into 2cm pieces

2 carrots, chopped into 2cm pieces

500ml water

chopped parsley, to serve

salt and pepper

Cut the slices of beef shin or brisket in half and add to the slow-cooker crock. Put the dried haricot and butter beans in. Drain the flageolet beans and rinse well. Add them in too. They are quite inauthentic, but I use them because they are a favourite of mine and they thicken the bean jar beautifully.

Add the onion and carrot. Season well and pour in the water. Put the lid on the slow cooker and cook your bean jar on low for 9–10 hours.

It should be thick and hearty with a real creaminess from the beans. The meat will have fallen apart into tender strands, so a little goes a long way. Sprinkle with parsley and serve in bowls. Try to serve this stew with good crusty bread and lots of Guernsey butter. I'll even let you read at the table if you ask nicely.

BRIXTON BAKED BEANS

When I was fifteen, I spent the summer with a family in Boston looking after their kids. No child in Boston doesn't like baked beans, which are a local tradition due to the city's connection with making molasses. This dark nectar is their secret ingredient. Unfortunately for my vegetarian teenage self, the other secret ingredient in Boston baked beans is salt pork and it was suggested I just pick the pork out and get on with it.

This biased me against baked beans until I got the slow cooker. Adding in some pomegranate molasses to give a savoury depth instead of meat converted me back to them and I love this Brixton version. I still don't do them on toast though. Try the Boston Brown Bread with them (see page 222) instead.

Pomegranate molasses is sweet, sour and savoury all at once compared to the regular version. If you can't get it, use some Fig and Pomegranate Relish from page 194 and add about a tablespoon of vinegar to replicate the layers of flavour it adds.

SERVES 4

200g dried haricot
  beans

1 onion, finely chopped

1 x 400g tin chopped
  tomatoes

4 tablespoons
  pomegranate
  molasses

3 tablespoons tomato
  purée

2 tablespoons brown
  sugar

2 teaspoons smoked
  paprika

½ teaspoon ground
  cloves

2 teaspoons mustard
  powder

500ml cold water

Put the dried haricot beans into the slow-cooker crock and add the onion and tomatoes.

Measure out the pomegranate molasses into a cup or bowl and add the tomato purée, sugar, paprika, cloves and mustard and stir it all together. This makes it easier to combine with the beans.

Pour this mix into the beans and stir well so that they are as evenly coated as possible. Add the water, put the lid on the slow cooker and cook on high for 7–8 hours.

The beans will swell and plump up and the sauce will thicken and intensify in flavour. It is rich and dark and much more grown-up than the tinned version. The beans reheat well and everyone loves them, no matter what their age.

CHORIZO BUTTER BEANS

If you are looking for a really tasty and easy dish, then let me introduce you to these butter beans. Cooking the beans from dried in the slow cooker lets you see exactly what they mean about them being buttery. You'll find it hard to believe pulses can be this good with so little effort. And if you have leftovers, they make wonderful Stuffed Tomatoes (see page 133).

SERVES 2 AS A
MAIN MEAL OR
4 AS A SIDE

200g dried butter beans

1 onion, diced

4 cloves of garlic, sliced

200g chorizo, cubed

1 heaped teaspoon smoked paprika

250g cherry tomatoes or 1 x 400g tin plum tomatoes

450ml water

salt and pepper

Put the dried butter beans into the slow-cooker crock, add the onion, garlic and chorizo and combine. Scatter the paprika and tomatoes over it all and add the water.

Put the lid on the slow cooker and cook on low for 8 hours. The beans will be so fattened up they are literally bursting out of their skins, the tomatoes will have collapsed into the beans and there will be a thick paprika-infused sauce studded with chorizo. Season well with salt and pepper and serve. This is one-pot food at its simple best.

ROSEMARY, GARLIC AND LEMON BUTTER BEANS

I just cannot get enough of the beautiful butter bean in the slow cooker. They are as grumpy as I am when woken on a Monday morning in November when they are cooked quickly on the stove – their skins wrinkle as if they are pulling their duvets round them and the flesh inside becomes chalky and dry in protest.

But slow cooked, they relax and soften as much as if they were sitting in the garden on a June afternoon with a long, cool drink and good company. They plump up and become smooth and velvety, allowing you to serve them as a side dish, mashed as an alternative to potatoes or squashed into a heavenly dip with pitta bread. Simple and summery all year round.

SERVES 2-4
(DEPENDING ON
WHEN YOU RUN
OUT OF PITTA
BREAD)

200g dried butter beans

6 cloves of garlic, finely chopped

2 sprigs of fresh rosemary

1 lemon, zested and juiced (if waxed, give it a vigorous scrub under the hot tap first)

650ml water

1 lemon, juiced, to serve

salt and white pepper

Put the dried butter beans in the slow-cooker crock and add in the garlic and rosemary. It really is best to use fresh rosemary here rather than the dried stuff in jars, which tastes thin in comparison. Strip it off the branches and chop the needles finely.

Add the lemon zest and juice of 1 lemon into the beans, then season. I like them with quite a generous hand with the salt and not too much pepper.

Pour the water over it all and put the lid on the slow cooker. Cook on low for 8 hours until the beans are falling apart and creating a thick, beany liquor. Taste and season again if needed. Squeeze the juice of the second lemon over them and serve.

If you want to make a mash to go with lamb, add a tablespoon of olive oil and crush with a potato masher to give a rustic feel rather than a purée.

To make a dip, add 2 tablespoons of olive oil and 2 tablespoons of water to begin with and use a hand blender to get a texture that you can scoop onto pitta bread. Add more water if needed. Theoretically it keeps well in the fridge, but it rarely lasts that long.

CHICKPEAS

Whenever anyone hears you are cooking on a budget, they extol the virtue and cheapness of dried pulses. This generally isn't news to anyone who is eating frugally and ignores the fact that soaking your own pulses requires a certain amount of forethought, a very large saucepan and a fairly endless capacity to eat them as it's impossible to do small portions.

I have to admit, I've rarely bothered with dried pulses despite years of living on a budget. The cost to faff ratio seemed skewed. Then I learned two things: you can cook pulses (*except* kidney beans) from dry in the slow cooker and you can freeze them once cooked. Sold to the lady with the bag of chickpeas in the cupboard.

This recipe makes enough for several meals and you can whip up a batch of hummus that's much tastier and cheaper than those wee pots in the chiller cabinet. The faff levels are extremely low…

**SERVES 4
(MAKES ABOUT
600G COOKED)**

200g dried chickpeas
500ml boiling water

Put the dried chickpeas into the slow-cooker crock. Add the boiling water. Don't add salt as it makes them tough and mealy.

Put the lid on the slow cooker and cook the chickpeas on high for 8 hours. You will have perfect plump chickpeas at the end of it.

You can now use these chickpeas the way you would the tinned ones or simply portion them into bags or containers and freeze until needed.

Note: One thing I'd caution is to check just how old your chickpeas are before cooking. The older they are, the less likely they are to plump up no matter which way you cook them. If they are older than a year, invest in new ones and check the sell-by-date in the store.

HUMMUS

If you use the slow-cooker chickpeas (above), making a batch of this will take less time and effort than queuing up with a small pot of the shop-bought stuff after work.

250g cooked chickpeas

**3 tablespoons tahini,
mixed with 2
tablespoons water
if thick**

2 lemons, juiced

**2 cloves of garlic,
crushed (optional)**

60ml olive oil

30ml water

salt and pepper

Put the chickpeas in a bowl. Add the tahini and blend until it's a dropping consistency.

Add the lemon juice, garlic and oil. Blend or smash until it's as smooth as possible. Add the water if it's too stiff. Season after you add the water.

FALAFEL

These little balls of chickpeas were my favourite vegetarian snack when I was meat free. I still love a falafel in a pitta bread or wrap after the pub. I've eaten many and the very best are light and almost fluffy. Making them in the slow cooker is foolproof for getting this perfect texture and skips the whole deep-frying stage. You can still come home to them from the pub and best of all, there's no queue in your kitchen, but you get the best falafel you'll eat this side of Jerusalem.

This recipe uses dried chickpeas you have soaked for 8 hours. They don't need to be cooked before you make the falafel. Tinned chickpeas aren't suitable for this recipe.

MAKES ABOUT 25
AND THEY KEEP
WELL IN THE
FRIDGE

200g dried chickpeas

**150g mashed pumpkin
or sweet potato**

**1 teaspoon ground
coriander**

**1 teaspoon ground
cumin**

**1 teaspoon red chilli
powder**

**2 tablespoons plain
flour**

salt and pepper

Soak the chickpeas for around 8 hours in cold water. Drain and rinse the chickpeas well and set aside.

I use leftover roast sweet potatoes or pumpkin here, but if you don't have any handy, steam them freshly to prevent them from becoming too watery. Squeeze any excess water from the pumpkin or sweet potato.

Put the soaked chickpeas, spices and seasoning in a large bowl. Use a hand blender to blend the chickpeas until they form what looks like a slightly powdery batter. Add the pumpkin and blend again briefly. It will look quite firm.

Add half the flour and mix well. Add the other half and stir until combined. The batter will now be firm and not sticky. Chill it for at least 30 minutes. Line the slow-cooker crock with baking liner or greaseproof paper.

Scoop a teaspoon-sized blob out of the batter with a spoon or your finger and thumb and roll it into a ball. Set each falafel into the lined slow cooker with a little bit of space between them. Once you have one layer in the crock, cover them with more greaseproof paper or baking liner and do a second layer if needed.

Put the lid on the slow cooker and cook the falafel as they are on low for 8 hours or high for 6 hours. They will develop a lovely crisp golden shell that makes a good contrast to the moist inner. I also sometimes cook them in Tomato Sauce (see page 132) to make them more like meatballs. The same cooking times apply.

PEASE PUDDING

Until I visited the Northeast of England, I thought pease pudding was something that you heard about in nursery rhymes and as unlikely to be served these days as pies with four and twenty blackbirds. I was wrong. Pease pudding, especially in a stottie or roll, is a way of life up there. And quite right too, because it's delicious.

Pease pudding is traditionally made with ham. I'm sure you could do a vegetarian version, but it's such a good excuse to cook a ham or gammon joint outside the Christmas season that I've never done it meat free. You can cook the peas alongside the ham in the same stock or use bacon or gammon pieces. So you have no excuses not to try 'pease pudding hot, pease pudding cold', without keeping it nine days in the pot.

SERVES 4–6

200g yellow split peas,
pinch of bicarbonate
   of soda
1 onion, diced
1 carrot, diced
2 bay leaves
2 whole cloves
¼ teaspoon ground
   nutmeg
¼ teaspoon salt
¼ teaspoon white
   pepper
750g (approx) ham or
   gammon joint
700-900ml cold water
1 egg, beaten

Soak the split peas overnight in lots of cold water with a pinch of bicarbonate of soda. Next day, drain and rinse them well.

Take a large, clean muslin cloth (found in the baby section of a supermarket) and put the soaked split peas, onion, carrot, bay leaves, cloves, nutmeg, salt and pepper into the cloth. Gather it up so that it makes a purse shape. Give it room to expand and then tie the top with string.

Place the ham joint into the slow-cooker crock and cover with the water. It doesn't matter if the very top of the ham pokes out a little bit. Dangle the muslin cloth into the water so it is completely submerged. Tie the string round the handle of the slow-cooker lid if you can, to keep it in place.

Put the lid on the slow cooker as snugly as you can and cook on high for 3–4 hours. At this point, check the ham. It should be cooked, but still nicely tender. Lift it out, set aside and continue to cook the pease pudding on high for another 3–4 hours to allow it to soak up the ham stock.

Take the muslin cloth of pease pudding out of the slow cooker and tip into a dish. Remove the bay leaves. Beat the egg through it quickly so the residual heat cooks it. This gives a lovely soft texture to the pudding.

Chop the ham into small chunks and add into the pease pudding before serving. Serve hot with steamed cabbage or spread cold on a stottie.

Note: If you don't have a ham joint, use 300g bacon or cooked, cubed gammon. Put the split peas, onion, carrot and the herbs and spices into the slow-cooker crock. Add the cubed ham or gammon and 250ml cold water. Put the lid on the slow cooker and cook the pease pudding on high for 6-7 hours. When you are ready to serve the pease pudding, fish out the bay leaves and beat the egg into it to loosen the texture.

MUSHY PEAS

My friend Glen and I have been known to frequent a certain popular peri-peri chicken chain where he can indulge his unlimited love of condiments and I can indulge my unlimited love of the bottomless soft drinks before we vibrate home on a mix of chilli and caffeine. We also always order the same dishes as we catch up. A confirmed hater of peas, he rolls his eyes at my love of the 'macho peas' they serve there. Or maybe it's my inability to eat them without having to push them onto my fork with my finger when I think no one is looking?

Here I've combined them with the easier to eat feel of the traditional mushy peas. Spiked with chilli and vinegar, everyone will fall in love with these peas. Even Glen.

SERVES 4–6 AS
A SIDE DISH

1 box or 250g dried
  marrowfat peas

½ teaspoon sugar

2 tablespoons mint
  sauce

1 teaspoon vinegar
  (cider, malt, white or
  white wine)

1 red chilli, deseeded
  and chopped

400ml cold water

1 Scotch bonnet
  pepper, whole

salt and pepper

Soak the marrowfat peas overnight in 850ml boiling water using both the tablets from inside the box. These help tenderise the peas so they soak up the water when cooking and become lovely and creamy. I soak mine directly in the crock.

Once the peas are plumped up, tip them into a colander and rinse well. Place back in the slow-cooker crock and add the sugar, salt and pepper, mint sauce, vinegar and chopped chilli. Pour the 400ml cold water over them. Float the Scotch bonnet pepper in it. Put the lid on the slow cooker and cook on low for 6–7 hours.

When you are ready to eat, remove the whole Scotch bonnet. It will have infused the peas with its fruity flavour and added some extra warmth without being unmanageably hot. Serve the peas with a dash more mint sauce or some fresh mint. I love these with some Brixton Chicken Wings (see page 62) or as a take on the ubiquitous hummus with pitta bread.

DAL MAKHANI

This is luxury dal. Invented in the five-star Moti Mahal Hotel in Delhi, its roots are in the dairy-loving Punjab. Based around the same spices and creaminess as the Butter Chicken on page 172, this is the dal to eat when you want to treat yourself. You just don't need to pay five-star prices for its unique slow-cooked texture, but don't be tempted to rush it. Things this luxurious take time even by slow-cooker standards.

SERVES 4 AS A MAIN

200g mung beans

100g yellow lentils

2 tablespoons ghee
(see page 173)

4 cloves of garlic

3–4cm piece of fresh
ginger

2 dried chillies, whole

4 tablespoons tomato
purée

2 teaspoons fenugreek
seeds

1 teaspoon cumin
seeds

1 teaspoon coriander
seeds

½ teaspoon chilli
powder

½ teaspoon salt

¼ teaspoon ground
mace

¼ teaspoon black
pepper

1 litre cold water

120ml cream

50g fresh coriander

1 teaspoon Garam
Masala (see page 168)

Traditionally, dal makhani uses urad sabot, or black lentils, but they are very hard to find in the UK unless you have a specialist shop nearby. I find the much more common mung bean does the trick beautifully.

This is incredibly simple to make in the slow cooker. Basically put all the ingredients except the cream, garam masala and fresh coriander in your slow-cooker crock.

Put the lid on and cook on low for 12–14 hours, checking about halfway through to stir it and add another 250ml water if needed. The texture should be quite loose rather than thick. The beans and lentils will thicken and collapse into a rich, glossy sauce and the aroma will be incredibly alluring.

When you are ready to serve, stir the cream into the dal and scatter with the fresh coriander and garam masala (I add the cream and the coriander to the serving bowls, rather than the crock, if I'm reheating any of the dal). It should be almost soup-like in its texture, so devour it with a spoon and maybe a chapatti to make sure you can wipe the bowl clean. Bet you can't do that in a five-star hotel!

TARKA DAL

People think lentils are dull or worthy, but they clearly haven't had a proper bowl of dal or they'd think again. Done properly, the lentils become creamy, bolstered with spices and slow-cooked to a heavenly texture. Adding the tarka, or spiced butter, adds a depth and intensity that will make you crave dal when you need comforting.

Make a big batch of this dal as you won't be able to resist a second helping and maybe a third. And dipping your spoon in every time you pass the fridge. There are never any leftovers when I make it for people, just dishes that have been scraped clean.

Dal is simply a term in India for the split version of peas, beans or lentils and chana dal is actually a type of split chickpea rather than lentils. These, or the yellow split peas, are better for the slow cooker than the usual red or brown lentils, which can become waterlogged.

SERVES 4 WELL

2 onions, sliced, or 150g Caramelised Onions (see page 122)

25g butter

2 large fresh tomatoes

200g chana dal or yellow split peas

4cm piece of fresh ginger, finely chopped

4 cloves of garlic, finely chopped

2 teaspoons paprika

1 teaspoon fenugreek seeds

1 teaspoon ground turmeric

½ teaspoon chilli powder

1 litre boiling water

1½ teaspoons Garam Masala (see page 168)

salt and pepper

If you don't have any of the Caramelised Onions from page 122, simply cook the 2 sliced onions in the butter over a low heat for about 25 minutes until they start to soften and brown round the edges, before proceeding with the recipe as below.

Start by peeling the tomatoes. The best way to do this is to cut a cross in the top and the bottom of the tomatoes and pour boiling water over the top of them. The skin will wrinkle and you can peel it off easily.

Then cut the tomatoes into quarters and remove the seeds. Cut each quarter in half again and chop roughly. They will dissolve into the dal in a tomatoey haze that tinned ones just can't quite replicate, so do use fresh ones if you can.

Put the chopped fresh tomatoes into the slow-cooker crock. Add the lentils and onions, including the butter if you've caramelised them specially. Add the ginger and garlic.

Measure the spices into the crock and add the butter if you haven't used it to soften the onions. Pour the boiling water into the crock and stir well so the butter starts to melt. Season the dal well. It needs a fair bit of salt to boost all the other flavours.

Put the lid on the slow cooker and cook on high for 8 hours minimum. I like it best stirred after 8 hours and given another hour or so to just come together completely. Add the garam masala just as you serve it.

Serve as a main meal with just a tiny smidgen more butter or on the side of a curry. If you don't eat butter, it works just as well with oil.

GARLIC AND HERB LENTILS WITH GOAT'S CHEESE

I know every vegetarian in the country is thinking 'more goat's cheese?' after eating their own body weight in the tartlets and risottos on every veggie menu in the nation's pubs and restaurants, but I promise this dish is really delicious. Equally popular with meat eaters, it uses those beautiful green Puy lentils from France.

A little bit more expensive than green lentils, these dappled little gems hold their shape well in the slow cooker and, as you'd expect from a Gallic delicacy, they love to be combined with garlic and onions for a nutty, rich flavour. The goat's cheese complements it all nicely. Use one as mild and creamy or strong and crumbly as you prefer.

SERVES 2 AS A
MAIN MEAL OR
4 AS A SIDE

200g Puy lentils
(uncooked weight)

1 red onion, finely
chopped

2 shallots, finely
chopped

4 cloves of garlic,
finely chopped

2 sprigs of fresh sage,
finely chopped

2 sprigs of fresh thyme

1 sprig of fresh
rosemary, finely
chopped

350ml water

1 tablespoon olive oil

1 tablespoon balsamic
vinegar

1 teaspoon Dijon
mustard

25g fresh flat-leaf
parsley, to serve

100g goat's cheese,
sliced, to serve

salt and pepper

Put the lentils in the slow-cooker crock along with the onion, shallot and garlic. Add the sage, thyme and rosemary and season well.

Pour the water over it all and put the lid on the slow cooker. Cook the lentils on low for 7–8 hours until they are tender and have absorbed most of the water, but have a lovely thick sauce coating them.

Make a quick vinaigrette by whisking the olive oil and the balsamic vinegar together with the mustard and pouring it over the hot herbed lentils. Allow to cool slightly and serve scattered with the chopped parsley and slices of the goat's cheese.

Note: If your tastes are more carnivorous, you can make this dish without the goat's cheese and with sausages instead. Simply brown a few plump pork sausages, such as sage-rich Lincolnshires, and nestle them into the lentils as you cook them. Drizzle with the vinaigrette and parsley and serve.

BEETROOT ORZOTTO

I'm on a mission to introduce more people to pearl barley. This chewy, nutty grain is an underrated ingredient that I just adore. Incredibly inexpensive, it works brilliantly in soups such as the Scotch Broth on page 146 or the Black Bean and Squash Stew with Kale and Barley on page 87, but it gets to dress up for the evening and show itself off when it comes to making an orzotto.

This is the Italian word for a pearl barley risotto and I think it works much better in the slow cooker than the traditional rice-based risotto, which can become mushy. Pearl barley retains some bite and texture while intensifying the flavours you add to it. This is the thing to cook when people come round and you want to impress with minimal effort.

Dried porcini mushrooms may seem expensive, but they are so packed with flavour than you will get five or six dishes from one packet, which makes them a great store cupboard ingredient. They are particularly rich in umami, or the fifth taste, which has the savoury tones usually associated with meat, making them many a vegetarian's secret weapon.

SERVES 2–4 (ANY LEFTOVERS ARE GREAT IN STUFFED TOMATOES OR CABBAGE LEAVES)

5g dried porcini mushrooms

100ml boiling water

1 onion, finely chopped

2 cloves of garlic, finely chopped

200g pearl barley

550ml hot stock

100ml vermouth or white wine

250g cooked pre-packed beetroot

50g Parmesan or another Italian hard cheese (to be vegetarian), grated

salt and pepper

Start by rehydrating the porcini mushrooms in the boiling water and allowing them to soak for 10 minutes.

Put the onion, garlic and pearl barley in the slow-cooker crock. Finely slice the rehydrated porcini and add them along with the soaking liquid. Pour the hot stock over it all and stir it well. Add the vermouth. Season with pepper and a cautious amount of salt if using a stock cube.

Put the lid on the slow-cooker and cook on high for 3 hours or low for 6 hours. The pearl barley will plump up and make a rich, chewy orzotto.

About 30 minutes before you are ready to eat, finely chop or purée the beetroot with a hand blender and stir it through the orzotto. Put the lid back on the slow cooker and allow it to heat through.

Stir the grated Parmesan through it all and serve with good company and a cold glass of wine. It is the most vividly pink meal you'll have eaten since you were about six and all the better for it!

You can also take inspiration from the porcini here and replace the beetroot with a selection of fresh mushrooms. White, chestnut and portobello ones all work well sliced and added at least an hour before the end of cooking.

BUCKWHEAT, CAULIFLOWER AND TAHINI SALAD

Buckwheat, despite the name, isn't related to wheat and is naturally gluten free and especially popular in Eastern Europe, where it is also known as *kasha*. Buy it toasted and it has a rich, nutty flavour. It is immensely filling and can be bought in Polish delis or supermarket sections cheaply under the name of *kasza*. It is especially good as a cold salad or mixed with Puy lentils to make them go further.

Tahini is sesame paste, often used to give hummus its nutty flavour. It may seem expensive to buy, but it keeps forever and a little goes a long, long way. Look for Lebanese brands like Al Nakhil, which have a loose texture, as these are even better value.

SERVES 2 WITH LEFTOVERS

500ml water

100g buckwheat

drizzle of olive oil

50g kale, finely shredded

dash of vegetable oil

pinch of sea salt

2 cloves of garlic

50ml plain yoghurt (see home-made Yoghurt page 202)

50ml tahini

½ lemon, juiced

50g feta or Greek-salad cheese, cubed

1 Whole Spiced Cauliflower (see page 118), cut into florets

salt and pepper

Start by cooking the buckwheat. If you are in a rush, you can do this on the hob. Boil 500ml water and salt it generously. Add the buckwheat and boil for 8–10 minutes until the grains start to puff up and there isn't much water left. Lower the heat to the lowest setting, put the lid on and cook for another 10–15 minutes until the buckwheat is puffed up, each grain is separate and the water totally absorbed.

To do it in the slow cooker, boil as above. Then pour the buckwheat and the remaining water into your slow cooker. Put the lid on and set it on low for 1 hour. This mimics the Eastern European method of putting your buckwheat into a special low oven to dry out.

When the buckwheat is ready, drizzle with olive oil and allow to cool slightly while you prepare the kale and make the dressing.

Mix the kale with a dash of vegetable oil and a pinch of sea salt. Using clean hands, massage the kale between your palms for about 3 minutes to soften it. This makes it tastier and gives it a delicious texture.

Crush the garlic and mix with the yoghurt and tahini. Add the lemon juice and about 25ml water if you have a thicker tahini like most British brands. If you have a looser Middle-Eastern version like the Al Nakhil brand, you don't need the water. You want the dressing to be pourable.

Toss the massaged kale, feta and the cauliflower florets through the buckwheat and season. Pour some dressing over it all and serve. This will keep for a day in the fridge, even when dressed, and makes a great packed lunch.

POLENTA

Pasta isn't the only carb in town in Italy. Northern Italians traditionally eat polenta, which is best (if a little unromantically) described as a slow-cooked porridge made from cornmeal. These days you can get all kinds of quick-cook or ready-made versions and they are as lacking in charm as my description of polenta. Nothing beats doing it slowly to get the correct creamy texture. And best of all, the slow cooker saves you the old-fashioned hassle of stirring and stirring to get it right like Nonna would have done. A generous knob of butter will finish it off in style.

Before you start, it's useful to know that in supermarkets anything labelled 'polenta' will cost twice as much as 'coarse cornmeal'. Hunt around, usually on the lowest shelf, and you will probably discover bags of cornmeal from a well-known Caribbean company, which is extremely good value. This bottom-shelf trick also works well with bags of pulses and soup mixes.

SERVES 4 WITH LEFTOVERS

175g coarse cornmeal

850ml boiling water or stock

50g butter

50g Parmesan, grated (optional)

salt and pepper

Pour your cornmeal into the slow-cooker crock and add the boiling liquid. Season well and put the lid on. Cook on low for 6–7 hours or high for 3–4. The polenta will have thickened and become creamy.

Stir in the butter and Parmesan, if using (omit the Parmesan or use another Italian hard cheese instead to make this dish vegetarian), and serve alongside the Meat Ragu on page 25 or the Squash and Spinach Ragout on page 125. It's spectacularly filling, so a little goes a long way and you'll have leftovers.

Note: To turn the leftovers into something special, line a baking tray with greaseproof paper and spread the remaining polenta out on it so it looks like a pizza base. Allow to cool completely. It will set firmly and you can then slice it up into chunks. Fry these cubes in olive oil so that the edges crisp up and go golden. Scatter over salads, like the Octopus, Polenta and Pepper Salad on page 81, stews or onto soups as a gluten-free take on croutons.

MACARONI CHEESE

I love macaroni cheese. It's the taste of simple childhood dinners where delicious food was the reason to gather round the table together and have a proper family dinner. Served piping hot from the oven with tomatoes on the top, it was a real favourite of Mister North and I when we were wee. It was also the source of a family joke that makes me giggle to this day, when my dad once made it and forgot the cheese. The laughter that provoked just made it taste all the better.

This is a simple way to make macaroni cheese for a large number of people (or those with big appetites) without all the various stages and pots and pans it usually requires. Don't be alarmed by the use of evaporated milk. It simply thickens the regular milk in the slow cooker without the sauce splitting.

SERVES 4 COMFORTABLY

350g cheese, grated

500g dried macaroni (not wholewheat or quick cook)

2 tablespoons cornflour

1 teaspoon mustard powder

¼ teaspoon white pepper

400ml unsweetened evaporated milk

600ml full-fat milk

I take a leaf from Mister North's book here and use a mixture of cheeses, usually about 200g Cheddar, 100g mozzarella and 50g Parmesan. You could simply use all Cheddar, but it needs to be quite mature to add flavour. I don't add salt to my macaroni cheese as I find the cheese salty enough. Your taste may vary.

Place the macaroni into the slow-cooker crock and sprinkle the cornflour over it all. Stir to coat it as evenly as possible. Add the mustard powder and the pepper.

Mix the evaporated milk with the full-fat milk and pour both over the macaroni. Scatter the grated cheese over it all and mix well so it is evenly distributed.

Put the lid on the slow cooker and cook on low for 2 hours. I often set my timer to turn the slow cooker on later in the day so I come home to bubbling hot macaroni cheese with no effort.

Serve the macaroni cheese immediately. I get my tomato fix with a splodge of the Easy Tomato Ketchup from page 188. There are never leftovers.

Note: If you'd like to make this for two people, simply halve the amounts and follow the same cooking time.

GRANOLA

This is a breakfast with a bit of bite and a lot of luxury. The recipe was given to my mum about twenty years ago when she had been unwell. She recovered completely and quickly and barely a month has gone by without a batch of this granola being made. I think that tells you how wholesome and healthy this is.

You need the oats, sesame seeds and wheatgerm as the basis, but you can adapt it anyway you like beyond that. Add nuts, seeds, dried fruit or even chocolate chips. No matter what you go for it works out much more affordable than the stylish boxes of granola you can buy. Serve this crunchy granola with yoghurt or milk or stir a handful into porridge. I rather like it dry as a snack in front of the telly. One batch is never enough.

MAKES AROUND
750G

85g jumbo oats
250g porridge oats
30g wheatgerm
45g sesame seeds
45g pumpkin seeds
45g sunflower seeds
45g flaked coconut
100g nuts of your
  choice (I favour
  broken Brazil nuts)
pinch of salt
120ml sunflower oil
120ml clear honey
1 teaspoon vanilla
  extract
100g dried fruit (added
  as the granola cools)

Measure out your oats, wheatgerm and sesame seeds into your slow-cooker crock. If you prefer you can use all jumbo oats or all smaller porridge oats, but I think this mix is the best texture.

Add in the seeds, coconut and nuts and mix well. If you go for hazelnuts and linseeds for example instead, use the same proportions so you get a spoonful of everything each time. Sprinkle with the pinch of salt.

Heat the oil and honey in a small pan on the hob over a medium heat until it is completely combined. Add the vanilla extract and pour this oil and honey mix into the slow-cooker crock and stir well. It will look like it isn't enough liquid for the dry mix, but keep mixing and it will coat it all perfectly without needing to add more.

Cover the top of the crock with kitchen roll and put the lid on. Cook on low for 2 hours. Remove the kitchen roll, stir well and give it another 30 minutes cooking.

Remove from the heat and spread out on a tray to cool. The granola will feel soft when it comes out of the slow cooker, but crisps as it cools, so don't be tempted to cook it longer to get it crunchy or it will burn. It should be a golden toasted colour.

Cool for an hour and then put into an airtight container to keep it crisp. If you move it carefully, you can keep it in little clusters of granola or you can break it up depending which texture you prefer. You'll get really good at knowing how you like it as you'll make this granola repeatedly.

Pub quiz fact: Granola is cooked to be crunchy. Muesli is kept raw to be soft.

PORRIDGE

Pretty much the first thing everyone asks me when they hear about my slow-cooking skills is 'Can you make porridge in the slow cooker?' The answer is yes, but just not the way you thought.

I had visions of putting oats and milk in the crock, turning it on to low and waking up to perfect piping hot porridge in the morning while avoiding the evils of washing the porridge pan. Instead I got burnt, gluey oats that tasted of powdered milk and failure. My brother experienced the same, unable to replicate our Scottish father's skills with the crock and a bag of oats.

Then I started, slightly obsessively, reading about the perfect porridge and my eye was drawn to the word 'porringer'. Not just a quaint term one hears in nursery rhymes, this is a double boiler or bain marie for cooking porridge slowly, using indirect heat to make it creamy and prevent it boiling. I had my slow-cooker porridge method...

Per person you need:

½ cup of porridge
   or jumbo oats
   (not the kind that
   come in sachets for
   microwaving)
1 cup water
   decent pinch of
   sea salt

I usually make my porridge half milk and half water on the stove, but this slow-cooked method makes water-based porridge incredibly creamy and you really don't need the milk. It can actually taste a bit like coffee creamer if you cook the milk for ages, so I stick to just water. Don't skip the salt. It really enhances the flavour of the oats and makes the porridge even tastier.

Put a 1.2-litre pudding basin in the slow-cooker crock. Put the oats and the water into it. Add the salt and mix well. You should be able to get up to four portions in this basin at a time, allowing you to make breakfast for several people.

Pour boiling water into the slow-cooker crock until it comes about two-thirds of the way up the side of the basin. Put a lid on the basin and put the lid on the slow cooker and cook on low for at least 5 hours. I like it best at about 7 hours, but it'll work if you leave it up to 12 hours.

As long as you put the lid back on the slow cooker, people can help themselves at different times once the porridge is cooked, allowing you to feed lots of people with only one porridge pot to wash. Three bears optional...

VEGETABLES

Vegetables get overlooked a little bit in the slow cooker, playing second fiddle to meat and pulses. If you pick the right kinds of veg and handle them well, you'll be pleasantly surprised just how well you can cook them in the slow cooker.

By a strange quirk, root vegetables actually take longer to cook in the slow cooker than meat. They need to be chopped small and to an even size to allow them to be cooked alongside meat or poultry so that they are ready at the same time. I peel all mine to aid the cooking process further. Don't use too much liquid to prevent them becoming waterlogged as you still want them to have texture despite the long cooking times.

Choose the right vegetables for your need. Sweet potatoes hold their shape and flavour, pumpkin has a higher water content and is more like to collapse, waxy or firm potatoes like Charlottes or Desirées won't break down and thicken stews like a floury Rooster or King Edward potato will. Many green vegetables like kale or peas aren't at their best after slow cooking, so add them at the end of cooking to retain bite.

Following this rule of the right vegetable for the right dish will open up possibilities for slow-cooker dishes only restricted by your imagination. You'll have no trouble getting your 'five a day' this way.

FUCHSIA-INSPIRED AUBERGINES

One of my favourite cookbooks is the wonderful *Sichuan Cookery* by Fuchsia Dunlop. Not only are her recipes mouthwatering, she writes beautifully, making it a treat to read as well as cook from.

This is my adaptation of the Sichuan classic of fish-fragrant aubergine for the slow cooker. The name refers to the style in which fish is often cooked and this dish is in fact fish-free and completely vegetarian and vegan.

It is extremely simple to make and is delicious alongside rice and a quickly wilted green leafy vegetable of your choice. I inauthentically serve it scattered with toasted sesame seeds instead of using expensive sesame oil.

SERVES 2-4 AS A SIDE DISH

- 2 aubergines
- 1 tablespoon sea salt
- 1 tablespoon vegetable oil
- 2–3cm piece of fresh ginger, finely chopped (or 1 tablespoon ground)
- 2 cloves of garlic, chopped
- 1 red chilli, chopped
- 1 teaspoon soy sauce
- 1 teaspoon sugar
- 100ml hot vegetable stock or water
- 1 teaspoon red wine vinegar
- 2 tablespoons toasted sesame seeds

While you no longer need to remove the bitterness from aubergines, I find they cook better in the slow cooker if you do. Top and tail the aubergines and then cut them into 2-3cm chunks. Put in a colander and scatter with about a tablespoon of sea salt. Cover the top of the colander with clingfilm and allow the aubergine to drain for 30 minutes. Rinse the salt off once the aubergine has developed moisture on its surface; the salting removes the bitterness in the aubergines, but you don't want to replace it with saltiness. Let the aubergine dry slightly.

Put the oil in the slow-cooker crock and allow it to heat slightly for about 10 minutes. Add the ginger, garlic and chilli. Stir and cook for about 2–3 minutes.

Add the aubergine, soy sauce, and sugar to the slow cooker. Stir well and then add the stock. Put the lid on the slow cooker and cook for 5–6 hours on low.

The aubergine flesh will turn a odd grey purplish shade to begin with. Don't worry. It will collapse into a silky loveliness by the end of cooking and its colour will be much improved.

About 20-30 minutes before you want to eat the aubergine, add the red wine vinegar and stir in. I do this as I'm putting the rice on to cook.

Serve with rice and some garlicky wilted greens (I favour spring greens or kale) and a scattering of sesame seeds. Any leftovers make a lovely packed lunch, especially with a flatbread of some description.

AUBERGINE RAGOUT

It's taken me a long time to get the hang of aubergines. In my vegetarian days, they haunted me with the regularity their bitter presence turned up in dishes when eating out. Then there was the time I tried to roast one and it exploded all over my oven. Or the occasion I blackened one to make a dip and burned my hand so badly it left a scar.

Gradually I learned to peel and salt them to remove the bitterness, then to prick them before they went in the oven and to wear rubber gloves when handling hot things and my hostility to the aubergine lessened, but I still didn't love them until I learned to slow cook them thanks to help from my friend Paola who inspired this dish.

Simmering them super slowly in a rich tomatoey sauce and a splash of olive oil makes them silky and smooth (and safe) and I always have some of this in the freezer for a quick dinner. Add it to the Lasagne on page 27 if you'd prefer a veggie version or serve it over pasta. It's true love after this dish.

SERVES 4 WITH LEFTOVERS

- 1 large or 2 medium aubergines
- 1 tablespoon sea salt
- 1 medium onion, finely diced
- 3 cloves of garlic, finely diced
- 1 x 400g tin chopped tomatoes
- 100ml water
- 2 tablespoons olive oil
- 15g torn fresh basil, to serve
- salt and pepper

I know people say you don't need to salt modern-day aubergines because the bitterness has been bred out of them, but I've tried foregoing this stage several times and it just doesn't work well for me.

Start by preparing your aubergine. Peel and cut it into 4cm cubes. Put in a colander and scatter with about a tablespoon of sea salt. Cover the top of the colander with clingfilm and allow the aubergine to drain for 30 minutes. Rinse the salt off once the aubergine has developed moisture on its surface. The salting removes the bitterness in the aubergines, but you don't want to replace it with saltiness. Let the aubergine dry slightly. Add to the slow-cooker crock.

Add the diced onion and garlic and tip the chopped tomatoes over them all. Pour in the water and drizzle half the olive oil over it all. Aubergines love a bit of oil and usually soak up so much when you're cooking them that the cost really adds up, so this version is a relief!

Season well, put the lid on the slow cooker and cook the aubergines on low for 8–9 hours. The dish is cooked when your aubergine is soft and silky. I sometimes squash mine down a little with a potato masher to help it out.

Add the torn fresh basil as you are ready to eat the dish, drizzle with the remaining olive oil and serve.

STICKY-GLAZED BALSAMIC BEETROOT

I adore beetroot. Doesn't matter whether it is pickled or grated or roasted. I love its earthy sweetness, but it always seems to take forever to cook in the oven or in a pot. Anytime I've tried to make it sweet and glazed, it has ended up singed and acrid round the edges, so it seemed sensible to make a virtue of cooking it slowly to prevent disappointment.

You will end up with tender beetroot with a beautiful glaze that enhances its natural attributes. I do a big batch this way and use it as a side dish on roasts, heap into salads with a sprinkle of goat's cheese or turn into soup like the Borscht on page 139 or the Orzotto on page 104. I think pink around dinner quite often in fact…

SERVES 4

- 1 bunch of beetroot, approximately 600g
- 1 teaspoon vegetable oil
- 2 tablespoons balsamic vinegar
- 1 teaspoon brown sugar
- 4 sprigs of fresh thyme

Remove the leaves and stalks from the beetroot if you are able to get them with the foliage still on. Keep these as the stalks make good pesto and the leaves can be eaten like spinach. Scrub the beetroot well under running water. Top and tail the beetroot and then cut them into quarters (or eighths if particularly large.)

Put the oil in the bottom of the slow-cooker crock and toss the chopped beetroot in it. Drizzle the balsamic vinegar over them evenly. I use the versions from the discount German retailers, which are excellent, inexpensive and last forever. If you don't have balsamic vinegar, use white vinegar with a dash of gravy browning and a tablespoon of brown sugar instead.

Scatter the sugar and the sprigs of thyme over the beetroot and coat well. Cook on high for 4 hours or low for 8 for tender, glossy beetroot that is utterly delicious and very similar in taste and texture to those pricey pots of rosebud beetroot from deli counters.

You can simply double the amounts to batch cook this. It will keep in a sterilised jar (see page 185) in the fridge for up to a week.

STUFFED CABBAGE LEAVES

This lovely dish is very popular throughout Eastern Europe, but for some reason hasn't gained the same fondness here. I am, of course, a bit obsessed with stuffing vegetables, but these are a particular favourite and one of the first things I wrote about when I started blogging. I make them frequently as they are very easy to make as well as frugal. The slow cooker also prevents any cabbage smells lingering in the house, which is an added bonus!

I like to use a Savoy cabbage for these as the leaves are big enough to roll easily and robust enough to cook well. I also think there are few more handsome veg than a crinkly green Savoy.

SERVES 4

8 cabbage leaves

75g pearl barley

100g lamb mince

1 onion, finely chopped

1 carrot, finely chopped

2 cloves of garlic, finely chopped

½ teaspoon ground cinnamon

150ml hot stock or water

1 teaspoon tomato purée

½ teaspoon sugar

1 teaspoon smoked paprika

1 x 400g tin chopped tomatoes

salt and pepper

Remove any tough or damaged outer leaves from the cabbage and then gently peel away each leaf separately. You want them to be whole, so go carefully. Cut the thick rib out of the base of each leaf to make them easier to roll.

Bring a pan of water to the boil and drop two leaves at a time into it and blanch the leaves for about a minute. Remove with tongs and lay them on a clean tea towel to dry out slightly.

Retaining the cabbage water, add the pearl barley to it and boil for about 10 minutes. Drain the barley well and tip in to a large bowl. Make the stuffing by adding the raw mince, chopped onion, carrot, garlic and the cinnamon. Mix it all through well and season generously.

Lay the cabbage leaves out flat and add about a tablespoon and a half of the stuffing to the middle of each one. Roll the leaves up from the base so that the opened end tucks under the top. Add a bit more stuffing in if you can and tuck the sides in too, making a little cabbage parcel. I find using uncooked mince keeps the stuffing in a better shape when lifting them out later.

Place the stuffed cabbage leaf parcels into the slow-cooker crock, making two layers if needs be. Pour the water or stock over the cabbage.

Mix the tomato purée, sugar and paprika into the chopped tomatoes (or simply add some paprika to a batch of the Tomato Sauce from page 132) and pour it over the cabbage as a sauce.

Put the lid on the slow cooker and cook the cabbage leaves on high for 5 hours. Serve them with some Pickled Beetroot from page 194 on the side and plenty of the paprika-infused sauce. They really are a fine one-pot meal!

BRAISED RED CABBAGE

Few vegetables say 'winter warmer' better than the red cabbage does. It adds colour and flavour to a plate in the grey months of winter and some festive cheer to a Christmas ham. It's economical, utterly fabulous and, unlike many vegetables, perfectly suited to the slow cooker. Once I had a slow cooker, I fell in love with this recipe all over again and make it all the time.

SERVES 2 WITH LEFTOVERS

1 red cabbage, approximately 1kg

1 onion (I like a red onion here, but I match my bag and shoes too)

2 cloves of garlic

1 large cooking apple or 4 tablespoons Apple Butter (see page 197)

100g cranberries (optional)

2 whole cloves

1 tablespoon brown sugar

3 tablespoons red wine or cider vinegar

150ml hot stock or water

salt and pepper

Remove the very outer leaves of the cabbage and cut it in half. Remove the core and then shred the cabbage a bit finer than a pound coin, but not tissue-fine.

Slice the onion and garlic cloves too. Cut the apple the same way. Put it all in the slow-cooker crock, along with the apple butter if you are using it.

Add the cranberries, if using, the cloves and brown sugar. Season well and add the vinegar and the stock or water. Put the lid on the slow cooker and cook on low for 7–8 hours.

The cabbage will darken as it cooks and soften down beautifully. The fruit will collapse into it all and the whole thing will reduce in volume, looking almost jam-like. It is delicious served hot or cold and it keeps for up to 3 days in the fridge.

WHOLE SPICED CAULIFLOWER

The humble cauli gets a bad rap. Seen as dull or just something to be drowned in cheese sauce, it has fallen out of favour. But treated well, it's a wonderful vegetable. It's racier than you'd expect and loves strong spices or curry flavours. I've rubbed it with yoghurt, aromatics and spices and steamed it whole.

I buy my spices in big bags from the Asian grocers near me and, to make them last better, I decant some into glass jars and keep the opened bags in the freezer. If you don't have access to an Asian grocer, look in the 'world foods' section of your supermarket and you'll often see bags of spices much cheaper than in the spice aisle.

SERVES 2-4 AS PART OF A MEAL

- 1 whole cauliflower, outer leaves removed
- 1 teaspoon cumin seeds
- 1 teaspoon coriander seeds
- 1 teaspoon caraway seeds
- 1 teaspoon onion seeds
- 1 teaspoon smoked paprika
- 1 teaspoon black pepper
- 1 teaspoon ground ginger
- ½ teaspoon salt
- ½ teaspoon chilli powder
- 2 tablespoons vegetable oil
- 150ml plain yoghurt (see home-made Yoghurt page 202)

Remove the outer leaves from the cauliflower. These can be eaten along with cabbage or greens, so you don't have to throw them out. Slice the base of the cauliflower so that it is still whole, but able to sit flat in the slow cooker.

Toast the cumin, coriander, caraway and onion seeds in a dry frying pan. This intensifies the flavour and softens them to become aromatic.

Add them in with the remaining spices and crush using a pestle and mortar or blend with a hand blender. Combine with the oil and the yoghurt. You want a texture that is easy to rub over the head of the cauliflower. Add a touch more oil if need be.

Line the slow-cooker crock with a piece of reusable baking liner. Set the cauliflower into it and then rub the spiced yoghurt over it all. Try to coat it evenly.

Put the lid on the slow cooker and cook on high for 3 hours or low for 5 hours. Lift the liner out when cooked and break the florets up with a knife to serve.

Serve with rice, plain yoghurt and flaked almonds or make the Buckwheat, Cauliflower and Tahini Salad on page 105.

LEEKS VINAIGRETTE

This is the kind of dish that was on every dinner party menu in the seventies, but has spent the last forty years being ignored and maligned. I'd forgotten about it until my friend Rebecca posted a recipe for it on her blog *Dinner Document* and I was reminded how simple it was to make. It was serendipity since I just bought a whole bunch of leeks for a pound in the market and wasn't quite sure what to do with them all beyond just soup. Rebecca is the vegetable whisperer and, thanks to her inspiration, I tweaked this dish for the slow cooker.

SERVES 2 AS A MAIN MEAL OR 4 AS A SIDE DISH

4 leeks

3 sprigs of fresh thyme

2 tablespoons cider vinegar

300ml hot vegetable stock or water

4 eggs

2 tablespoons olive oil

1 tablespoon balsamic vinegar

1 teaspoon Dijon mustard

salt and pepper

Start by making sure your leeks are spotlessly clean. Peel off the very outer leaves and then split the green tops along the natural creases with a sharp knife. Gently pull the layers back and wash inside them well, shaking them upside down to dry them out.

Trim the very tips of the green part of the leek and remove the root. Cut each leek in half from top to bottom and then cut each half across to make quarters with a flat base. Layer the leeks into the slow-cooker crock, flat base downwards. You will probably have two layers.

Season the leeks well. Sprinkle the fresh thyme and the cider vinegar over them all. Cover with the stock or water so none of the leeks are poking out. You may need more or less liquid depending on how hefty your leeks are. Put the lid on the slow cooker and cook the leeks on high for 6 hours or low for 8 hours.

While your leeks are cooking, hard boil your eggs on the hob. Lower the room-temperature eggs into a pan of boiling water. Bring the water back to the boil and cook the eggs for about 8 minutes. Lift out of the water and run under cold water, then allow to cool enough to be able to peel the eggs, then chop them into small pieces.

Make your vinaigrette by pouring the olive oil and the balsamic vinegar into a jam jar. Season well and add the mustard. Put the lid on the jam jar nice and tightly and shake to emulsify it all.

Lift the cooked leeks out of the slow cooker with a slotted spoon. Put on a plate or into a serving dish and drizzle with the vinaigrette. Top with the chopped hard-boiled eggs and eat warm.

SKIRLIE-STUFFED MUSHROOMS

I was first drawn to the traditional Scottish dish of skirlie because it's just the most glorious word to say as it dances across your tongue. But like all the best things, it's substance over style as well. Made from toasted cooked oats, it's a little like a chewy, nutty risotto, if you can imagine risotto made from brown rice. Warm, filling and very easy, it's a great alternative to breadcrumbs and the texture is lovely here with the soft mushrooms. Even the most mushroom-jaded vegetarian will enjoy this dish.

**SERVES 2 AS A
MAIN MEAL OR
4 AS A SIDE DISH**

4 large flat mushrooms

1 leek

4 spring onions

25g butter

2 sprigs of fresh thyme

4 leaves of fresh sage

**1 sprig of fresh
  rosemary**

200g oats

400ml water

salt and pepper

Begin by preparing your mushrooms. Scrub them clean, if needed, but don't peel them, then remove the stalk. Chop this finely and set aside. Line the slow-cooker crock with baking liner and set the mushrooms on it.

Finely slice the leek and spring onions. Melt the butter in a frying pan over a medium heat and soften them in it for 3–4 minutes. Add the chopped mushroom stalk and herbs. Stir to coat well and add the porridge oats. Allow them to toast for about 3–4 minutes until they smell slightly nutty.

Stir in the water about 50ml at a time. The skirlie should absorb it and become slightly swelled up, but not sticky and wet. Stop adding water if it begins to look gloopy or porridge-like. Remove from the heat. Season well with salt and pepper.

Spoon the skirlie into the mushrooms, packing it down slightly round the edges to keep it in place. Add about 100ml water to the crock and put the lid on. Don't worry if they are slightly on top of each other rather than snugly settled in. Cook the mushrooms for 2–3 hours on high or 4 hours on low.

The skirlie will plump up further, the leeks become soft and flavoursome and the mushrooms tender and incredibly savoury because the method of cooking barely dilutes their taste, creating the ultimate mushroom. Serve with a green salad or some cabbage or kale on the side.

MUSHROOM STROGANOFF

This is one of those dishes that's just ripe for a bit of a revival. Done well with lots of flavour, this is a very simple and delicious meal. This was the dish when I was vegetarian that won me over to the mushroom's humble charms. It works well in the slow cooker with its spacious crock making it much easier to cook a large number of mushrooms than any saucepan.

I've used a small amount of dried mushrooms to add depth here. A packet can look expensive, but I get five or six recipes from it, making them a frugal store cupboard standby.

SERVES 4
(SEE BELOW FOR
A LEFTOVERS TIP)

5g dried porcini
mushrooms

60ml boiling water

250g chestnut
mushrooms

250g white
mushrooms, fresh or
frozen

250g large flat
mushrooms

1 leek, sliced

1 onion, finely diced

2 cloves of garlic,
finely diced

1 tablespoon smoked
paprika

75ml vermouth or
white wine

10g fresh tarragon

1 tablespoon Dijon
mustard

100ml plain yoghurt
(see home-made
Yoghurt page 202) or
sour cream, to serve

salt and pepper

If you are using frozen mushrooms, make sure you defrost them before using. Drain off any water they give off. Don't worry if you only have one kind of fresh fungi. The mixture just looks nicer, but use any sort you have, along with the dried ones, and it'll still be great.

Soak the dried mushrooms in the boiling water and allow to rehydrate for about 10 minutes while you chop the fresh mushrooms. I quartered the chestnut and white mushrooms and cut the flat ones into thick slices. Put all the vegetables in the slow-cooker crock.

Season well and add the paprika. Mix it all well and then put in the soaked porcini with their soaking liquid. Splash in the vermouth and add half the fresh tarragon. Stir in the mustard.

Put the lid on the slow-cooker crock and cook on high for 4 hours or low for 6 hours. The onions and garlic will caramelise and add lots of flavour and the mushrooms become soft and delicious, creating their own stock.

Stir through the yoghurt or sour cream before serving and sprinkle with the remaining fresh tarragon. The stroganoff is excellent on pasta, gnocchi or with steamed rice.

Note: Any leftovers can have a little vegetable stock added and be blitzed with a hand blender to become a quick mushroom soup. Add a dash of Worcestershire sauce if you aren't vegetarian and heat gently to prevent the yoghurt curdling. Serve with crusty bread.

CARAMELISED ONIONS

Ever seen those recipes that say 'cook the onions for 10–15 minutes until caramelised' and been slightly disappointed when your onions are still *Twilight*-pale after that time? That's because onions do not caramelise at speed. They need butter, time and love to achieve that sticky tangle of caramelisation. Generally this is not something you can do for a quick weeknight dinner. Except in a slow cooker.

Don't worry, there's method in my madness here. I'm not suggesting you get the slow cooker out after work and start from scratch. No, I'm suggesting you do a big batch of slow-cooked caramelised onions in the slow cooker at some point and then keep them in the fridge for up to 3 weeks or freeze them in portions. Defrost as needed and put slow-cooked flavours into fast meals any time.

You can also add some sausages or frankfurters in here to cook alongside them when you are out and about, like on Bonfire Night, before coming back to the ultimate hot dogs and onions.

MAKES ABOUT 600G

25g butter

1 tablespoon olive or vegetable oil

1kg white onions

1 teaspoon brown sugar (optional)

salt and pepper

Warm the slow-cooker crock while you prepare the onions. Add the butter and oil so that it has time to melt.

Peel your onions and top and tail them. Cut in half from top to bottom, then cut each half onion down the centre so you have four pieces per onion. Slice each quarter to the thickness of a pound coin.

Toss the onions in the oil and butter. Add the sugar, if using. Season well, put the lid on the slow cooker and cook on low for 8 hours or high for 4–5 hours. The onions will collapse gently, giving out a rich oniony juice and becoming golden and gorgeous.

I freeze them in 100g portions in small freezer bags or make the French Onion Soup on page 144. I defrost them as needed for gravies, soups, sauces or anywhere an onion improves the situation.

BLACK PUDDING-STUFFED ONIONS

My life is not too short to stuff vegetables. I attribute it to my fascination with *The Good Life* when I was a nipper. I wanted the frocks and formidable attitudes of Margot Leadbetter and the stuffed vegetable meals of Barbara Good. I stuff every fruit and veg possible, but particularly love making stuffed onions. They are sweet and delicious and they look like you've done something very tricky. They suit the slow cooker especially well.

If you prefer, use the vegetarian version of black pud, which is a bit more expensive, but utterly lovely.

SERVES 2–4 AS
EITHER A SIDE
OR A MAIN

4 medium white onions

75g breadcrumbs

**1 teaspoon fresh
  tarragon, chopped**

125g black pudding

**1 small apple or
  50g Apple Butter
  (see page 197)**

**1 teaspoon Dijon
  mustard**

25g butter, melted

squeeze of lemon juice

50ml water

salt and pepper

You've read the ingredients and your mouth is watering, but you're wondering: how exactly do you stuff an onion? It's very easy...

Chop the pointed top and about another 1cm off the onion. Peel your onion, taking off the first inner layer of the onion if it is discoloured or uneven. Leave the root intact, but trim it down if the onion doesn't sit flat. Take a small sharp knife and cut round the inner layers of the onion, leaving at least one or two outer layers. Dig the core of the onion out with the tip of the knife and it will all come out easily, leaving the root as it is, but the centre ready to stuff. Repeat with each onion. Reserve the middles of the onions and finely chop them up. Put them in a large bowl and add the breadcrumbs and tarragon.

Peel any casing from the black pudding and crumble it into the bowl. It doesn't matter if it's chunky or fine as the texture will vary depending what variety of black pudding you use. Dollop the apple butter and mustard in or add the apple, which has been peeled and chopped small.

Melt the butter and add it to the bowl with the lemon juice and mix everything well to turn it into a rough, slightly crumbly stuffing. Season it and then squash it together slightly with your hands.

Pack the stuffing into the onions so that they are very well filled. It doesn't matter if a bit pokes out the top. Put the onions directly into the slow-cooker crock, packing them in tightly so they touch the sides. Add the water, pouring it between the onions rather than directly over the top.

Put the lid on the slow cooker and cook them for 7 hours on low so the onions are translucent and the stuffing is golden. The sides should be getting sticky and caramelised around the edges. They are gorgeous as a main dish or served reheated with Garlic, Anchovy and Mint Lamb Shoulder (see page 49).

LATE SUMMER SUCCOTASH

A Native American invention, succotash is one of those dishes that everyone has a different recipe for. I like this late summer version that is light enough to eat when there is still warmth in the evenings, but that makes the most of the abundant harvest produce.

Fresh corn makes this dish something special, but it works just as well with frozen or tinned. It is especially good finished off with some cream or you can keep it dairy-free. You can cook the black-eyed beans from dried, making this very straightforward. I freeze Parmesan rinds for use in soups and stews where they add a deep flavour. Just add a little more seasoning if you don't have any.

SERVES 2 WITH LEFTOVERS

350g corn, fresh, frozen and thawed or tinned

1 onion, chopped

2 carrots, chopped

2 celery stalks, chopped

100g dried black-eyed beans

4 cloves of garlic, chopped

1 teaspoon dried oregano

1 tablespoon smoked paprika

1 x 400g tin chopped tomatoes

1 whole Scotch bonnet pepper

1 Parmesan rind (optional)

500ml hot vegetable or chicken stock

200g green beans, fresh or frozen and thawed

100ml double cream, to serve

salt and pepper

Shuck the ears of corn if you are using fresh corn. Do this by running a sharp knife down each side of the cob to loosen the kernels. If you are using frozen corn, make sure it is thawed. Drain the tinned corn and rinse.

Chop all the vegetables to the same 1cm size and place in the slow-cooker crock with the dried black-eyed beans, garlic and the corn. Add the oregano and paprika and stir to coat well. Pour the tomatoes over it. Stir again. Put the whole Scotch bonnet in to allow its flavour to infuse. Also add the Parmesan rind, if using (omit the Parmesan rind or use another Italian hard cheese instead to make this dish vegetarian), and pour the stock over it all.

Put the lid on the slow cooker and cook on high for 5–6 hours or low for 8–9 hours. Add the topped and tailed and halved green beans an hour before the succotash is ready to eat to steam lightly.

Remove the Scotch bonnet and the Parmesan rind. Ladle into bowls and stir in the cream to serve. Don't add it to the main crock if you want to reheat the succotash for lunch or it will curdle. Add after heating.

This is a hearty, tasty and filling dish, packed with vegetables and flavour, even if the Native Americans didn't eat Parmesan...

SQUASH AND SPINACH RAGOUT

I find it hard to believe that when I was a kid, you couldn't buy a squash or a pumpkin for love nor money in the UK. They were weird orange things that you saw in American movies, usually around Hallowe'en, but no one I knew had eaten one. And then one day, the shops were full of butternut squash and Britain had taken them to their heart in no time.

Now with the advent of farmers' markets and veg box schemes, you can buy all kinds of shapes and sizes of squashes and the seeds are available to grow your own. I always keep one in the cupboard as my emergency vegetable and you can even buy it frozen. Combined here with celeriac, parsnip and fresh herbs, I've put some frozen spinach in at the last minute to add lashings of colour to this simple vegetarian dish.

SERVES 2 AS A
MAIN MEAL OR
4 AS A SIDE DISH

1 medium butternut
  squash

1 large parsnip

¼ celeriac

2 tablespoons plain
  flour

1 large onion, chopped

1 sprig of fresh
  rosemary

1 bay leaf

500ml hot vegetable
  stock

75ml vermouth

200g frozen spinach

salt and pepper

Peel your squash, parsnip and celeriac and cut them each into cubes of about 3–4cm. Place in the slow-cooker crock, scatter with the plain flour and toss well to coat them fairly evenly.

Add the onion and herbs and season well. Pour the hot vegetable stock and the vermouth over it all and stir so that all the vegetables are as submerged as possible. Put the lid on the slow cooker and cook for 7–8 hours on low.

As you put the ragout on to cook, take your frozen spinach out to defrost. Place in a sieve over a bowl or the sink until needed.

After 7–8 hours, your vegetables will be soft and tender and starting to break up gently. Fish out the rosemary and the bay leaf and give the vegetables a helping hand with a potato masher. You want it chunky, but mashed.

Squeeze all the excess water from the frozen spinach, add it into the vegetables and put the lid back on the slow cooker. Give it all half an hour longer and then serve in bowls with some crusty bread on the side.

STUFFED PUMPKIN

It has become much easier to get hold of edible pumpkins and most supermarkets and veg box schemes will have them around late autumn now. Here I've hollowed it out, filled it with sausages and white beans and then baked it in the slow cooker with its lid on like a slow cooker within a slow cooker. When it's ready to serve, I scatter the reserved seeds over it having lightly toasted them with salt and cayenne pepper. Serve it by cutting out wedges of the pumpkin and scooping the flesh off the skin. It makes a great centrepiece to gather round on a cold night!

SERVES 4

1 edible pumpkin, approximately 800g to 1kg

6 sausages

1 x 400g tin cannellini beans or 150g dried

150g cherry tomatoes or 1 x 400g tin chopped tomatoes

1 teaspoon tomato purée

1 teaspoon smoked paprika

½ teaspoon cayenne pepper, plus a pinch for the pumpkin seeds

200ml hot stock

1 tablespoon Worcestershire sauce

Note: If you can't get a pumpkin to fit your crock, or want to use a different kind of squash, just chop it into 3–4cm pieces and cook for 6–7 hours. You can scatter the pumpkin or squash with fried breadcrumbs for crunch instead of pumpkin seeds and even leave out the sausages to make it meat-free.

Check your pumpkin fits the slow cooker. For a 3.5-litre slow cooker, I used a 20cm pumpkin. Line the slow-cooker crock with double thickness greaseproof paper or reusable baking liner (which looks like thicker, stronger baking paper, but is heat resistant and washable. I got mine in the pound shop).

Take the top off the pumpkin with a sharp knife. You want it to resemble a lid. If needs be, trim the stem down so it doesn't protrude and stop the slow-cooker lid from fitting. Hollow out the seeds and fibres of the pumpkin. Reserve the seeds, but discard the slippery bits.

Cut the sausages into 2–3cm pieces and lightly brown them in a pan for about 3 minutes. I don't think it improves the flavour especially, but they look unappetising otherwise.

Drain the cannellini beans and rinse them well. Mix them in a large bowl with the tomatoes, tomato purée, spices and the now browned sausages. Combine well so it is all evenly distributed. Season well.

Put the pumpkin into the lined crock and carefully put the sausage and bean filling into the pumpkin. Top up with the stock and the Worcestershire sauce. Put the lid on the pumpkin and then the lid on the slow cooker. Cook for 8–9 hours on low. The pumpkin will darken in colour and become soft and tender without collapsing.

While it is cooking, wash and dry the seeds from the pumpkin by laying them on a baking tray lined with kitchen roll for a couple of hours. About 15 minutes before you are ready to serve the pumpkin, toast them in a dry frying pan over a low heat. Watch them carefully so they don't burn.

Take them off the heat when golden brown. Scatter with salt, a pinch of cayenne and some black pepper and serve sprinkled over the wedges of pumpkin for some crunch.

THANKSGIVING STUFFING

As an Americanophile teenager, I was obsessed with the idea of Thanksgiving. I loved the idea of a midwinter get-together solely based round food, friends, family and contemplation. However, the lack of presents meant I stayed loyal to Christmas and I only attended my first Thanksgiving lunch while I was writing this book. This stuffing was inspired by that, combining pumpkin and cranberries and would be amazing with the Vermouth-brined Turkey on page 55 that I learned there too.

SERVES 2-4

2 medium onions, sliced, or 150g Caramelised Onions (see page 122)

50g butter

1 teaspoon olive oil

½ teaspoon brown sugar

100g cranberries

1 onion squash or medium pumpkin

180g breadcrumbs

50g kale, finely shredded

1 egg

salt and pepper

You want to caramelise the onions for this dish, so if you have any of the Caramelised Onions from page 122, use those. Otherwise, add the sliced onions to a pan with the butter and olive oil and cover with a lid. Cook slowly over a low heat for about an hour. Add the sugar halfway through and stir well. Replace the lid and leave to become soft and golden.

About 15 minutes before you are ready to use the onions, add the cranberries into the pan, putting the lid back on. This will soften them slightly.

Cut your squash or pumpkin open, scoop the seeds out and set them aside. Chop the pumpkin into large chunks and peel them. Chop the flesh into small pieces.

Wash the seeds well and dry in a clean tea towel. Put them in a hot dry frying pan and toast them so they are a bit golden and crunchy on the outside. Keep shaking the pan to stop them burning easily.

Pour them into a large bowl. Add the breadcrumbs and shredded kale. Tip in the caramelised onions and the cranberries, along with all the butter from the pan. Season and mix it all well. Beat the egg in so the stuffing comes together. It shouldn't be sticky, but it should form one lump.

Put the stuffing into a disposable loaf tin or small ramekins. Place in the slow cooker and pour boiling water into the crock so it comes about halfway up the side of the dish you are using. Cover the crock with folded kitchen roll, put the lid on the slow cooker and cook the stuffing on high for 5-6 hours.

If you are cooking the stuffing to go with the turkey, simply cook it in advance and reheat when needed. Serve in slices. You can also use the stuffing in the onions on page 123. Either way, it will taste sensational and make you give extra thanks for the presence of gravy...

BAKED POTATOES

I know you are probably rolling your eyes and thinking a recipe for baked potatoes? Really? But these are a little slow-cooker secret. You can turn a big old spud into a crisp-skinned, buttery-centred beauty with very little effort and some long slow cooking while you're at work. So, if like me, you love a proper jacket potato and find the flabby microwaved ones make you sad, but don't have time after work for real ones, today is your lucky day!

First, find your large potato. I never buy those labelled 'baking potatoes' as they seem to charge twice the price that way. I simply root about in the loose spuds until I find something the size of a dinosaur egg and use that instead.

Give it a good wash and dry it well. A dry skin crisps up better, so there is method in the madness of giving your potato a rub down. Follow this by massaging a tiny drop of oil into the skin. You want the kind of gloss you get on a Hollywood starlet's legs, but not greasiness.

Pull enough foil off the roll to wrap your potato up. Value foil is fine for this. The metal allows the heat to conduct better and this is what crisps the skin. Put the potato on the foil and then rub the potato with a tiny scattering of salt and some black pepper. Then wrap your spud up. As long as no skin is showing, it doesn't matter what technique you use.

Place your potato parcel in the slow cooker. Cook without liquid or lifting the lid for 8 hours on low or 4 hours on high. Carefully remove when ready and unwrap.

Definitely worth the wait as you can do three or four at a time and then freeze the cooked potatoes until needed. Simply defrost them and warm gently in the microwave.

I usually do these the day after I've batch-cooked a stew and fill it with that. These are the best baked potatoes I've ever eaten. They taste like you've always wanted the ones cooked in the embers of a fire to, but without the burned bits. Rediscover the jacket potato today!

JANSSON'S TEMPTATION

This is a lovely Scandinavian name for my favourite things all combined in one dish. Thinly layered potatoes cooked with sticky caramelised onions, salty little anchovies and a splash of cream until the potatoes go crisp round the edges – it's perfect winter food.

In Scandinavia, they use *ansjovis* for this dish, which are actually pickled sprats, not anchovies. If you have an IKEA nearby, grab a few tins and be authentic. Otherwise, use my recipe with anchovies. I adore their umami flavour and would put them in anything and everything I'm cooking. I'm *this* close to needing a meeting with Anchovies Anonymous. I think you'll fall in love after trying this too.

SERVES 2-4 (REHEATS BEAUTIFULLY)

750g potatoes

25g melted butter or vegetable oil

4 anchovies, chopped

2 onions, chopped or 150g Caramelised Onions (see page 122)

1 tablespoon sugar

500ml hot vegetable or chicken stock

150ml white wine or cider vinegar

75ml double cream, to serve

pepper

Start by preparing your potatoes. I use big baking-style potatoes for this dish so that the slices are large enough to crisp without burning. If you have a mandolin, use that to turn them into whispers of potato or use a sharp knife to cut them as thinly as possible.

Brush the slow-cooker crock with the butter or oil and then start layering the potatoes into the crock. I usually do two layers and then add one chopped anchovy, some black pepper and a quarter of the onions and then repeat until everything is used.

Dissolve the sugar in the hot stock and add the vinegar. If you happen to always have a jar of gherkins in sweet vinegar in the house or a pot of rollmop herrings, use the liquid from them instead. Adding this little bit of bite is more like the original dish and stops it being too rich.

Pour the liquid over the potatoes. The very top layer of spuds shouldn't be covered, but the rest should be submerged. Add a last sprinkle of black pepper, but don't add salt as the fish are enough.

Put the lid on the slow cooker and cook on high for 6 hours or low for 8–9 hours. Everything melds together beautifully and tastes fabulous. Serve with the cream poured over the top so it soaks in.

This is a perfect one-pot meal, although I love the leftovers the next day with a fried egg on top for breakfast.

ROOT VEGETABLE PAN HAGGERTY

A few years ago Mister North and I went to Alnwick in Northumberland for the weekend and I fell madly in love with the Northeast of England. The people, the beaches and the scenery were all fantastic. The beer was brilliant, but the food was the best bit. Simple, but very flavoursome, it used fantastic ingredients and we ate incredibly well. It's given me a longing to try more food from that area, but possibly when the good folk of the area realise I've tweaked their classic dish of pan haggerty, I won't be invited back.

Usually made of thinly sliced potatoes layered with onions and bacon with melted cheese on top, it makes the most of simple ingredients. I've adapted mine to use all those root veg you buy and then wonder what to do with instead of just mashing them – and it's fantastic. I get really quite excited about bags of stew vegetables now.

SERVES 4 (BEST EATEN FRESHLY COOKED)

4 rashers of bacon

20g melted butter

1 large sweet potato

¼ celeriac

1 swede (or turnip if you're Northern Irish or Scottish)

1 large potato

1 carrot

1 onion, chopped, or 150g Caramelised Onions (see page 122)

100g grated cheese, such as Cheddar or mozzarella

salt and pepper

Start by cubing your bacon and frying it lightly in a small pan over a medium heat to crisp the edges. Set aside when you get a little bit of crunch on it. Butter the slow-cooker crock well.

Peel and slice your sweet potato, celeriac, swede and potato as thinly as possible. If you have a mandolin, that's perfect. If you don't, just cut them as thinly as you can. Peel and dice the carrot.

Begin layering up your vegetables. I tend to start with the sweet potato and then add some of the bacon, onion, carrot and some salt and pepper. Next I do the swede and more of the bacon, onion and carrot. Repeat with the celeriac. I usually get six layers and end with a mix of celeriac and potato having used up all the bacon, carrot and onion.

Brush the potatoes with a tiny bit more butter and put the lid on the slow cooker. Cook on low for 8–9 hours. About 10–15 minutes before you are ready to serve, sprinkle the grated cheese on top and replace the lid so that it melts evenly.

Serve spoonfuls of the pan haggerty with some peas or Savoy cabbage on the side.

POTATO AND OLIVE STEW WITH PRESERVED LEMONS

This stew combines the flavour of those lovely Preserved Lemons on page 186 with potatoes and plump cannellini beans and adds olives to enhance their savoury flavour. I originally made this dish with goat, but my friend Jamey veganised it with the white beans and it's a stunner of a dish. It's great if you are cooking for a crowd and it's so packed with flavour, no carnivore will miss the meat.

SERVES 4

1 x 400g tin cannellini beans or 200g dried beans

4 large potatoes, peeled and cut into 2cm chunks

1 large onion, chopped

3 cloves of garlic, chopped

2 sprigs of fresh thyme or ½ teaspoon dried

1 teaspoon ground ginger

50g black olives, pitted

450ml hot vegetable stock or water

1 Scotch bonnet pepper or 1 teaspoon Tabasco sauce

½ Preserved Lemon, chopped (see page 186)

handful of fresh parsley, chopped

pepper

If you are using tinned beans, open and drain them. Wash the water off them well. You can use dried beans without having to soak them if you prefer.

Put the beans in the slow cooker along with the potato, onion and garlic. Add the fresh or dried thyme, ginger, black pepper and the olives. I love those tinned black olives you get in supermarkets that are actually dyed green ones, but feel free to use little wrinkled, oil-infused ones if you have more refined tastes.

Pour the stock over it all and add the whole Scotch bonnet or Tabasco. Now add the chopped preserved lemon and stir well. Put the flesh and skin in for an intense flavour.

Put the lid on the slow cooker and cook for 8 hours on low or 6 hours on high until the potatoes are collapsing slightly round the edges and the beans are plumped up and falling apart.

Serve in deep bowls with some chopped fresh parsley. It needs no more accompaniment than that.

TOMATO SAUCE

You will never be at a loose end in the kitchen if you have a batch of tomato sauce to hand. We grew up on it as children, heaped over pasta for a quick meal or baked with fish or chicken. It is perfect for the slow cooker as it takes simple ingredients, adds the magic element of time and turns it into something amazing with very little work.

The tomatoes are the star of this show. You want it to have that intense tomatoey essence you get in a warm greenhouse full of vines on a summer day, so pick your chopped tomatoes well. The very cheapest cans tend to be full of stalks and thin watery juice. Go up a level or two to supermarket own-brand or even branded ones when on offer. It works out better value in the long run and you'll enjoy the flavour much more.

I make a big batch and freeze some of it ready for those nights when you want the minimum of cooking. It also works beautifully with stuffed cabbage leaves (see page 116) or to make a vegetarian lasagne (see page 27) with some courgettes sliced into it.

SERVES 6
GENEROUSLY
OR ALLOWS YOU
TO STOCK THE
FREEZER

1 tablespoon butter (about 20g)

2 stalks of celery, finely chopped

2 carrots, peeled and finely chopped

2 cloves of garlic, finely chopped

1 large onion, finely chopped

½ bulb fennel, finely chopped (optional)

½ bunch fresh parsley stalks, finely chopped

2 x 400g tins chopped tomatoes

1 teaspoon sugar

100ml red wine (optional)

1 tablespoon tomato purée

salt and pepper

Warm the butter in a preheating slow-cooker crock and add all the finely chopped vegetables, including the parsley stalks. These have the flavour of parsley, but are more robust than the leaves for long slow cooking. Stir well and season with salt and pepper. Allow to cook for about 5 minutes, if you can.

Add the chopped tomatoes and any juice from the tins. Stir well and add the sugar. This helps mellow the acidity in the tomatoes and makes the sauce smoother. Don't be tempted to skip it for health or to add more than this. You shouldn't be able to taste it, but simply miss it if it wasn't there.

Pour in the red wine, if you're using it. Stir in the tomato purée and add a pinch more salt. Tomatoes love a bit of salt and it's best cooked into it rather than added at the end. Put the lid on the slow cooker and cook the sauce on low for 8 hours.

You can add in the Lemon and Olive Meatballs on page 31 at the same time if you choose or leave it vegetarian.

The sauce will reduce and thicken and become much darker. The vegetables will collapse into it and you can leave it chunky if you like the texture or you can blend it all with a hand blender for a smooth feel (or if you are trying to disguise the five a day!)

Serve with pasta and Parmesan or portion up and freeze. Defrost and use as needed.

GREEK-SALAD STUFFED TOMATOES

When it comes to stuffing vegetables, I'm less Shirley Conran, who doesn't stuff a mushroom, and more Deirdre Barlow, who stuffs a marrow at a moment's notice. I love any ingredient you can stuff and tomatoes are a real favourite of mine. Slow cooking them is a particularly good way to add the flavour those big beef toms often lack when eaten raw. There's something so delightfully retro about them too that you can't help but smile when you're eating them.

SERVES 4

4 large or beef tomatoes

100g Chorizo Butter Beans (see page 95)

1 small onion, chopped

2 cloves of garlic, chopped

75g roasted red peppers or Confit Peppers (see page 134), diced

1 teaspoon paprika

30g black olives, pitted

50g feta or Greek salad cheese, diced

120ml tomato juice

salt and pepper

Start by cutting the tops off the tomatoes. Cut low enough to ensure a solid lid for your toms, but not so low that you can't put much filling in them. Then scoop the inside of each tomato out into a large bowl and reserve it.

Add the beans, chopped onion, garlic and the peppers to the same bowl. You can use jarred ones here as often the discount supermarkets do great deals on them or I use the Confit Peppers from page 134. Mix them all together with the paprika, reserved tomato flesh, black olives and feta cheese and season with black pepper.

Line the slow-cooker crock with reusable baking liner. Spoon the bean mix into the tomatoes and then gently lower them into the crock. Put their lids on. They'll probably only fit at a jaunty angle. Pour the tomato juice round the tomatoes and season the closed tomatoes lightly with salt.

Put the lid on the slow cooker and cook the tomatoes on low for 7 hours. The tomatoes will collapse nicely. Serve with a pile of steamed broccoli drizzled with the sauce for a great take on the Greek salad.

CONFIT TOMATOES

One of the things I love most about my slow cooker is that I can use it to preserve foods or add details to quick stove top meals that lift them from basic to brilliant. These tomatoes are a fantastic example of this. Suggested by my friend Nicholas from Salon in Brixton, they are a great way to use up a glut of home-grown tomatoes or preserve proper summer ones that taste of sun.

They are covered with olive oil in the slow cooker along with your choice of herbs and spices and then keep beautifully in a jar in the fridge for months. They can be used anywhere you'd pop a grilled tom or two or make a quick pasta sauce. Spiked with chilli they go well with a chunk of cheese and I make a fabulous creamy, coconutty soup with them too.

You can reuse the olive oil mixture for salad dressings since it's now packed with flavour and you don't have to buy extra virgin or anything. I buy stuff when it's on offer and simply mark the bottle so I don't get confused.

MAKES 500G

500g tomatoes

choice of woody herbs, such as rosemary, oregano, thyme, bay or marjoram (about a teaspoon each of whatever you choose to use)

choice of caraway seeds, coriander seeds, cumin seeds, fennel seeds (about a teaspoon each of whatever you choose to use)

1 dried red chilli, whole or flaked (optional)

1 teaspoon sugar

1 teaspoon black peppercorns

5 cloves of garlic, peeled and bashed

150ml olive oil

200ml white wine or cider vinegar

sea salt

You don't want anything as large as beefsteak tomatoes for this, but medium ones are fine. Baby plums or cherry tomatoes work well too.

If using medium tomatoes, cut in half crosswise. Layer them into the slow-cooker crock, no more than two layers deep. If you are using baby toms, layer the same way, but leave them whole. Season with the sea salt. Add your choice of herbs and flavourings. Scatter the sugar and peppercorns over them. Tuck the garlic in around them.

Cover with the olive oil and the vinegar. The tomatoes should be as near to covered as possible. Don't worry if the very tops poke out. You may need a bit more oil or vinegar depending on the size and shape of your tomatoes.

Put the lid on the slow cooker and cook on low for 4–5 hours until the tomatoes are soft, but still holding their shape. Allow to cool for about 10–15 minutes and then lift the tomatoes out with a slotted spoon.

Put in a sterilised jar and drizzle enough of the oil over them to keep them moist. They will keep in the fridge for up to 3 months. Completely submerged in the oil they should last longer than that, but I've always managed to eat mine by then! Pour the remaining oil and vinegar in a bottle and use as needed.

Note: You can also adapt this recipe to confit peppers. Simply cut the peppers in half and remove the seeds. Cut them in half again and sear on a griddle pan for about 3–4 minutes until they are slightly char-grilled. Follow the rest of the recipe for the tomatoes and use in salads, soups or chillies.

SHAKSHUKA

One of the most popular dishes throughout the Middle East, this tomato and pepper rich stew makes eggs the star of the show and is absolutely perfect to make in the slow cooker. Cook the vegetables low and slow, cook the eggs fast and serve it all with lots of bread to soak up the juice and the runny yolks. There are always clean bowls at the end of this and a friend told me it's the best shakshuka she's had. She used to work for Ottolenghi, so I definitely trust her judgement.

Traditionally served as a breakfast dish, make the sauce overnight and crack the eggs into it the next morning. They won't take that much longer than a kettle will take to boil, making this a great way to wake up and the only way tinned tomatoes are acceptable in my breakfast…

SERVES 4

1 large onion

1 red pepper

1 yellow pepper

1 x 400g tin chopped tomatoes

2 red chillies (optional), finely sliced

1 teaspoon cumin seeds

1 bay leaf

2 sprigs of fresh thyme

pinch of cayenne pepper

2 tablespoons tomato purée

200ml water

6–8 eggs

chopped fresh parsley, to serve

salt and pepper

Start by slicing your onion and peppers into half moons and adding to the slow-cooker crock with the chopped tomatoes. Add the red chillies if you like a bit of heat with your eggs.

Toast the cumin seeds in a dry frying pan over a medium heat until aromatic and then add to the tomato mixture along with the bay leaf, thyme and cayenne. Stir in the tomato purée and add the water. Season well, bearing in mind tomatoes love a bit of salt. Put the lid on the slow cooker and cook on low for 7–8 hours.

When you are ready to eat, take the lid off the slow cooker and stir the sauce. Make small dents in the now thick sauce with the back of a serving spoon and break the eggs into these dents. Put the lid back on the slow cooker and turn the heat off.

Allow the eggs to cook for 10 minutes for a set white and runny yolk or 15 minutes for a set yolk as well. Serve the tomatoey sauce with an egg in the middle of it and some chopped parsley. Don't forget the bread on the side. I am equally fond of white crusty loaf as I am of a puffed-up pitta bread here.

SOUP

The possibilities for soup in the slow cooker are endless. Think of a style of soup. Think of an ingredient and wait 8 hours and you can make anything you could possibly imagine. I particularly love it for big robust soups and broths that traditionally take lots of nurturing over a low heat to give up their nourishment.

Pots of slow-simmered bone broths and pulse-rich soups are perfect in the slow cooker, helping economical ingredients go even further while giving them a new lease of life. Many of the soups create their own stock, but do try to use the best stock you can with those that don't. Stock cubes can be great, but watch your seasoning as they can be very aggressively salty.

I freeze my own Chicken Stock from page 61 or make a vegetable version with leftover ends and peels simmered in the slow cooker for 4–5 hours. I then pour it all into freezer bags and lay them flat on a baking tray that goes into the freezer. You'll end up with flat packs of stock that stack easily and defrost quickly to allow you to reach for them without too much forethought. You can also freeze the cooked soups this way for a speedy slow-cooked lunch. No matter what the question is, soup is probably the answer…

BORSCHT

I have never quite lost my childhood fascination with pink and thus I have a very soft spot in my heart for beetroot with its vivid fuchsia hue. I've never met a way to serve it that I don't love, but I have a particular adoration for borscht. An Eastern European classic, this flavoursome tangy beetroot soup is perfect at any time of the year. I make mine vegetarian and use dried mushrooms to add depth. Topped with a splodge of sour cream, it's a very grown-up way to remind me of childhood loves.

This recipe is an amalgamation of Polish, Ukrainian and Russian traditions. They all do borscht brilliantly and it's a shame not to combine their talents!

SERVES 2 AS A MAIN OR 4 AS A STARTER

3 large beetroot

1 carrot

2 medium potatoes

1 onion

1 leek

5g dried mushrooms

3 cloves of garlic

3 allspice berries

2 tablespoons cider vinegar

750ml boiling water or vegetable stock

½ white or sweetheart cabbage

sour cream, to serve (optional)

fresh dill, to serve (optional)

salt and pepper

This soup is very easy to make. Start by peeling the beetroot and cutting it into 1.5cm cubes. You may prefer to wear gloves for this in case you stain your hands.

Peel and chop the carrot and the potatoes to the same size as the beetroot. Dice the onion finely and shred the leek and put all these vegetables into the slow-cooker crock. Add the dried mushrooms, whole cloves of garlic, allspice and vinegar. Season well.

Cover it all with the water or stock. Put the lid on the slow cooker, reserving the uncooked cabbage. Cook the borscht on low for 6–7 hours until all the vegetables are tender and the stock is beautifully scarlet.

Shred the cabbage very finely and add to the slow cooker. Replace the lid and cook for another 30 minutes. Serve ladlefuls of the soup in deep bowls with a dollop of sour cream and some fresh dill, if you have it.

CELERIAC REMOULADE SOUP

Celeriac will never win any prizes for the prettiest vegetable in the garden, but underestimate them taste wise at your peril. Like a richer, creamier version of celery, they love strong flavours.

Both my mother and the French adore making remoulade with them. Celeriac is thinly shredded before being dressed with mayonnaise, mustard, crème fraîche and parsley and served as a winter salad. The tanginess is perfect with the gentle flavour of this humble root. This soup omits the mayonnaise, but keeps the essence in a much more warming way.

SERVES 2 WITH LEFTOVERS (REHEATS WELL FOR LUNCH)

- 1 whole celeriac, peeled and chopped into 5mm chunks
- 1 onion, finely diced
- 2 stalks of celery (optional)
- 2 tablespoons wholegrain or Dijon mustard (not English)
- 500ml hot vegetable or chicken stock
- 3 tablespoons crème fraîche or cream cheese
- handful of chopped fresh parsley, to serve
- salt and pepper

Peeling a celeriac is easier than you'd think from looking at its *Doctor Who* villain-like visage. I usually look for the smallest, least knobbly one I can find, but if I can only get a tendril-y one, I chop them off. I then double peel, taking off the outer layer and then the first layer of the naked celeriac to get rid of any persistent lumps or bumps and give it a good wash after peeling. Use a heavy knife to chop it into even pieces.

Put the celeriac chunks into the slow-cooker crock along with the onion and the celery. I love the extra oomph of flavour these add, but if you don't have any handy, don't worry. My friend The Skint Foodie drew my attention to just how tricky the '1 stalk of celery' in recipes is on a budget. I got round that for a while by growing celeriac and using the shoots and leaves until my neighbour 'tidied' up and threw them out.

Season well with salt and pepper. Add the mustard, stir well and cover with the stock. This soup works well as a vegetarian dish as long as you use a good veggie stock. Cook on low for 7–8 hours or high for 5–6 hours.

The celeriac will be slightly darker in colour when it is cooked and tender, but don't worry about this. Using a hand blender, blitz the soup until as smooth as possible and then add the crème fraîche or cream cheese and allow to melt in. Blitz briefly again to make the soup light and creamy. If you are a mustard fiend, add a touch more, but I like the mellow note from slow cooking it. Serve garnished with the chopped parsley.

SWEET POTATO CORN CHOWDER

One of my favourite quick standby dinners is a bowl of steaming hot chowder. Basically a chunky soup rich with potatoes and milk, it's both easy to make and incredibly fortifying. It uses store cupboard and freezer essentials to the fullest effect, all with very little effort and when cooked in the slow cooker, very little washing up. I think this might be my favourite everyday soup recipe.

SERVES 2 WITH JUST ENOUGH FOR LUNCH LEFTOVERS

2 sweet potatoes

1 medium potato

1 carrot

200g frozen and thawed sweetcorn

1 dried chilli

½ teaspoon ground mace

500ml hot vegetable or chicken stock

200ml milk

salt and pepper

Peel your sweet potatoes and cut into 2cm cubes. Do the same with your potato and carrot and place them all in the slow-cooker crock along with the thawed sweetcorn. Add the salt, pepper, chilli and mace and pour the hot stock over it all.

Put the lid on and cook on low for 7–8 hours. At this stage, ladle about one-third of the soup out of the crock and set it aside. Blend the remaining two-thirds of the soup with a hand blender or mash well with a potato masher.

Add the reserved soup back into the crock to give a lovely balance between a smooth and chunky texture. Pour the milk into the soup, put the lid back on the slow cooker and warm the soup through for another 30 minutes. Serve.

The soup is very filling so you won't need anything with it. You'll feel a bit like your dinner has given you a hug.

FRENCH ONION SOUP

This soup was just made for the slow cooker. Slow-cooked onions, rich beef stock, a warm kick of brandy and soft melted cheese all mingle together to create the kind of meal that makes simple ingredients into something that feels very luxurious and decadent. I always used to make a big pan of this on Christmas Eve and I now can't think why I stopped because it's one of the best winter soups around.

SERVES 4

500g onions (not red)

25g butter

1 teaspoon brown sugar

2 cloves of garlic, finely chopped

2 tablespoons plain flour

½ teaspoon mustard powder

900ml hot beef stock

100ml vermouth

25ml brandy (optional, but excellent)

4–6 round slices of baguette, about 3cm thick

150g Emmental or mature Cheddar cheese, grated

salt and pepper

Start by caramelising your onions. Peel, halve then slice them into half moons about the thickness of a pound coin and add to the slow-cooker crock with the butter and sugar. Put the lid on the slow cooker and cook on low for at least 4 hours, or up to 6 hours.

At this stage, add the chopped garlic, plain flour, mustard powder and salt and pepper and stir well to combine with the melted butter and lovely oniony juices from the caramelising onions.

Pour the stock and the vermouth over the onions and stir well to make sure there are no lumps. Put the lid back on the slow cooker and allow it all to cook for 4 hours.

About 20 minutes before you are ready to eat, add the brandy (if using), put the rounds of bread in the crock, sprinkle the grated cheese over them, then put the lid back on to allow the cheese to melt and the bread to soak up some of the soup as is traditional. They don't sink!

Scoop the bread out with a slotted spoon into bowls and ladle some of the soup over it. Serve with a generous helping of the soft sticky onions from the base of the crock. A glass of chilled white wine on the side doesn't go amiss.

TOMATO AND PEPPER SOUP

This is the kind of soup you don't say very much about save a contented sigh or two while you eat it. But then you make it at least once a week because it's just so good and so simple and actions speak much louder than words.

SERVES 2 (REHEATS BEAUTIFULLY FOR LUNCHES)

1 red pepper

1 yellow pepper

1 medium red onion

1 sweet potato

1 small fresh red chilli or ½ teaspoon chilli powder

1 teaspoon brown sugar

1 teaspoon paprika

1 x 400g tin chopped tomatoes

1 heaped tablespoon tomato purée

500ml hot chicken or vegetable stock

50ml single cream, to serve (optional)

Start by preparing your peppers. Cut the tops off and then halve. Scoop the seeds out and remove any of the white pith remaining as this can make them bitter. Cut the peppers into slices about 2–3cm wide and then cut each slice in small chunks of about 3cm. Dice the onion and the sweet potato to the same size.

Add them all to the slow-cooker crock. Cut the fresh chilli in half and remove the seeds if you don't want too much heat. Add into the crock and sprinkle the sugar and paprika (and chilli powder, if using) over them all. Stir well to combine. Tip the chopped tomatoes, tomato purée and the hot stock over it all and stir again.

Put the lid on the slow cooker and cook the soup on low for 4–5 hours. When you are ready to serve, use a hand blender to blend the soup in the crock. The vegetables should be smooth without any lumps. Add the cream, if using, stir and serve with crusty bread on the side.

RIBOLLITA OR TUSCAN BEAN SOUP

We spent time in Tuscany on holiday when we were kids and one of the best things we used to do was attend the *sagras*, or local food festivals, in the town near our friend's house. We tried delicacies such as frog (like very, very small chicken legs), trout and wild boar, but my favourite was the *zuppa Etruscan*. It was a rich, tasty bean soup, thickened with stale bread and served with a generous scattering of Parmesan. I loved it, had two bowls and became a convert to bean soup forever as nobody does beans better than the Tuscans.

This soup is cooked twice, hence the name, meaning 're-boiled'. It can be made thick and stew-like to begin with and then loosened with water to go even further. Just don't use fresh bread or it will become sticky. Stale bread is essential here.

SERVES 4 AND GETS
BETTER WHEN
COOKED AGAIN

1 onion

1 leek

2 carrots

2 stalks of celery

3 cloves of garlic

1 heaped tablespoon
  tomato purée

1 x 400g tin chopped
  tomatoes

1 teaspoon dried
  oregano

1 litre hot vegetable or
  chicken stock

1 x 400g tin or 200g
  dried haricot, borlotti
  or butter beans

175g cabbage, kale or
  cavolo nero, finely
  shredded

150g stale bread

1 Parmesan rind
  (optional)

50g Parmesan, grated

salt and pepper

Start by chopping your vegetables to the same size so they all cook evenly. You want a dice of about 2cm. Chop the garlic as finely as possible, then add to the crock too. Put all the diced vegetables into the slow-cooker crock.

Add the tomato purée and the chopped tomatoes. Scatter in the dried oregano and the salt. I find the black pepper is best added toward the end here. Pour the hot stock over it all and add the beans.

Put the lid on the slow cooker and cook the soup on low for 6–8 hours. About 45 minutes before the end of the cooking time, add the shredded cabbage and the black pepper. You could eat the soup at this stage, but it's so worth the second cooking to give it the rich flavour associated with the dish.

Allow the soup to cool down in the crock. You can leave it in there with the lid on and outside the fridge for about 6 hours. If you are leaving it longer, put the cooled soup in the fridge and transfer it back to the crock when you are ready to cook it again.

For the second heating, or 're-boiling' as the name suggests, tear the bread into the soup and add the Parmesan rind to impart a savoury flavour (omit the Parmesan rind or use another Italian hard cheese instead to make this dish vegetarian). Put the lid on and cook on high for 2–3 hours. Do not cook for longer or the bread will be soggy. Serve in deep bowls, scattered with the grated Parmesan.

If you don't have time to cook it again, cut the bread into rounds, place in the base of the bowl, ladle the soup over it and sprinkle with grated Parmesan.

DUTCH SPLIT PEA SOUP

I am one of the few people I know who came back from Amsterdam having really enjoyed the food. Most people dislike Dutch food's reputation for stodge and cabbage, but I loved it. Similar to Irish food, but with more canals and pork, it enhanced my trip hugely. I came home with a particular love for this *erwtensoep*, or thick split pea and pork soup. Incredibly filling, very frugal and simple to make, it is the most effective antidote I know to cold and damp winter days. Kids especially love it, particularly when it's called 'hot dog soup'.

**SERVES 6
AND REHEATS
BEAUTIFULLY
FOR LUNCH**

2 pigs' trotters

200g yellow split peas

1 pork spare rib chop

2 stalks of celery

2 potatoes, peeled

1 leek

1 onion

1 carrot

1 parsnip

½ celeriac

75g bacon, cubed

**½ smoked pork
    sausage or 4–6
    frankfurters, sliced**

1 litre water

**fresh flat-leaf parsley,
    to serve**

salt and pepper

This dish is so simple to make. Start by putting your pigs' trotters in a large pan of cold water on the hob and bringing it to the boil. Boil for 10 minutes and then drain and rinse any froth off them.

Layer half the split peas on the bottom of the slow-cooker crock and set the pigs' trotters on top of them at each end of the crock. Nestle the pork chop in between both of them. Season well.

Prep your vegetables. You want them all finely diced to 2cm cubes so they cook evenly and at the same rate before breaking down to thicken the soup. Put half of them on top of the trotters, then layer the bacon and smoked sausage on top of the vegetables. Finish the layering with the remaining vegetables. Season well.

Pour the water over it all. The meat in the soup will create a wonderful thick, glossy stock so you don't need to add any cubes or equivalent. Put the lid on the slow cooker and cook the soup on low for 8–9 hours.

Lift the lid off when you are ready to serve and remove the trotters. I discard mine as I love the flavour they impart, but don't like the texture of the skin and cartilage. You may like it. Stir the soup together. The pork chop will have become so tender it collapses into the soup. Press the peas and the vegetables with the back of a spoon to break them up more and make sure the soup is lovely and thick.

Serve with a scattering of flat-leaf parsley. You don't usually need any bread to accompany this soup as it is incredibly filling.

SCOTCH BROTH

Of all the recipes in this book, this one gives me the greatest excitement to put in print. Not just a recipe for soup, it's a little piece of family history for me as it originated with my great-grandmother, passing down through my granny Connie to my dad and then on to me. There's something quite touching about a recipe that started off orally, then progressed to being scribbled on scraps of paper, making it into a proper published book. This is the only dish I remember my granny making as she died when I was six and it's nice to have the connection with her.

The recipe has lasted this long because it's really good. Thickened with pearl barley and split peas, it's hale and hearty as well as frugal and filling. I make a big batch of this and have it for lunch in cold weather. It's as comforting as pulling the curtains and curling up on the sofa on a cold winter's night.

This soup is so simple to make in the slow cooker I'm sure my family won't mind too much that I've tweaked it a little bit to be specific to this way of cooking.

SERVES 4 AND REHEATS WELL IF SERVING FEWER PEOPLE

400g beef shin

1 leek, sliced in half moons

1 onion, diced

1 carrot, diced

2 stalks of celery, diced

2 spring onions, sliced

1 bunch of fresh flat-leaf parsley

1 teaspoon Worcestershire sauce

100g pearl barley

100g yellow split peas

750ml water

salt and white pepper

Cut the slices of beef shin (or boiling beef as it tends to be known in Scotland and Northern Ireland) in half and place in the slow-cooker crock.

Add your prepped vegetables. Cut the stalks off the parsley and chop finely and add these too. Reserve the leaves. Sprinkle the Worcestershire sauce and the salt and pepper over it all.

Tip in the barley and the split peas. Neither of these needs to be soaked or pre-cooked before adding them here. Pour the water over it all and put the lid on the slow cooker. Cook the broth on low for 8–9 hours.

The beef shin will create a rich, beefy stock while it flakes apart into tender morsels of meat dispersed evenly throughout the soup. It will all be thick with the peas and barley; you'll probably be able to stand a spoon up in it. Add a wee bit more water if you like it a looser texture.

Add the chopped flat-leaf parsley leaves through it and serve piping hot. It will warm your cockles in no time.

GUMBO

This is one of the most famous soups in the world with its legend spreading far beyond the coasts and swamps of Louisiana. Packed with chicken, okra and smoked sausage, it can be served very hearty like a stew or slurped up with a spoon, depending on your preference. I like it somewhere in between both, like my friend Richard serves in Kaff Bar in Brixton.

Cajun food from Louisiana has an enduring charm and is based round the 'trinity' of celery, onion and green peppers, which are sautéed to form the base of nearly every dish. The addition of garlic lifts it to become the 'holy trinity'. The use of a roux, where flour and butter are cooked together like the beginning of a white sauce, is very traditional here too. The roux in Cajun food gets cooked for longer to make it dark and toasted and it gives your dishes a real depth.

SERVES 4–6 AND
REHEATS WELL

50g butter

50g plain flour

750ml hot chicken stock

1 green pepper, diced

1 onion, diced

2 stalks of celery, diced

4 cloves of garlic, finely chopped

1 teaspoon celery salt (use more celery and salt if you don't have it)

½ teaspoon black pepper

2 dried red chillies

1 teaspoon dried oregano

1 bay leaf

½ bunch of fresh parsley

150g smoked pork sausage

4–6 chicken thighs

150g okra, topped, tailed and cut into 3 pieces

hot sauce, to serve

Start by making your roux. Melt the butter in a saucepan over a medium heat and add the flour, beating it together with a whisk to prevent any lumps. Cook the roux for about 10 minutes until browned and nutty smelling. It's best if you can stir as it cooks as this actually speeds it up.

Once the roux is browned, add about 150ml of the chicken stock, whisking constantly to prevent lumps. Keep adding the stock about 150ml at a time until you have a glossy golden brown sauce. It should be slightly too thick to pour without having to really tip the sauce to one side.

Add the sauce into the slow cooker, making sure you run a spatula round the saucepan to catch it all. Mix in the green pepper, onion, celery and garlic. Stir the celery salt, pepper, dried chillies, oregano and the bay leaf into it. Chop the stalks of the parsley finely and add these too. Slice the smoked sausage into half moons about 2cm thick and add them in, stirring well.

Skin the chicken thighs and remove the bones. Cut each thigh into quarters and add the meat to the crock. Tie the bones together with some string and place them in the crock as well to help add flavour.

Add the okra to the crock. (These soft, velvety pods have a reputation for being slimy, but this is a sign that they are old. Pick firm-feeling pods that aren't leaking any liquid. You can use fresh or frozen and thawed okra here.)

Put the lid on the slow cooker and cook the gumbo on low for 6–7 hours until the chicken is soft and tender and the flavours have all infused. Remove the parcel of chicken bones, serve the soup in deep bowls with some hot sauce.

SLOW-COOKED CHICKEN DUMPLING SOUP

This is my favourite one-pot meal for when I've got a batch of chicken stock and a big appetite. These are Caribbean-style dumplings from Trinidad taught to me by my friend Brian. I serve the soup hot-and-sour style and it never fails to warm my stomach and my soul.

SERVES 4

750ml Chicken Stock (see page 61)

250g plain flour

1 teaspoon sugar

½ teaspoon salt

500ml water

200g cooked chicken

1 red chilli, chopped

1 tablespoon soy sauce

1 teaspoon brown sugar

3cm piece of fresh ginger, finely sliced

1 tablespoon white wine vinegar

25g fresh coriander, chopped

25g fresh mint, chopped

salt and white pepper

Put the chicken stock in the slow-cooker crock and heat on high for 1 hour if you are heating it from cold. If you've just made it and it's still hot, simply strain the bones out through a muslin cloth-lined sieve and return to the crock.

Mix the flour, sugar and salt together in a bowl with your hand and then add a little water at a time to knead into a soft, but not sticky dough.

Using some extra flour on your work surface, roll the dough out to a 1cm-thick sausage shape and then cut into 5cm lengths.

Put in the slow cooker along with the cooked chicken, red chilli, soy sauce, brown sugar and the fresh ginger. Cook on high for 2 hours.

When you are ready to serve, taste the soup and season it as needed with salt and white pepper. Add the vinegar. Ladle the soup into bowls, making sure you have lots of dumplings, and serve scattered with the coriander and mint.

Note: If you don't have very much chicken left, bulk the soup out by sieving two beaten eggs into the hot stock for a Chinese-egg-drop style finish. It's a quick, economical way to add protein.

GHANAIAN PEANUT SOUP

I was introduced to this by a Ghanaian friend for whom it was the taste of home. She couldn't cook, so she challenged me to learn to make it from the internet. I have adapted the original recipe over the years and then adjusted it for the slow cooker. You can serve this thick – like stew over rice – or as a soup.

Very filling and satisfying, you can get away with using very little meat or omitting it completely. I wouldn't advise making it completely vegetarian though as the anchovies really add depth. West African cooks use dried prawns or crayfish, but these are very expensive here. It is also very good with the fish and I use defrosted fillets of pollock. Ghanaian cooks use a smooth groundnut or peanut paste, but sugar-free peanut butter works extremely well and is very economical.

SERVES 4

250g chicken thighs

150g groundnut paste or peanut butter

1 litre cold water

1 heaped teaspoon ground ginger

1 heaped teaspoon smoked paprika

½ teaspoon cayenne pepper

2 anchovy fillets, chopped

1 x 400g tin chopped tomatoes

1 red pepper, diced

½ butternut squash or 2 sweet potatoes, peeled and chopped

2 medium onions, chopped

4 cloves of garlic, chopped

2 cobs of corn, chopped into 3cm chunks

1 Scotch bonnet pepper (optional)

150g white fish fillets, such as pollock

chopped fresh coriander, to serve

Start by skinning and boning your chicken thighs. Cut the thighs into quarters. Reserve the bones and tie them into a little bundle with some kitchen string. Season the meat and set aside.

Preheat the slow cooker to high with the lid on and once it heats up, put the peanut butter into it and add about a third of the water, stirring until it is smooth and a pourable consistency. It may look at one point as if it is about to split, but don't worry. It comes back together.

As it does so, add the ginger, paprika, cayenne and the chopped anchovy fillets, stirring them in well. Tip in the chopped tomatoes.

Then add in the pepper, squash, onion, garlic and the chicken and stir to coat. Drop in the little bundle of chicken bones. These will add flavour as the stew cooks. Pour the remaining water in and mix it all well. Don't be tempted to skimp on the water, the peanut paste thickens and you need more liquid than in most slow-cooker recipes.

Place the corn cob chunks on top of it along with the whole Scotch bonnet, if you are using it. Put the lid on, turn the slow cooker down to low and cook for 6–7 hours.

An hour before you want to eat, lay the pollock fillets on top of the soup, turn the slow cooker back to high and cook for 1 hour. The soup is ready when these are flaking apart. Stir the fish and the corn into the stew and serve in deep bowls scattered with fresh coriander. This is very filling so you will only need a small amount of rice if you are having it as a stew.

LAKSA

Laksa, a popular soup from Malaysia, is one of my favourite pick-me-ups. Something about the fresh clean taste and perfect combo of fat, carbs and protein means it always hits the spot. Plus something about slurping up noodles always makes me feel better about life. Coconut milk can be expensive if you buy Western versions, but international brands are often half the price. You can also buy blocks of creamed coconut cheaply and mix it with water if you can't get tinned easily.

SERVES 2–4

4 chicken thighs

2 dried chillies

50g cashew nuts

4 cloves of garlic

1 onion, sliced

3cm piece of fresh ginger

1 teaspoon Thai fish sauce (or 3 anchovies)

1 lime, juiced

1 teaspoon sweet paprika

1 teaspoon ground turmeric

1 stalk of lemon grass (optional)

1 teaspoon coriander seeds

1 x 400ml tin coconut milk

200ml water

½ teaspoon brown sugar

4 curry leaves

½ teaspoon black pepper

250g bean sprouts

100g thin noodles (rice vermicelli)

squirt of lime juice, to serve

fresh coriander, to serve

Start by skinning and boning the chicken thighs. (I use kitchen scissors to do this.) Discard the skin, but reserve the bones. Cut each thigh into three pieces and set aside.

Put the chillies, cashews, garlic, sliced onion and fresh ginger into a bowl and blend with a hand blender, or use a pestle and mortar and blend to a purée with the Thai fish sauce, lime juice and a drop or two of water. Add the paprika, turmeric, lemon grass, if using, and coriander seeds and blitz until you have a loose paste.

Rub half of it over the chicken and, if you can, allow to marinate overnight. Otherwise, pop the chicken into the slow-cooker crock along with the chicken bones and pour the coconut milk over it all. Add the water, brown sugar, the curry leaves, black pepper and the remaining paste. Stir well.

Put the lid on the slow cooker and cook the soup on low for 8 hours or high for 6. The chicken will create a rich, creamy stock with the flavoursome paste and become very tender. Add a touch more water if the soup is very thick.

Put the bean sprouts and the thin rice vermicelli noodles into the bottom of each bowl and ladle the steaming hot soup over them, making sure you don't add the chicken bones or the curry leaves. The hot stock will blanch the noodles and bean sprouts without extra cooking. Serve the soup immediately with a squirt of lime juice and some fresh coriander.

SPICED CARROT AND PARSNIP SOUP

Few vegetables go better together than carrot and parsnip. It wasn't Sunday lunch at my granny's house unless there was a tureen of it on the table, all speckled with orange and white and dappled with butter. So imagine my excitement when I discovered that both the carrot and the parsnip love a bit of spice to accompany their sweetness. If you've never combined the two vegetables before, this is the way to start.

SERVES 2 AS
A MAIN OR 4
AS A STARTER

1 teaspoon cumin
  seeds

1 teaspoon coriander
  seeds

½ teaspoon fennel
  seeds

3 carrots

3 parsnips

½ teaspoon ground
  ginger

¼ teaspoon ground
  cloves

750ml hot vegetable
  or chicken stock

1 teaspoon Garam
  Masala (see page 168)

50ml double cream
  (optional)

salt and pepper

Toast the cumin, coriander and fennel seeds in a dry frying pan until they smell lightly aromatic. Remove from the heat immediately so they don't burn and grind them lightly using a pestle and mortar.

Peel the carrots and parsnips and cut them into 1cm cubes. Put in the slow-cooker crock along with all the spices except the garam masala, seasoning and the stock and put the lid on.

Cook on low for 7–8 hours or high for 5–6 hours. About 30 minutes before you are ready to serve, sprinkle in the garam masala and replace the lid.

Before serving, purée the soup with a hand blender until it is smooth. Add the cream if you like and serve with a scattering of black pepper.

PHO

The Vietnamese national dish, this soup is just the ticket when you feel you've overindulged or need fortifying. A rich, deep broth made from meat bones and filled with rice noodles, aromatics and fresh herbs, we've started a lovely trend in our house, encouraged by Mister North's girlfriend Emma, to use the leftover bones and meat from a Sunday lunch or Christmas Day to make it.

It's traditionally a beef broth, but it works very well as a pork version too. I've made both several times and like them equally well. Pho (which is actually pronounced more like 'fuhr') is a great dish for lots of people as you can each customise your bowlful to your own tastes, making it very sociable.

SERVES 4

For the broth:

2 onions, quartered

5 spring onions, whole

5cm piece of fresh ginger, peeled

5 cloves of garlic, peeled

500g pork ribs or beef bones

3 star anise

5cm cinnamon stick

3 whole cloves

1 tablespoon Thai fish sauce

2 teaspoons brown sugar

1.5 litres cold water

For the bowls:

4 bunches of rice noodles or rice vermicelli

1 carrot

370g bag of bean sprouts

3 spring onions

50g fresh coriander

50g fresh mint (optional)

1–2 red chillies

1 lime

The pho requires a few steps before it goes into the slow cooker, but it's still very easy.

Put the onion, spring onions, ginger and whole garlic cloves into a very hot, dry frying pan or under the grill and allow them all to char and blacken slightly for about 5–7 minutes. This charring adds fabulous flavour to the broth. If you have a gas hob, carefully use the flame to char them. Don't allow them to cook and soften. Put in the slow-cooker crock and set aside at this stage.

If you are using cooked bones from a roast, you can put them directly into the slow cooker. If you are using raw bones, put them into a large saucepan on the stove and cover with cold water. Bring the water to the boil and boil vigorously for 10 minutes. Skim as much froth and scum from the surface as possible.

After 10 minutes boiling, drain the bones into the sink and rinse well with cold water so that you remove any impurities from the bones or the water you boiled them in. Remove little gristly or red bits and put the rinsed bones in the slow cooker.

Add the star anise, cinnamon, cloves, Thai fish sauce and sugar and add the cold water. Put the lid on the slow cooker and cook the bones and aromatics together on low for 8–9 hours.

At this stage, keep the heat on the slow cooker and remove the bones from the stock. If you are using pork bones, set them aside to cool so you can remove the meat from them. You don't need to do this with beef bones. Remove and discard all the charred aromatics and star anise and cinnamon.

Taste the broth. It should be rich with a meaty taste and a salty-sweet background flavour. Add some sea salt or a drop or two more Thai fish sauce, if needed. The long, slow cooking will have made the broth incredibly clear and tasty without accidentally boiling and becoming cloudy.

Put the rice noodles into the still-warm stock. These are very thin, almost translucent noodles, which you can often buy for mere pence in the 'world foods' section of the supermarkets. They may be easier to find online if you don't live near a large store. Put the lid back on the slow cooker and leave for 10 minutes to allow the noodles to cook.

Slice the leftover beef into the bowls or strip the pork off the ribs into the bowls. Peel the carrot and, using the peeler, peel off thin ribbons of carrot. Put these in a small bowl. Add the bean sprouts to a small bowl too. Slice the spring onions and put in a small bowl. Shred the coriander and the mint and put in small dishes. Chop the red chilli and do the same. Cut the lime into wedges. Put all the bowls on the table in the centre.

Ladle out some of the broth and the noodles into the bowls with the cooked meat in. Allow everyone to customise theirs with herbs, chilli and vegetables. Squeeze the lime over it all and slurp up your noodles with gusto. The soup is surprisingly filling, but incredibly satisfying and fortifying. I can't eat mine with any decorum, only great joy.

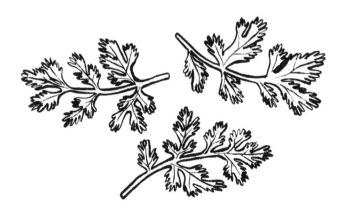

RAMEN NOODLE SOUP

For something so fundamentally simple as soup there seems to be a version for every community and culture in the world. Some become celebrities of the soup world, known and loved beyond their own region. Ramen, or Japanese noodles in broth, is definitely in this category. Big bowls of it fuel not just Japan, but thousands of wooden-benched noodle bars around the world on a daily basis.

Its secret is the broth, which is cooked for up to 18 hours, bursting with the flavour of meat and bones. This can be very time consuming when done on the stove, but the slow cooker makes it very simple to get a broth of such flavour you'll almost swoon when you taste it.

Japanese and Asian stocks differ from European ones in that they are usually white and creamy compared to the clear Continental versions. Getting that creamy, rich, white version requires one extra step, which is very worthwhile. Few dishes in my life have made me happier than this one. It's like cuddling up on a cold night with someone you love.

SERVES 4-6 AND FREEZES WELL

- 250g chicken wings or chicken bones
- 250g pork ribs, cut individually
- 2 pigs' trotters, cut in half
- 2 onions
- 8 cloves of garlic
- 5cm piece of fresh ginger
- 4 spring onions, whole
- 100g brown mushrooms, left whole
- 2 litres cold water
- salt and pepper

To serve (per person):
- 1 egg
- 1 heaped dessertspoon peanut butter or tahini
- 1 block of ramen or instant noodles
- 1 spring onion, sliced
- ½ teaspoon soy sauce

To get the creamy white Asian-style stock, start by putting the bones, ribs and trotters in a large pan of cold water on the hob and bringing them to the boil. Boil for 10–15 minutes. You'll notice some froth come to the top.

Drain the boiling water out of the pan and then run cold water over the bones. Using a chopstick, if needed, remove any blood or dark spots from the bones, ribs and trotters and clean all the froth off them well. Layer the cleaned bones, ribs and trotters into the slow cooker.

Peel your onions and take the top and bottom off them with a sharp knife. If you have a gas flame on your hob, stick a fork in the base of the onion and carefully blacken it in the flame until the outside is softened and charred. Leave it to cool and then slice into rings.

If you don't have a gas flame, slice the onions thickly and cook in a dry pan on a high heat until the rings begin to char. Move them around to make sure they don't actually burn and become acrid. You just want colour on the onions. This increases the savoury flavour of the onions and thus the stock.

Peel your garlic cloves and ginger. Leave them both whole and drop into the slow-cooker crock. Add the onion, spring onions and the mushrooms. Season well and add the cold water. Cook on low for between 12–18 hours without opening the lid, depending on how much time you have.

After 2 hours, the stock will smell so good you will be tempted to stand by the slow cooker breathing in deeply. It will have a darkish tinge up until about the sixth hour and then it will soften and mellow in the lighter, creamier Japanese style. This is further enhanced by starting the stock from cold and bringing it to a rolling boil.

About 30 minutes before you are ready to eat, put the desired number of eggs into a pan of boiling water. Bring back to the boil and cook for 5 minutes. Remove from the heat and lower into a bowl of iced water to stop them cooking further.

Take the lid off the slow cooker and, using a slotted spoon, remove the bones, ribs and trotters from the stock. If you are using chicken wings, remove as much meat as possible and reserve. Do the same with the pork ribs. Discard the chicken bones, rib bones and the trotters.

Whisk the tahini or peanut butter into the hot stock, setting aside any you want to freeze for later. This helps add creaminess and to emulsify the fat from the meat to make the soup feel even more luxurious in your mouth. Put the noodles in the stock and put the lid back on. Allow to cook for about 5 minutes.

As the noodles soften, peel the eggs and slice in half. Your yolks should still be nice and soft in the middle. Put one egg in each bowl. Ladle the stock and noodles on top. Scatter the sliced spring onion on top. Add the reserved meat and drizzle over the soy sauce. Eat and feel the soup's warm embrace.

Note: I've also made this soup with leftover turkey bones, making it a great post-Christmas dish.

CURRY

You'll be amazed how well some curries work in the slow cooker. Low slow cooking can help create layers of flavour. Meat-based curries tend to work best this way, but some root vegetables also work well.

Using whole spices really adds an extra dimension of flavour to your curries. I lightly toast them and then grind them to release those wonderful aromas and flavours. This takes only a minute or two before putting everything in the slow-cooker crock.

You may worry that the spices for a curry will be very expensive to buy or be difficult to source. I've deliberately used the same selection of spices in a variety of ways so you can maximise your spice cupboard to its full potential.

If you can look for spices in the 'world foods' section of a supermarket or visit your local Asian grocer, you'll get big bags of spices for a fraction of the cost of buying jars. Simply decant what you will use to sealed jars and store the spare spices in the freezer to keep them fresh. You can also buy big bags online at a well-known auction site, which is how I got my dried chillies!

Just to give you a sense of how far spices (and herbs) go, I tested everything in the book multiple times and didn't have to replace any of them except the coriander seeds, which I dropped on the kitchen floor. Build your collection up gradually, starting with your favourites. I didn't use ready-made pastes as they tend to be specific to one dish and much more restrictive than buying the basic spices long term.

BEEF RENDANG

Rendang is a Malaysian dish full of spices and coconut. It is slow cooked until it is incredibly flavoursome and the coconut is thick. I've tweaked it a bit here because it usually involves buying ingredients specially, which often I'm not organised enough to have done. However, if you do have lemon grass and fresh chillies, use them. You should be able to get tins of coconut milk for a good price in the 'world foods' section of the supermarket. If you can only find expensive branded ones, use creamed coconut from a block and mix with warm water to make your own version at a fraction of the price.

Cook this one for a long time, up to 12 hours, and then if possible leave overnight to absorb the flavours. This is a very easy dish and a lot of the work can be done the night before if you want to make it for dinner.

SERVES 2-4

2 onions, finely diced

3 cloves of garlic, finely diced

1 stalk of lemon grass or 1 tablespoon fresh lemon zest (if waxed, give the lemon a vigorous scrub under the hot tap first)

1 fresh red chilli, chopped (or 2 dried red chillies, whole)

2 tablespoons brown sugar

1 teaspoon tamarind syrup or lemon juice

½ teaspoon ground ginger or 2–3cm piece of fresh ginger, grated

1 teaspoon coriander seeds

1 teaspoon cumin seeds

½ teaspoon ground cloves

½ teaspoon ground mace

1 teaspoon vegetable oil

500g stewing steak, cut into 3cm chunks

1 tablespoon soy sauce

1 tablespoon Thai fish sauce or 2 anchovies

1 x 400g tin coconut milk

200ml water

salt and pepper

Blend the onion, garlic, lemon grass, fresh chilli (if using), sugar, tamarind, fresh ginger (if using) and all the spices in a hand blender or pestle and mortar. Don't add the dried chillies. Add the oil to make a paste. Rub into the cubed stewing steak and leave to marinate overnight in the fridge.

Put the marinated meat in the slow-cooker crock. Add the dried chilli. Drizzle the soy sauce and Thai fish sauce over the meat and stir to coat well. Pour the coconut over the meat and add the 200ml water so that the meat is just covered.

Cook on high for 10–12 hours. In the early stages of cooking the coconut milk will look curdled and lumpy. Don't panic. Like adolescence, it's just a stage. By the time 8 hours are up, it will be well rounded and smooth as the sauce thickens and reduces. At 10 hours, it will have almost completely reduced to barely coat the tender meat. By 12 hours, it's so beautiful you'll be putting it all over Instagram to show it off.

Serve with steamed rice. It reheats very well so is even better the next day when the flavours have developed even more. The oil in the coconut may rise to the top and you can skim the excess off if you prefer.

Note: If you can't find tinned coconut milk, use a quarter of a block of creamed coconut mixed with 300ml of warm water instead.

FISH CURRY

I have to admit I used to be quite sceptical about fish curry as it summoned up ideas of those seventies-style curries with sultanas in and I couldn't quite get my head round it. Then my friend Zoe cooked me a fish curry one night and I was smitten. Creamy coconut milk, aromatic spices and flavoursome fish, it's become a real favourite. This recipe was inspired by Felicity Cloake's 'perfect' fish curry in *The Guardian*.

I'm lucky enough to have a superb fishmonger's near my house so I make this often. I've used fish that anyone should be able to get if they aren't as lucky to have such a choice. White fish is best, but salmon works well too. My fishmonger Donna ate some of the curry for lunch and felt I'd definitely done justice to her stock, which is one of the best compliments I've had of my cooking!

Don't be startled by the inclusion of conger eel. It is less like the small eels people think are slimy (but aren't) and more like a firm white version of salmon. Its flesh is perfect for slow cooking as it is quite robust and it soaks up flavour well.

SERVES 4

2 teaspoons coriander seeds

1 teaspoon cloves

1 teaspoon cumin seeds

2 dried red chillies

2 star anise

½ teaspoon ground turmeric

2 teaspoons brown sugar

1 green chilli

1 teaspoon sea salt

4 cloves of garlic

1 onion

4cm piece of fresh ginger

1 tablespoon white vinegar

1 x 400g tin plum tomatoes

1 x 400ml tin coconut milk

2 thick conger eel steaks, about 300g

2 thick coley steaks, approximately 200g

Don't be put off by the relatively long ingredient list; this curry is very easy to make. Start by toasting the coriander seeds, cloves, cumin, red chillies and star anise in a dry frying pan until they smell aromatic. Remove from the heat immediately so they don't burn. Bash them up a bit using a pestle and mortar and put in the slow-cooker crock.

Purée the turmeric, brown sugar, green chilli, salt, garlic, onion, ginger and white vinegar together using a hand blender or a pestle and mortar. It should be a thick paste, but it doesn't have to be smooth. Add to the spices in the slow cooker and stir together.

Squash the plum tomatoes a little bit with your hands and add to the slow cooker along with the coconut milk. Put the lid on the slow cooker and cook on high for 3 hours. The fish needs less cooking so it goes in later.

The coconut milk should be bubbling round the edges at this stage. Take the lid off and pop the fish in. Steaks rather than fillets of fish work better here as they cook slowly while absorbing all the flavour of the spices.

Make sure the fish is submerged in the coconut milk and replace the lid on the slow cooker. Cook on high for a further 2 hours.

If you are using the mussels, scrub and de-beard them under cold running water. Discard any mussels that don't close when tapped as they are already dead and not safe to eat. Add the mussels to the curry 1 hour before the end of cooking to allow all the lovely flavours to mingle in.

**2 handfuls of fresh
mussels (optional)**

**1 tablespoon
vegetable oil**

5 curry leaves

**½ teaspoon black
mustard seeds**

About 5 minutes before you are ready to eat, heat the vegetable oil in a small pan on the hob and fry the curry leaves and mustard seeds until they smell aromatic and the mustard seeds start to pop. Remove from the heat as soon as that happens.

Serve the curry in deep bowls with steamed rice and lots of the lovely coconut-rich sauce and the fried mustard seeds and curry leaves on top of it all.

CURRY GOAT

Goat might not be particularly well known in Britain, but if you have a halal butcher in your area, they will sell this tasty meat at a reasonable price. Almost never intensively reared, goat is slightly gamier and less greasy than the cheaper cuts of lamb. It always needs long, slow cooking to make it tender and bring out the flavour. You could use mutton or stewing lamb if you can't get your goat easily.

I usually cook goat curry in a Caribbean style as the hint of heat really suits the meat, but it also works well in with the Potato and Olive Stew with Preserved Lemons on page 131 instead of beans.

My friend Brian at Fish, Wings & Tings in Brixton serves his goat curry along with pumpkin stew in a buttery soft roti or flatbread, and I've taken to putting pumpkin into the stew to make this a one-pot meal as the two are fabulous together.

SERVES 4 GENEROUSLY

1kg goat, either leg or shoulder on the bone, in 4cm chunks

3 cloves of garlic, chopped

1 lime, juiced

1 teaspoon cumin seeds, lightly crushed

1 teaspoon ground allspice

1 tablespoon Madras curry powder

1 Scotch bonnet pepper (or 4 shakes of Tabasco sauce)

1 small butternut squash or large wedge of pumpkin (about 400g)

1 large onion, chopped

1 teaspoon Worcestershire sauce

600ml hot chicken stock

salt and pepper

Ask the butcher to cut the goat into chunks for you. I prefer it on the bone as it adds flavour to the stew.

Marinate the goat in 1 clove of the garlic, lime juice, cumin, allspice and curry powder for 24 hours. If you want a bit of heat in the dish, chop your Scotch bonnet pepper and add it to the marinade. Otherwise, keep it whole and add later when the stock goes in.

Add the marinated goat into the slow cooker along with any remaining marinade. Peel and chop the butternut squash or pumpkin into 1cm cubes and add in with the goat. Add the onion and remaining garlic. Sprinkle in the Worcestershire sauce. Stir to make sure everything is mixed.

Pour the chicken stock over it all. Add the whole Scotch bonnet pepper if you haven't used it earlier. It will infuse the curry with flavour without too much heat. Put the lid on the slow cooker and cook on low for 8 hours or high for 6 hours. The meat will be tender and the pumpkin will have cooked down to the point of collapsing.

Serve with rice or flatbread to soak up the lovely flavoursome juices.

PORK VINDALOO

If ever a dish has suffered due to reputation and bravado, it's the vindaloo. A traditional vindaloo is rich with chilli and vinegar and hails from the Portuguese-influenced area of Goa in southern India. British vindaloos tend to be just overwhelmingly hot and lacking the layers of flavour it needs. This version gives you that chilli buzz people mention, but with all the other flavours you need to keep it tasty. Don't be afraid of the long list of ingredients, this is a very simple curry to make.

SERVES 4

- 2 teaspoons cumin seeds
- 2 teaspoons coriander seeds
- 1 heaped teaspoon coarse ground black pepper
- 1 teaspoon ground cinnamon
- 1 teaspoon ground turmeric
- 1 teaspoon brown mustard seeds
- 1 teaspoon fenugreek seeds
- ½ teaspoon ground cloves
- 6 dried red chillies
- 1 teaspoon brown sugar
- 3 tablespoons vinegar
- 500g pork shoulder, diced
- 2 onions, finely sliced into half moons
- 2–3cm piece of fresh ginger or 1 heaped teaspoon ground ginger
- 1 large green chilli, sliced
- 6 cloves of garlic, sliced
- 250ml water

Using a pestle and mortar or a hand blender, make a paste of the spices, dried chillies and sugar with the vinegar. Pour this over the pork and mix well. Marinate overnight if you can.

Add the pork to the slow-cooker crock with the sliced onion, ginger, green chilli, garlic and water. Put the lid on the slow cooker and cook the pork on high for 6 hours or low for 8 hours. The pork will become meltingly tender and the flavours will come together in many layers.

Serve it with some fluffy naan bread and a cooling drink on the side.

Note: A mango lassi would be just perfect with it. Use some of my home-made Yoghurt from page 202 to make a batch by blending about 50g fresh or tinned mango with 100ml yoghurt and 50ml water.

KASHMIRI-STYLE LAMB LEG

This is a show-stopper of a meal and a particularly good dish to do with frozen lamb. A leg or half leg from the freezer cabinet will become something really special here. The only effort is a bit of time it takes to marinate. I have all these ingredients in the house anyway and this is a favourite Easter dish or when I have lots of guests. I usually serve it with flatbreads or naan and it makes a leftover sandwich to rival even a Boxing Day number!

SERVES 4–6
WITH SCOPE FOR
SANDWICHES

1 half leg lamb,
   approximately 1kg
5cm piece of fresh
   ginger
4 cloves of garlic
1 teaspoon ground
   cumin
1 teaspoon ground
   turmeric
1 teaspoon ground
   cinnamon
½ teaspoon sea salt
½ teaspoon ground
   black pepper
½ teaspoon red chilli
   powder
¼ teaspoon ground
   cloves
2 cardamom pods
1 lemon, juiced
250ml plain yoghurt
   or my home-made
   Yoghurt (page 202),
   strained (see note)
2 tablespoons
   desiccated coconut
2 tablespoons ground
   almonds
1 tablespoon clear
   honey

If you are using frozen lamb, make sure the meat is completely defrosted before you begin cooking. A half leg fits nicely into a 3.5-litre slow cooker and a whole leg should fit a 6.5-litre one, but do check your proportions first!

Start by making your spice paste. Grate the ginger and garlic together into a bowl and add the cumin, turmeric, cinnamon, salt, pepper, chilli powder and cloves. Remove the seeds from the cardamom pods with the tip of a sharp knife and crush them slightly using the side of the knife. Add them to the garlic and ginger spice mix and combine it all into a paste with the lemon juice.

Take a sharp knife and make deep slits into the lamb. They should be big enough to wiggle the end of your little finger into. Rub the garlic and ginger spice mix over the lamb, poking it into the slits in the meat to really infuse the flavour. Allow the lamb to marinate overnight in a cool place.

Mix the strained yoghurt with the desiccated coconut, ground almonds and honey to make a thick, slightly lumpy paste. Spread this paste over the marinated lamb and place in the slow cooker.

Put the lid on the slow cooker and cook the lamb for 7–8 hours on low. The meat will be falling off the bone and the yoghurt will have tenderised it all while the spices and nuts add flavour and texture. Serve with flatbreads or rice. I like an extra drizzle of yoghurt with a little chopped chilli on the side too.

Note: Strained yoghurt sounds like a specialist ingredient, but it's extremely easy to make. Also known as labneh, it simply involves straining yoghurt through a cloth to remove the watery whey and make it thicker, creamier and less likely to curdle when cooked. Make it by spreading a clean J-cloth or muslin square in a sieve over a bowl and pouring some plain unsweetened yoghurt into it. Gather the cloth up into a purse-like shape and allow the yoghurt to strain for at least 15-20 minutes. The whey will drain into the bowl and you will be left with thick, creamy yoghurt. Store the whey for up to a week in the fridge for use in the Lamb Nihari on page 176.

ROGAN JOSH

I remember my dad making rogan josh when I was a very small child and I think it was probably my first introduction to Indian food. It seemed like a very long, involved procedure that went on all day and thus we didn't have it very often, but I loved it when we did. I have no idea how authentic it could have been back in 1980s Belfast and I'm not sure how authentic this modern-day version is either. But it's not involved at all and it tastes absolutely amazing. My inner child and I make this one a lot.

SERVES 4

200ml plain yoghurt, strained or my home-made Yoghurt (page 202), strained, (see note, page 164)

500g lamb chops

1 teaspoon chilli powder

1 large onion

6 cloves of garlic

5cm piece of fresh ginger

1 teaspoon sea salt

4 green cardamom pods

1 stick of cinnamon, broken up

1 teaspoon black peppercorns

4 whole cloves

2 teaspoons coriander seeds

2 teaspoons cumin seeds

½ teaspoon ground mace

1 dried red chilli

1 x 400g tin chopped tomatoes

200ml water

Begin the rogan josh by straining your yoghurt. Reserve the whey in a shallow bowl and keep the thickened yoghurt in the cloth until needed.

Coat the lamb chops with the chilli powder and add them to the bowl of whey. Marinate overnight if you can to really tenderise the lamb. If you don't have time, you can skip this step as you're actually cooking the lamb in the whey.

Blend the onion, garlic and ginger together using a hand blender or a pestle and mortar or grate them together into a thick paste. Add this to the slow-cooker crock and combine with the chilli-coated lamb and the whey and mix well. Season with the sea salt.

Toast the cardamom, broken-up cinnamon stick, peppercorns, cloves, coriander and cumin seeds in a dry frying pan until they smell aromatic. Remove from the heat and bash them up a bit using a pestle and mortar or put them in a cloth and whack with a rolling pin.

Stir the toasted spices into the slow cooker along with the mace, dried chilli and the tomatoes, making sure the meat is evenly coated. Add the water to go with the roughly 100ml of whey you have.

Put the lid on the slow cooker and cook for 8 hours on low. When you are ready to serve, take the lid off and turn the slow cooker off. Allow to sit like this for about 10 minutes and then stir the strained yoghurt into it all. If you do it too quickly, the yoghurt curdles and looks unpleasant.

Serve with rice or naan bread and maybe an extra dollop of yoghurt on the side. This tastes even better the next day.

SQUASH CURRY

This is a really, really good basic curry that even confirmed veggie sceptics love. It uses butternut squash and courgettes, which are of course part of the summer squash family. It's the perfect way to use up leftover odds and ends from the fridge and feel very virtuous while secretly being a little bit lazy...

SERVES 2–4 WITH LEFTOVERS

- 1 medium butternut squash (about 450g)
- 2 courgettes (about 450g)
- 1 onion, finely diced
- 4cm piece of fresh ginger, finely diced
- 3 cloves of garlic, finely diced
- 1 teaspoon fenugreek seeds
- 1 teaspoon ground turmeric
- 1 teaspoon mustard seeds
- 1 teaspoon ground coriander
- 1 teaspoon black pepper
- 1 teaspoon tamarind syrup (see note)
- 100ml boiling water
- 1 x 400ml tin coconut milk
- spinach or fresh coriander, to serve (optional)

Peel and deseed your butternut squash. Cut into 2.5cm chunks. Top and tail the courgettes and cut into 3.5cm chunks.

Pop the squash, courgette, onion, ginger and garlic into the slow-cooker crock with the spices. Mix the tamarind syrup with the boiling water and pour it into the crock. Stir it all together well, add the coconut milk and put the lid on.

Cook on low for 8 hours. The vegetables will be soft and tender and the sauce will have thickened slightly. I usually stir some spinach or fresh coriander through it just as I serve to add an extra splash of colour.

Note: The tamarind syrup is very easy to make. You need a block of tamarind pulp, which you can buy for well under a pound in the 'world foods' section. Break it up and pour about 300ml boiling water over it. Allow it to steep for about 20 minutes and then drain through a sieve. Throw the pulp away and keep the syrup. A little goes a long way and you can keep the leftover in the fridge for 4–6 weeks in a sterilised jar.

SWEET POTATO, SPINACH AND PANEER CURRY

I love sweet potatoes. Adding their lovely orangey flesh to any dish just adds a splash of cheerful colour as well as their delicious sweet flavour. They are often a very good price when sold loose and keep much better than regular potatoes, so you always have something in the house for whipping up an easy tea.

This tasty curry adds paneer, that Indian cheese that soaks up flavour and enhances any dish. It can be bought in blocks and it also keeps for ages in the fridge, suiting the casual nature of this dish, or what my friend Claire calls 'kitchen surprise', made using whatever you have in the house around payday!

SERVES 2 WITH LEFTOVERS OR 4 AS A GENEROUS MAIN

- 1 teaspoon mustard seeds
- 1 teaspoon fenugreek seeds
- 1 teaspoon onion seeds
- 1 teaspoon coriander seeds
- 1 teaspoon cumin seeds
- 1 dried red chilli
- 1 x 400g tin chopped tomatoes
- 200ml water
- 1 x 400ml tin coconut milk
- 2 sweet potatoes
- 1 onion, finely diced
- 4 cloves of garlic, finely diced
- 1 x 400g tin spinach or 250g frozen and thawed spinach
- 125g paneer, cubed

Start by roasting all the spices and the dried chilli in a dry frying pan over a medium heat until the mustard seeds start to pop and they all smell very aromatic. Make sure they don't burn or they will become bitter, so keep a beady eye on them. Take off the heat immediately. Crush lightly using a pestle and mortar.

Add the chopped tomatoes to the slow-cooker crock and purée them using a hand blender so they are very smooth. Add the water and the coconut milk along with the toasted spices.

Peel the sweet potatoes and cube into 4cm chunks. Add to the slow cooker with the onion and garlic.

Put the lid on the slow cooker and cook on low for 6–7 hours. About 20 minutes before you are ready to eat, add the spinach and the cubed paneer. Stir well and put the lid back on for 20–30 minutes to heat through and allow the cheese to soak up the flavours. Serve with rice or naan breads.

GARAM MASALA

The first few times I made curries in the slow cooker they were a bit flat, but with some detective work from my friend Kavey and her mum, who are the food-blogging royalty behind *Mamta's Kitchen*, I learned I was using my garam masala wrong.

They taught me that cheaper brands of ready-made garam masala are often bulked up with cumin and coriander, diluting the impact of the spice blend. It should be made in small batches as needed and stored in an airtight jar or the freezer until needed. Added towards the end of cooking, it adds flavour and a little goes a long way, making it surprisingly economical.

MAKES ABOUT 50G

- 1 tablespoon black peppercorns
- 1 teaspoon whole cloves
- 1 teaspoon fennel seeds
- ½ teaspoon cumin seeds
- 5–6 cardamom pods
- 4–5 bay leaves
- 7cm piece of cinnamon stick or cassia bark
- ⅓ nutmeg, grated
- 1 star anise

Toast the spices in a dry frying pan until they smell aromatic. Take off the heat the moment that happens so they don't burn.

Finely grind all the spices using a pestle and mortar. It is surprisingly easy to do. I simply waited until *The Archers* omnibus and vented some irritation with a particular character — ground spices in no time.

Sieve the spices to remove any large pieces and store in an airtight jar in the freezer. Use in recipes that call for garam masala and add towards the end of cooking.

BUNNYCHOW

Nothing to do with rabbits, bunnychow is a South African curry, particularly popular in Durban, served in a hollowed-out loaf or bread rolls. It's a meal where you get to eat the container as well as the filling. It appeals to my love of putting anything in bread to make it even tastier and it's a lovely change from having curry with rice. Kids especially love having a bunny to themselves.

Having never been to Durban (even though the city bizarrely boasts a replica of Belfast's City Hall), I have no idea if this dish is their exact style, but it's fantastic all the same. I like the curry to be slightly fruity here and the meatballs make it much easier to eat since I'm not graceful when faced with a street-food-style dinner. A heap of napkins on the side are not optional!

SERVES 2-4 WITH LEFTOVERS

450g Beef Meatballs (see page 30)

1 x 400g tin sliced peaches

1 onion, finely diced

4 cloves of garlic, finely chopped

1 carrot, finely diced

2cm piece of fresh ginger

1 teaspoon chilli powder

1 teaspoon Madras curry powder

1 x 400g tin chopped tomatoes

200ml tomato juice or water

1 lemon, juiced

1 teaspoon Garam Masala (see page 168)

4 white crusty rolls or white batch loaf

20g chopped fresh coriander, to serve

salt and pepper

This is a very simple recipe to make. Follow the directions for the meatballs and ensure they are chilled for at least 30 minutes before you put them in the slow-cooker crock.

Rinse the syrup off the sliced peaches and break them up with a potato masher so they still have a bit of texture, but aren't whole. Mix in the chopped onion, garlic and carrot. Grate in the ginger and add the spices. Stir in the tomatoes. Season well.

Pour the peach and tomato mix into the slow-cooker crock and add the tomato juice or water. The meatballs will be covered. Squeeze the lemon juice all over it.

Put the lid on the slow cooker and cook the meatballs on low for 8 hours until the sauce thickens nicely and the flavours are combined. Scatter the garam masala over it all as you are ready to serve.

If you are using the white batch loaf, cut into four equal-sized pieces and use your hand to scoop out the middle, making sure you leave enough of a base to support the meatballs like a dish. Spoon the meatballs and sauce into each hollowed-out 'bunny' and sprinkle with coriander. Place the remaining bread on top to help you eat the filling and soak up the sauce.

Do the same with the rolls if using them, cutting off a lid first. A big Belfast bap would be perfect here with its robust crust, but use this as an excuse to tour through the regional variations of barms, butteries, stotties or teacakes. Maybe experiment with a Staffordshire oatcake, but don't use baguettes or it becomes a meatball sub! I always set it all on a plate, so don't worry if your bread leaks a bit. It's just so much fun to eat this way.

BEEF MADRAS

This is one of those dishes that's very simple to make, but that the slow cooker really excels at because the meat becomes so tender and the flavours intensify. I make this curry whenever I want something simple but easy to make from store cupboard ingredients. It has also gone down very well with my editor on occasion…

SERVES 2-4

500g stewing steak

1 onion, roughly chopped

4 cloves of garlic, diced

1 red chilli

1 tablespoon coriander seeds

2 teaspoons cumin seeds

1 teaspoon ground turmeric

1 teaspoon ground ginger

1 teaspoon black pepper

4 tablespoons tomato purée

1 tablespoon ghee (see page 173)

1 green chilli, sliced

300ml hot beef stock

1 tablespoon Garam Masala (see page 168)

salt

Chop the stewing steak into 5cm pieces and place in the slow-cooker crock.

Using a pestle and mortar or hand blender, blitz the roughly chopped onion, garlic and the red chilli into a purée. Add the coriander, cumin, turmeric, ginger, black pepper and tomato purée and blend together.

Pour the purée over the meat and toss it all to mix it well. Add the ghee and the sliced green chilli. Season well with salt and pepper. Pour the beef stock over it all.

Put the lid on the slow cooker and cook the beef on low for 7-8 hours. About 30 minutes before you are ready to serve, sprinkle the garam masala over the madras. Serve the curry with steamed rice or naan breads. Or get on the bus and come to mine…

TANDOORI CHICKEN

Few things make meat tastier and more tender than marinating it in yoghurt and as soon as I marinate meat in yoghurt, I think of the Indian tradition of tandoori chicken. Usually baked in a very hot oven, this style of chicken actually works very well adapted to the slow cooker, keeping the flavours and melt-in-the-mouth texture of the meat, but easier to make than building your own brick oven.

Don't be tempted to marinate the chicken for longer to make it more tender. The lactic acid in yoghurt can make the meat feel a bit woolly in texture if you do. Even an hour marinating works well, but overnight is best.

SERVES 2–4 WITH
LEFTOVERS
DEPENDING ON
THE SIDES YOU
SERVE IT WITH

4 cloves of garlic

**2 dried red chillies or
1 fresh red chilli**

**6cm piece of fresh
ginger**

**200ml plain yoghurt,
or home-made
Yoghurt (see page
202), strained (see
note, page 164)**

**½ teaspoon mustard
seeds**

**1 teaspoon caraway
seeds**

**4 tablespoons malt
vinegar**

**4–6 chicken thighs,
skin on and bone in**

**1 teaspoon Garam
Masala (see page 168)**

salt and pepper

Blend the garlic, chillies and the ginger together in a blender or use a pestle and mortar and stir it into the yoghurt along with the mustard and caraway seeds and vinegar.

Season the chicken well and then pour the spiced yoghurt all over it. Mix it well with your hands to coat both sides of the chicken. Allow to marinate for up to 10 hours.

When you are ready to cook the chicken, remove it from the marinade and scrape any excess yoghurt back into the dish. Sear the chicken, skin side down, for 5 minutes in a hot frying pan on the hob.

When the skin is crisped up, place the chicken thighs in the slow-cooker crock and add the remaining marinade as well. Put the lid on the slow cooker and cook the chicken on low for 7–8 hours. About 20–30 minutes before you are ready to eat, sprinkle the garam masala over it all.

The chicken and yoghurt will give off quite a lot of liquid and fat that will essentially poach and steam the meat so that it falls cleanly off the bone. Eat this tender, juicy meat with flatbreads and some cucumber and mint chopped into yoghurt. It makes wonderful cold chicken leftovers.

BUTTER CHICKEN

Everyone loves this dish with its rich combination of spices. It's particularly appealing on a Friday night when most people go out to eat it or dial in. This is a fabulous slow-cooker version that requires only slightly more effort than finding the takeaway menu. I can't claim it's super authentic, but it is so delicious no one has ever queried my methods when I've served it.

Ghee is basically clarified butter, which means butter that has been heated until the cloudy milk solids separate and can be skimmed off. This leaves a clear butter that solidifies when cooled and doesn't go off when stored, allowing it to keep well. It is common in Indian cooking and it's worth making one batch and storing it if you like your curries.

I use chicken thighs I've skinned and boned for this. This is the most economical way to buy chicken and you can freeze the bones to add to a stock or stew in the future.

SERVES 4 WITH
LEFTOVERS

400g chicken thighs, skinned and boned

2 tablespoons ghee (see note)

2 teaspoons Garam Masala (see page 168)

60ml double cream (optional)

fresh coriander, to serve

salt and pepper

For the marinade:

5cm piece of fresh ginger, finely chopped

3 cloves of garlic, finely chopped

2 dried chillies

1 teaspoon ground cumin

½ teaspoon ground turmeric

1 tablespoon lemon juice

150ml plain yoghurt (see home-made Yoghurt page 202)

Place the chicken thighs in a bowl or freezer bag.

Put the ginger and garlic in the bowl of a hand blender or use a pestle and mortar. Add the dried chillies, 1 tablespoon water and the cumin, turmeric and lemon juice and blitz or pound into a paste.

Stir the yoghurt through and then coat the chicken with this spiced yoghurt. Marinate in the fridge for at least an hour or up to overnight.

I prepare the rest of the ingredients for the butter chicken sauce at the same time as they can be left in the fridge in a container until needed:

Purée the chopped tomatoes with the hand blender, making sure they are really smooth.

Add in the lemon juice, tomato purée and all the spices from the second list, along with the additional chopped garlic and ginger. Refrigerate until needed.

When you are ready to cook, put the chicken into the slow-cooker crock, leaving any excess marinade behind. Pour the tomato sauce over the chicken pieces and stir well to coat evenly. Add the ghee.

Put the lid on the slow cooker and cook on low for 8 hours. The sauce will thicken and become glossy with the ghee, while the chicken becomes very tender.

Before you are ready to eat, tease the chicken apart slightly with two forks and stir into the sauce. This mimics the 'chopped' texture of traditional butter chicken and thickens the dish. Sprinkle the garam masala over it all this point too.

For the sauce:

- 1 x 400g tin chopped tomatoes
- 1 tablespoon lemon juice
- 2 tablespoons tomato purée
- 1 cardamom pod (optional)
- 1 teaspoon ground turmeric
- 1 teaspoon coriander seeds
- ½–1 teaspoon chilli powder
- ¼ teaspoon ground cloves
- 2 cloves of garlic, finely chopped
- 2–3cm piece of fresh ginger, finely chopped

If you like your butter chicken really creamy, add the double cream and mix through. Check the seasoning. Serve the curry with rice and a sprinkling of fresh coriander if you have it. Enjoy!

Note: To make ghee, heat about 200g unsalted butter in a pan over a medium heat until it is just starting to bubble. Pour it into a clean dish and allow it to sit for a moment or two. You'll see some froth on the top. Skim this off with a spoon. You'll also see some sediment gather at the bottom of the butter. Pour the clear butter into a clean jar, leaving the sediment behind, and allow to cool. This is ghee and it will keep for up to 6 months in the fridge.

CHICKEN KORMA

Everyone sniggers at the korma when they go out for a curry. It's become a byword for blandness and I'm not standing for it any longer. A well-prepared korma is absolutely packed with flavour and is a soothing, soul-enriching dish. I rarely order it when I'm out because of its reputation, but I have a real soft spot for it at home and love making this version. Not only does it taste fabulous, you don't have to listen to anyone judging you for this guilty pleasure.

SERVES 4 COMFORTABLY

400g chicken thighs, skinned and boned

5cm piece of fresh ginger, peeled and finely chopped

2 cloves of garlic, finely chopped

100ml plain yoghurt (see home-made Yoghurt page 202)

2 red onions, chopped

1 dried red chilli

1 tablespoon coriander seeds

2 tablespoons ground almonds

1 teaspoon ground turmeric

200ml coconut milk or 75g creamed coconut with 200ml warm water

1 tablespoon ghee (see page 173)

2 teaspoons Garam Masala (see page 168)

salt and pepper

Cut the thighs into 6cm pieces and put them in a bowl or freezer bag with the ginger, garlic, yoghurt and salt and pepper. Marinate overnight or for up to 24 hours in the fridge.

To make the sauce for the korma, purée your onions using a hand blender along with about 1–2 tablespoons water. They should be just thick enough to scoop rather than pour. Blitz the dried chilli in with them and add the coriander seeds to break them up a bit.

Tip the chicken pieces into the slow-cooker crock, leaving any excess marinade behind. Cover with the onion and spice mix and sprinkle the ground almonds over them. Mix well to coat the pieces, adding the turmeric. Grate the creamed coconut over it all, if using, and add the water or pour the coconut milk into the crock. Add the ghee.

Put the lid on the slow cooker and cook the chicken for 8 hours on low. The sauce will thicken and the flavours will intensify. About 30 minutes before you are ready to eat, add the garam masala over the top of it all. Serve with rice or a hot fluffy naan bread and rediscover the joys of the korma.

LAMB DOPIAZA

I had a friend who always used to order this when we went out for Indian food and I used to sneak a very large taste when they weren't looking, but never ordered it myself because it was 'their' dish. When I got the slow cooker, I realised this dish, with its onions two ways, could be enhanced by using the super-slow-cooked Caramelised Onions on page 122, which the slow cooker does so well, and now I like to think this is 'my' dish...

SERVES 2–4

3 tablespoons coriander seeds

2 tablespoons cumin seeds

4 cloves of garlic, roughly chopped

5cm piece of fresh ginger, roughly chopped

½ teaspoon ground turmeric

1 teaspoon sea salt

500g lamb chops

2 onions, caramelised (see page 122)

1 onion, finely chopped

1 heaped tablespoon cornflour

250ml cold water

2 teaspoons Garam Masala (see page 168)

This is one of the easiest curries around. Lightly toast the coriander seeds and cumin seeds in a dry frying pan for 1–2 minutes until they become very aromatic. Watch them closely so they don't burn.

Take them off the heat immediately and put them in the bowl of a hand blender, or use a pestle and mortar, along with the garlic, ginger, turmeric and sea salt and blend to a purée.

Place the lamb chops in the slow-cooker crock. Pour the garlic and ginger paste over the meat and mix well. Add the caramelised onions and the chopped onion.

Mix the cornflour with about a tablespoon of cold water and add it to the slow-cooker crock along with the rest of the water. Put the lid on the slow cooker and cook the lamb on low for 7–8 hours.

About 30 minutes before the end of the cooking time, sprinkle the garam masala over the curry and put the lid back on to warm it through. Serve with rice or hot chapattis and a cucumber salad. It's onion heaven.

LAMB NIHARI

As I've mentioned before, frozen lamb works very well in the slow cooker. Here I've used lamb chops, which I always keep a bag of in the freezer as they defrost quickly and are surprisingly flavoursome. They have just enough bone to make this dish velvety smooth. I also tenderise it all by using any whey I have left over from straining yoghurt. Don't worry if you don't have any whey, the meat will still be fabulous without it.

This dish is so well suited to the slow cooker that it was the very first dish Mister North suggested to me when I got mine. He's got very good taste...

SERVES 2-4
DEPENDING ON
SIDE DISHES

500g lamb chops

2 onions, cut into half moons

5cm piece of fresh ginger, grated

1 tablespoon ghee (see page 173)

1 teaspoon fennel seeds, crushed

¼ nutmeg, grated

2 teaspoons ground cinnamon

¼ teaspoon cayenne pepper

150ml whey (see page 164) (optional)

1 tablespoon cornflour

350ml water

1 tablespoon Garam Masala (see page 168)

squeeze of lemon juice

fresh coriander, to serve (optional)

salt and pepper

I cook my chops whole on the bone to allow them to be very tender and, of course, to save on preparation time. Put them into the slow-cooker crock and add the onion, ginger and ghee. Toss the chops to coat it all well.

Add in the fennel seeds, nutmeg, cinnamon and cayenne and mix well. Add about a tablespoon of the whey or water to the cornflour to make a loose paste. Add to the meat. Pour the remaining whey and the water over the spiced meat. If you don't have whey, make up the liquid with more water. Season well.

Put the lid on the slow cooker and cook the meat for 7-8 hours on low. About 30 minutes before you are ready to serve, sprinkle the garam masala over the lamb and warm through with the lid back on.

Serve the lamb with rice and a squeeze of lemon juice to lift all the flavours. A scatter of fresh coriander also works well.

LAMB KEEMA

I think I've spoken before about my love of mince and it was a happy day when I was introduced to keema at a local Pakistani restaurant, Elephant, to expand those horizons. Lamb mince cooked with spices and peas is perfect 'Friday night food'. It cries out to be eaten from a big bowl while wearing your pyjamas and knowing you don't have to get up early the next day.

It's also simple enough to pop in the slow cooker before work on Friday morning, so you can get home to dinner without being tempted to get a takeaway. If a meal could be described as relaxing, it's this one.

SERVES 2 AS A
MAIN OR 4 AS
PART OF A MEAL

1 large onion, diced

4 cloves of garlic,
  roughly chopped

5cm piece of fresh
  ginger

2 teaspoons ground
  coriander

1 teaspoon ground
  turmeric

2 teaspoons ground
  cumin

2 green chillies,
  chopped

500g lamb mince

2 cardamom pods

¼ teaspoon ground
  cloves

½ teaspoon black
  pepper

1 small cinnamon stick
  or 1 teaspoon ground
  cinnamon

3 tablespoons tomato
  purée

200ml water

½ teaspoon salt

200g frozen peas

1 tablespoon Garam
  Masala (page 168)

This is so simple to make. Using a hand blender, purée the onion, garlic, ginger, coriander, turmeric, cumin and chilli. Stir through the lamb mince and add to the slow-cooker crock.

Add the cardamoms, cloves, black pepper and the cinnamon stick along with the tomato purée and water. Season well with salt.

Put the lid on the slow cooker and cook it for 7–8 hours on low or 6 hours on high. About 30 minutes before the end of cooking, when you go to put the rice on, add the frozen peas and sprinkle the keema with your garam masala. Replace the lid and cook for another 30–40 minutes.

Serve with rice or hot fluffy naan bread to make sure you don't miss a drop of the tasty spice-infused juices this lovely dish makes.

AUBERGINE AND SPINACH CURRY

As I've mentioned earlier in the book, slow cooking is what's made me a fully fledged aubergine fan after my prior indifference. Cooked until they are soft and silky, they are a wonderful alternative to meat, especially when teamed with their nightshade cousin, the tomato, for a deep savoury flavour. I've brightened the curry with some spinach stirred in at the end and while it's not a showy dish, it's one you'll make time and time again.

SERVES 2-4 AND
MAKES GREAT
LEFTOVERS

1 large aubergine

1 tablespoon sea salt

1 teaspoon fennel
seeds

1 teaspoon fenugreek
seeds

½ teaspoon mustard
seeds

1 teaspoon coriander
seeds

1 teaspoon cumin
seeds

5 curry leaves

4 cloves of garlic

1 onion

4cm piece of fresh
ginger

1 tablespoon tamarind
syrup (see page 166)

1 x 400g tin chopped
tomatoes

200ml water

1 teaspoon Garam
Masala (page 168)

200g fresh, frozen and
thawed or tinned
spinach

salt and pepper

Many people insist you don't need to salt modern-day aubergines to remove the bitterness as they are bred to be milder. I don't know if it's the slow cooker or me generally, but I have found them unpleasantly bitter without it, so I recommend you do so.

Peel the aubergine and cut into 3cm cubes. Put in a colander and scatter with about a tablespoon of sea salt. Cover the top of the colander with clingfilm and allow the aubergine to drain for 30 minutes. Rinse the salt off once the aubergine has developed moisture on its surface. The salting removes the bitterness in the aubergines, but you don't want to replace it with saltiness. You can do this stage the night before to save time. The aubergine will discolour a little overnight, but it doesn't affect the taste and it isn't noticeable after slow cooking it. Let the aubergine dry slightly.

Toast the fennel, fenugreek, mustard, coriander and cumin seeds along with the curry leaves in a dry frying pan until they smell aromatic and the mustard seeds are just starting to pop. Remove from the heat immediately. Crush the seeds lightly using a pestle and mortar to release the flavours.

Put the aubergine in the slow-cooker crock along with the toasted spices. Blend the garlic, onion and ginger using a hand blender or the pestle and mortar, adding the tamarind syrup as well to make a purée. Stir this through the aubergine and add the chopped tomatoes.

Season well and add the water. Put the lid on the slow cooker and cook the curry on low for 8-9 hours until the aubergine is soft and glossy. About 30 minutes before you are ready to eat, break the aubergine up slightly with a spatula to make it a bit smoother. Stir the garam masala and the spinach into the curry and replace the lid to allow it to warm through.

Serve with rice or naan breads for a very simple and tasty slow-cooked curry.

BOMBAY POTATOES

My love of potatoes is well known. I have never met a spud I didn't like and one of the best things about them is their versatility. Equally comfortable as a main meal or a side dish, these spiced potatoes are a particular favourite of mine when I want something simple but tasty. I like them with a little bit of red chilli chopped over the top and some yoghurt on the side. Leave the skins on the spuds for extra bite and tuck in!

**SERVES 2 AS A
MAIN MEAL OR
4 AS A SIDE DISH**

750g potatoes

1 onion, finely chopped

**3 cloves of garlic, finely
chopped**

**5cm piece of fresh
ginger, finely chopped**

1 teaspoon cumin seeds

**1 teaspoon mustard
seeds**

**1 teaspoon coriander
seeds**

1 dried chilli

1 teaspoon onion seeds

**½ teaspoon ground
turmeric**

**1 tablespoon ghee
(see page 173)**

3-4 curry leaves

**1 x 400g tin plum
tomatoes**

200ml water

**1 heaped teaspoon
Garam Masala (see
page 168)**

**1 red chilli, chopped
(optional)**

Chop the potatoes into 3cm cubes and place in the slow-cooker crock along with the onion, garlic and ginger.

Put the cumin, mustard, coriander and onion seeds in a dry frying pan along with the whole dried chilli and toast for 1–2 minutes until they are all very aromatic. Don't let them burn or they will become bitter. Take off the heat immediately and grind roughly using a hand blender or pestle and mortar.

Add the toasted and ground spices to the crock along with the turmeric, ghee and curry leaves. Roughly break up the plum tomatoes with a knife or your hands and add in along with any juice. Pour 200ml water over it all.

Put the lid on the slow cooker and cook the potatoes on low for 8 hours. About 30 minutes before you are ready to serve, sprinkle the garam masala over it all. I often make some strained yoghurt (see page 164) at this point and then serve the potatoes with that and the chopped red chilli to both soothe me and fire me up at the same time.

SAAG ALOO

When I first moved to London, I had very little money and shared a tiny kitchen with seven other people. We had one small freezer and everyone was allowed one item each. Mine was always frozen spinach because it was so much more versatile than peas.

These days I don't really buy the stuff having overdosed on it for over three or so years, but I cannot cope with the price of the fresh leaves in supermarkets. Pillow-sized packets steam down to nothing and leave you hungry. Luckily the tinned version is fantastic and suits slow cooking beautifully.

I make this tasty saag aloo with tinned or frozen spinach and potatoes. You could add in any spring greens or even beetroot tops. I've also made it with a bit of leftover swede or a sweet potato. It's delicious and a great use of store-cupboard staples.

SERVES 4

1 teaspoon mustard
  seeds
1 teaspoon vegetable
  oil
1 onion, diced
3 cloves of garlic,
  chopped
1 teaspoon ground
  ginger
5 curry leaves
50g creamed coconut
2 x 400g tins chopped
  spinach, drained,
  or 800g frozen and
  thawed spinach
6 potatoes, peeled and
  cut into 1cm cubes
250ml water
1 teaspoon Garam
  Masala (see page 168)
dollop of plain
  yoghurt, to serve
handful of fresh
  coriander, to serve

Lightly toast the mustard seeds in the vegetable oil until they start to pop. This adds lots of flavour to the dish. Remove them from the heat as soon as the popping starts. Add them to the slow-cooker crock.

Add the onion, garlic, ginger and curry leaves to the slow cooker and stir well. Grate the creamed coconut over them. Tip in the spinach and the potatoes and then pour the water in. Stir and put the lid on the slow cooker and cook for 6–7 hours on low or 3–4 hours on high. Sprinkle the garam masala over it all about 20 minutes before you are ready to eat.

Serve with a big dollop of plain yoghurt and some chopped fresh coriander. I particularly enjoy this with some spiced rice.

TOMATO CURRY

A friend made me this curry a while back and I fell madly in love with its charms, but getting the scribbled recipe home, I decided to double the tomatoes and add just a hint of sweetness from caraway seeds to give it a fresh summery flavour all year round. It's amazing served as it is or it loves some flaky white fish or plump prawns cooked in it for about 15 minutes at the end when you spy a bargain in the freezer aisle.

It's also a good way to use up a tomato glut in the summer. I make a batch of the spices and keep them in a jar until needed, making this even easier.

SERVES 2–4
COMFORTABLY

1 tablespoon cumin
  seeds

1 tablespoon coriander
  seeds

1 teaspoon black
  mustard seeds

1 teaspoon caraway
  seeds

1 teaspoon fenugreek
  seeds

1 teaspoon onion seeds

½ teaspoon ground
  turmeric

½ teaspoon ground
  cloves

4 cardamom pods,
  seeds scraped out

1 x 400g tin chopped
  tomatoes

300g cherry tomatoes

1 teaspoon sugar

6 curry leaves

1 x 400ml tin coconut
  milk

1 tablespoon tamarind
  syrup (see page 166)

2 star anise

salt and pepper

This is about the easiest curry ever. Measure all your spices, except the curry leaves and star anise into the slow-cooker crock and add the chopped tomatoes. Stir it all well so it is evenly combined.

Toss the whole cherry tomatoes in and sprinkle the sugar and curry leaves in. Pour the coconut milk over it all and add in the tamarind syrup with about a tablespoon of water. Drop the star anise in and season well. Tomatoes love salt.

Put the lid on the slow cooker and cook on low for 8–9 hours. The cherry tomatoes will burst into the chopped tomatoes and it will all cook down into something extraordinarily full of flavour. Serve with rice or a healthy dollop of Tarka Dal from page 102 and be reminded that sometimes simple is best.

PRESERVES AND PANTRY STAPLES

I adore making preserves. Few things please me more than an afternoon pottering round my kitchen, peeling, chopping and simmering things to be put in jars using a jam funnel. The only thing better is sitting on the sofa with a good book while things simmer and preserve, which is what happens when you make them in the slow cooker.

If you've ever wanted to do your own yoghurt or try making lime pickle just the heat you like or give home-made jam or curds for Christmas, then the slow cooker will allow you to do it without all the standing over a hot pan the traditional way entails. I had so much fun creating jams, chutneys and preserves in mine I ran out of people to give them all to. But luckily everyone loves home-made condiments.

Get yourself a good jam funnel, source a supply of glass jars and be amazed at what you can create in the slow cooker with a minimum of fuss. I might have to join the WI to keep up with my desire to experiment with foraged autumnal goodies and garden gluts at this rate.

A NOTE ON STERILISING JARS

To make all the goodies in this chapter, you will need sturdy glass jars with well-fitting lids or cellophane circles. You'll need to sterilise the jars before you fill them to ensure your preserves last well and safely. There are multiple ways to do this to suit each kitchen. Do not eat preserves that have not been stored this way.

By oven: This is a good way to do large batches of jars at once. Preheat the oven to 140°C or Gas Mark 1. Wash the jars in hot soapy water and dry well. Place them in a deep roasting tin just far enough apart that they aren't touching each other. If you are using rubber-sealed preserving jars like Kilner jars, remove the rubber first or it may perish.

Heat the oven for 25 minutes. Lift the whole tin out with the jars in it and without touching the jars, fill them with the piping hot preserves and seal with clean lids you've boiled for 10 minutes, rubber seals or cellophane circles.

By microwave: This is a great way to sterilise just a few jars very quickly. It is not suitable for metal-rimmed jars. Wash the jars in hot soapy water and dry slightly. Put each slightly wet jar into the microwave one at a time and heat for 30 seconds on full heat. Remove carefully with oven gloves, making sure you don't touch the rim or inside of the jar. Fill with the hot preserves and seal with clean lids you've boiled for 10 minutes or cellophane circles.

By boiling water: This is a good way to sterilise jars if you don't want to turn the oven on in summer weather. I particularly like it for rubber-sealed Kilner jars. Remove the rubber seals or lids from the jars and put them in a small pan of cold water. Put the glass jars in a large pan of cold water. Bring both pans to the boil and boil them for 10 minutes. Lift each jar and lid or rubber seal out of the boiling water with clean tongs and fill with the hot preserves. Seal with the lids, rubber seals or cellophane circles.

By dishwasher: Remove any rubber seals or lids from the jars and lay them out in one layer on the upper or cutlery racks of the dishwasher. Stack the clean jars into the dishwasher and turn on the hottest cycle without any detergent or cleaning products. Don't open the dishwasher until you are ready to fill the jars with preserves. Don't touch the rim or inside of the jar. Fill with hot preserves and seal with the lids, rubber seals or cellophane circles.

Notes: Never fill a hot sterilised jar with cold preserves as this may cause the glass to shatter; preserves should also be hot when the hot jars are filled to prevent any bacteria growth. Never take them out of your sterilising method before they are needed. Allowing them to cool first undoes the act of sterilising them. I always sterilise more jars than needed just in case I've misjudged my amounts. Fill the jars to the very top to prevent anything awful from growing in there while you are storing it; allow the jars to settle for 15 minutes before sealing. Store your preserves in a cool, dark place until opened and then store in the fridge and eat within 10 days.

PRESERVED LEMONS

You probably think these are very expensive and difficult to make due to the price of them in those tiny jars in the posh aisle of the supermarket, but in all honesty, they are easier to make than falling off a log. You need lemons, salt and about three weeks' waiting time, but they are incredibly simple to prepare. Make a jarful and use them any time you want to perk up a roast chicken or a stew.

Don't be freaked out by the amount of salt. You are creating a brine to essentially pickle the lemons and you aren't eating it all. I use coarse sea salt, which you can buy in any supermarket cheaply. You don't need a fancy version.

FILLS A 500ML
KILNER JAR

12 lemons

4 tablespoons sea salt

1 dried chilli

**1 tablespoon black
  peppercorns**

**bottled lemon juice,
  as needed**

Prepare the lemons for preserving by splitting 4 of them from top to bottom, making sure you leave about 1cm of the base intact. Repeat so you have four splits, but the lemon is still held together at the base.

Holding the lemon over a plate, pour a tablespoon of sea salt crystals into the lemon. Don't worry if some drops onto the plate. Squash the lemon tightly into a Kilner jar. Repeat with the other 3 lemons. You want them wedged tightly in the jar. Put the chilli and the peppercorns in as well.

Juice the remaining 8 lemons over the salt-filled ones. You need them to be covered with the lemon juice to allow them to be preserved. Top up the jar with bottled lemon juice if needs be.

Close the lid on the jar and leave to preserve for at least 3 weeks. The flesh and peel will soften and you can dip into the jar as needed. The flavour is intense so a little goes a long way. They will last up to 6 months non-refrigerated in the jar as long as the lemons are submerged in the lemon juice.

BANANA KETCHUP

Traditionally from the Philippines, banana ketchup is sweet, sour, salty and savoury all at once. I cannot remember how I first discovered it, but I fell in love immediately. This is what I want on a bacon butty and luckily it's really easy to make since you can't get it very easily – unless you also happen to frequent the shop in Guy's Hospital in South London with its extensive Filipino grocery section…

The secret is to cook half the bananas to get the texture right and then mash the other half in right at the end. I've seen people eat a whole jar of this in one sitting with a meal and then ask for the recipe.

MAKES 5 X 300ML JARS

6 very ripe bananas

1 onion, finely diced

4 cloves of garlic, finely chopped

1 Scotch bonnet pepper, finely chopped (or 2 red chillies)

4cm piece of fresh ginger, finely chopped

1 teaspoon ground turmeric

2 teaspoons ground allspice

½ teaspoon ground cloves

1 teaspoon tamarind syrup (see page 166)

1 teaspoon soy sauce

1 tablespoon tomato purée

3 tablespoons brown sugar

150ml vinegar

200ml water

This ketchup is a great savoury way to use up the over ripe bananas in the fruit bowl as the fruit needs flavour. Peel half the bananas and chop them roughly into the slow-cooker crock. Add all the other ingredients, reserving 3 bananas for later.

Put the lid on the slow cooker and cook everything on low for 5 hours. It will all soften and collapse together at this stage. Mash it all together with a potato masher so it is smoother, but with enough texture to keep it interesting.

Mash the remaining 3 bananas together well and mix them into the hot ketchup. Spoon it all into sterilised jars and seal immediately. The ketchup will keep in a dark place unopened for 3–4 months and the flavours will intensify. It will keep for 4 weeks in the fridge when opened.

Note: See page 166 for an explanation of how to make the tamarind syrup. The concentrate versions are too sharp here with the delicate bananas.

EASY TOMATO KETCHUP

One of my favourite books as a child was called *Mrs Pig's Bulk Buy*. Mr and Mrs Pig had ten little piglets and those piglets were ketchup fiends. Mr Pig had to buy the stuff in catering jars and feed it to them in lieu of actual meals to keep up. It taught me a thing or two about good ketchup.

Good ketchup lifts a chip to something sublime and takes a bacon sandwich to brilliance. I've even been known to use a potato waffle as a vehicle for good ketchup after a night out when I was a student. Ketchup should be intensely tomato-rich with the mellowness of sugar and the tang of ketchup. It shouldn't just be artificially red and gloopy.

This is a recipe for the home-made ketchup you've always wanted to make, but thought you needed tonnes of toms to do so. It uses ordinary tinned plum tomatoes and if your family are as ketchup crazed as the little pigs, then you can make it in bulk for much less than the branded versions. It's so good, you'll be pigging out in no time.

MAKES 5 X 300ML JARS

- 1 small onion, finely diced
- 2 stalks of celery, finely diced
- 2 x 400g tins plum tomatoes
- 1 tablespoon paprika
- 1 tablespoon celery salt
- 1 tablespoon mustard powder
- 4 tablespoons brown sugar
- 1 teaspoon tamarind syrup (see page 166) (optional)
- 2 tablespoons tomato purée
- 100ml vinegar (any will work)
- 1 teaspoon chilli powder (if liked)

This is ridiculously simple to make.

Put the onion and celery in the slow-cooker crock along with the plum tomatoes and any juice from the tins. Using a spoon or spatula, break the tomatoes up into rough chunks. I use the best-quality plum tomatoes for this, which I buy when they are on offer.

Add in the spices and sugar. Dollop the tamarind syrup in along with the tomato purée and mix well. Pour the vinegar over it all. I use cider vinegar as that's what I have, but even malt will work well. Balsamic will make the ketchup darker and works well if you aren't using the tangy, savoury tamarind.

Put the lid on the slow cooker and cook the ketchup on low for 7–8 hours. The ketchup will have reduced and darkened slightly.

Now blend the ketchup in the crock using a hand blender. Make sure there are no lumps of tomato at all. The ketchup will be velvety and should be halfway between thickened and liquid in texture. If you'd like it a little bit thicker, turn the heat up to high and give it another 2 hours to reduce it a little more.

When the texture is as desired, pour the ketchup into sterilised jars or bottles and allow to cool before storing. It will last for about 6 months unopened and up to 3 months in the fridge once you open it.

TOMATO CHUTNEY

Who doesn't love a bit of chutney on the side of their cheese plate? It adds some delicious tangy taste while using up those seasonal gluts of fruit and veg. They are a great British tradition, as is the pervasive smell of hot vinegar throughout the house when you make it. Luckily though, when you make chutney in a slow cooker, this aroma is minimised while the flavour is kept to a maximum. When chutney is this easy to make you, you'll find yourself experimenting with all kinds of flavours and impressing people with your home-made varieties. Much better than buying small jars of it for large prices.

MAKES 6 X 300ML JARS

1kg tomatoes

2 red onions, finely chopped

2 apples

4 cloves of garlic, chopped

1 red chilli, chopped

4cm piece of fresh ginger, finely chopped

1 teaspoon smoked paprika

1 teaspoon mustard seeds

½ teaspoon black peppercorns

½ teaspoon mustard powder

5 whole cloves

3 allspice berries

150g brown sugar

500ml red wine or cider vinegar

salt

Start by skinning your tomatoes. Cut a cross into the top and bottom of each one, place in a bowl and pour some boiling water over them. Allow to sit for 1–2 minutes and then lift out with a slotted spoon. Once cool enough to handle, you can just peel the skins off.

Cut each tomato into quarters, removing the stem at the top. Cut each quarter in half and add them all to the slow-cooker crock along with any juice from the tomatoes. Add the chopped onion. Peel and core the apples and then cut them into 2cm cubes, mixing them in with the onion and tomatoes.

Toss in the garlic and the chilli, adding the seeds if you like a little warmth to your chutney. I scatter the ginger and spices into the chutney directly as I don't mind finding the odd clove in my chutney. Stir in the sugar (brown sugar is less sickly sweet than white here).

Cover it all with the red wine vinegar. I like the rich but mellow taste of a wine or cider vinegar here. Chutneys made with white or malt vinegar are just too astringent for my tastes and something like balsamic is too overpowering.

Season it all well and put the lid on the slow cooker. It will seem like an enormous amount of chutney, especially if you are using a 3.5-litre slow cooker, which will be full almost to the brim. Don't worry, the tomatoes will reduce in volume as they cook, but I give mine 2 hours longer than most recipes to allow for the crock being so full as this can reduce the heat of the slow cooker.

Cook the chutney on high for 10 hours. It will reduce by about half and become darker in colour without too much liquid. Spoon it into sterilised jars along with any remaining liquid and seal quickly. It can be eaten immediately, but is best left to mature in a cool, dark place for 1–3 months.

Don't forget to label each batch with dates and the main ingredient as you'll make so many kinds in the slow cooker you'll get confused!

LIME PICKLE

I find it very hard to hold back from the poppadoms and pickles when I go out for Indian food. There's just something about the mixture of crunchiness and softness along with all those flavours that means I almost always spoil my appetite, scooping up every last scrap. Lime pickle goes down especially well with its mix of tanginess and spice and this recipe combines the two perfectly. It's a little stickier and more marmalade-like than some versions of this as the spices slow-cook down beautifully. I guess it's an Irish-Indian version of this famous pickle.

This is a serious slow-cooking recipe. You start by salting the limes for several days to pickle them and then slowly cook them together with the spices, so you can't rush this one!

MAKES 5 X 300ML
JARS

8 limes

2 tablespoons sea salt

3 cloves of garlic

5cm piece of fresh ginger

2 teaspoons mustard
  seeds

1 teaspoon cumin seeds

1 teaspoon coriander
  seeds

1 teaspoon onion seeds

1 teaspoon fenugreek
  seeds

1 teaspoon chilli flakes

100g sugar

250ml cold water

Begin by preparing your limes. Cut each one in half from top to bottom. Cut each half in half again. Then cut those halves in half so each lime becomes 8 pieces. Put them in a non-metallic dish (your slow-cooker crock is perfect if you don't need it for a day or two) and cover with the sea salt.

Put the lid on the crock or cover it with a tea towel and leave the limes to pickle for 2 days. Try and put them somewhere that isn't too warm or in direct sunlight. After 2 days, drain off the liquid the limes will have given off, but don't rinse them.

I purée up the garlic and ginger or you can finely chop it. Put both in the crock with the pickled limes. Add the spices and sugar. Pour the water over it all. Put the lid on the slow cooker and cook the pickle on low for 10 hours. You want the flesh of the limes to collapse into the pickle to thicken it all and the rinds to become soft enough to squash with the side of a spoon.

Put the hot pickle into sterilised jars and seal as quickly as possible. The pickle will store unopened for up to 6 months in a dark place. Keep it in the fridge once opened.

Not only is it excellent with poppadoms or curries, it perks a cheese sandwich right up!

SWEET-AND-SOUR ONION RELISH

Few things make a sandwich or a cold cut better than a dollop of this sweet-and-sour onion relish with its hints of mustard. All the flavours combine together in the slow cooker and it keeps for up to 3 months in the fridge, making sure any tears from slicing the onions will be dried in next to no time.

MAKES 4 X 200ML
JARS

8 medium red onions

2 tablespoons olive oil

**3 tablespoons brown
  sugar 2 tablespoons
  wholegrain mustard**

**1 tablespoon black
  treacle**

1 teaspoon soy sauce

**160ml balsamic
  vinegar**

This is very simple to make. Peel your onions and cut them in half. Cut each half in half again so you have quarters and then cut these into slices just slightly thinner than a pound coin.

Put the sliced onions in the slow-cooker crock and stir the olive oil through. Add the sugar, mustard, treacle and soy sauce into the crock as well and stir so they coat the onions evenly.

Pour the balsamic vinegar over them all and put the lid on the slow cooker. Cook the onions on low for 8–9 hours until the onions are a soft, sticky tangle of tangy sweetness. They will have given off just enough liquid to keep everything moist and easy to scoop up with a spoon.

Spoon the hot relish into sterilised jars and seal immediately. Store in the fridge until needed.

FIG AND POMEGRANATE RELISH

Nothing sets a nice bit of cheese off better than a good relish on the side and this fig and pomegranate molasses version is one of the best I've tasted. I had barely given my first batch away when people started requesting more. It made excellent Christmas gifts and was a favourite with the Christmas night cheeseboard. It's especially good with a soft goat's cheese and, best of all, it's incredibly easy to make.

MAKES 4 X 250ML
JARS

800g dried figs

**75ml pomegranate
molasses**

**2 tablespoons
wholegrain mustard**

**2 tablespoons red wine
or balsamic vinegar**

75g brown sugar

**1 teaspoon fresh or
dried thyme**

500ml boiling water

200ml cold water

Remove any stalks still on your figs. You can use any dried figs for this, even those very hard ones sometimes sold in blocks in health food shops, because the slow cooking will make them so soft and tender it's unbelievable.

Cut the figs in half and place them in the slow-cooker crock. Drizzle the pomegranate molasses, mustard and vinegar over them. Scatter the sugar and thyme evenly over it all. Pour the boiling water ino the slow cooker and put the lid on. Cook the figs for 7–8 hours on low. They will have plumped up hugely and started to collapse around the edges.

Carefully lift the hot crock out of the slow cooker and place it on a chopping board.

Blitz the figs using a hand blender, adding in the cold water as you go. You should end up with a lovely soft relish that is easy to pour from a spoon. Add more water, 50ml at a time, if it's still a little stiff.

Pour the still-hot relish into sterilised jars and seal immediately. Allow the jars to cool. The relish will keep for up to 6 months in a dark place, unopened. I'm not entirely sure how long it will keep when opened because a jar has never lasted more than 2 weeks in my fridge...

GREEN FIGS IN SYRUP

What could be more luscious than a meltingly ripe fig where the purple skin splits at the merest touch to reveal the succulent flesh inside? You'll be surprised when I say slow-cooked green figs, won't you? But trust me, you can turn those green figs from the tree in the garden you didn't even plant into something truly mouthwatering.

Cooking the figs in a beautiful sticky syrup will add the warmth to them that the sun hasn't and turn them into a wonderful preserve that can be kept in the fridge for months. Richly spiced, they work equally well on the Granola from page 108 or baked in the Spiced Chicken on page 64.

FILLS A 1-LITRE KILNER JAR

750g green figs

500g sugar

2–3cm piece of fresh ginger, sliced

peel of 1 lemon

2 whole cloves

1 star anise

3 allspice berries

750ml boiling water

1 lime, juiced

50ml dark rum (optional)

The figs take a little bit of preparation before they are ready to cook. Pick your figs, checking them for any holes or insects. Remove the stalks and poke a hole in the base of each one with a chopstick. This allows the sap to drain out more easily, which prevents the figs from being bitter. (They exude a milky white sap, which is a form of latex. You should wear gloves when handling them even if you aren't allergic as it makes your fingers sticky and itchy.)

Put the figs in the slow-cooker crock, cover with cold water and soak them for about an hour. Drain, rinse and soak again, this time overnight. The water will turn white with sap.

Drain the figs again and rinse both them and the crock well to remove any traces of the sap. Place the figs back into the crock. I set them on their bases so they pack in tightly. Scatter the sugar over them evenly.

Add the fresh ginger, lemon peel and spices and then pour the boiling water over them. They should be pretty much submerged with only the very tops poking out. Add about 100ml water and 50g more of sugar if they need a top up. Squeeze the lime juice over them then cover with the lid.

Cook for figs on low for 10 hours. This will give them time to soften in the syrup and infuse with the flavours and preserve in the sugar. Don't be tempted to reduce the sugar beyond the amount given or they will not preserve, but instead boil into a pulp.

The figs will keep their shape as they cook, but the colour will darken to a deep purple. They will be softened, but still firm. Don't be tempted to keep cooking them.

Allow the figs to cool for about 10 minutes and then spoon them into a large sterilised jar. Pour the still-warm syrup over the figs to cover them. Add the dark rum for an extra kick of flavour, if liked. Store in the fridge.

PICKLED BEETROOT

I know lots of people are a bit scared of pickled beetroot after having it on every salad as kids, doused in malt vinegar and served with one lettuce leaf and half a hard-boiled egg. I never minded this delicacy as I associate it with my grandpa Bert, who loved its pink pickled charms. He even sneaked it into a cheese sarnie to give it some edge.

This version uses a smoother-tasting vinegar and a scattering of sugar and spices to create a slightly candied flavour that everyone loves when they sample it. I heap it on the side of everything I can, especially a cheese sandwich.

MAKES 3 X 300ML JARS

650g beetroot

2 cloves of garlic

2 sprigs of fresh thyme or ½ teaspoon dried

2 allspice berries

½ teaspoon caraway seeds

200g sugar

300ml cider vinegar

300ml water

salt and pepper

Peel your beetroot and cube into 2.5cm pieces. You may prefer to wear gloves when doing this to protect your hands from being stained. Put the beetroot into the slow-cooker crock along with the garlic, thyme, allspice and caraway. Season it well.

Put the sugar in a small saucepan on the hob and add the vinegar and water. Bring to the boil and stir the sugar until it dissolves.

Pour the hot vinegar over the beetroot, making sure that the cubes are submerged. Add a little more vinegar and water if needed. Put the lid on the slow cooker and simmer the beetroot on low for 7–8 hours or high for 4–5 hours.

When the beetroot is tender, spoon it into sterilised jars and cover with the hot vinegar. Leave the flavourings behind. Seal immediately and store for up to 3 months. Once opened, it should go in the fridge.

Single salad leaf and half a hard-boiled egg, optional.

CRANBERRY SAUCE

I will probably find myself not invited for Christmas back home when I tell you this story, but my main memory of cranberry sauce is my mum burning it. I don't know if it only happened once and because it was so unlike her, we laughed and made it legendary in the process. But I've never made it for fear of repeating the mistake. But you can't really burn stuff in the slow cooker, so I just had to try it.

MAKES 200G

200g fresh or frozen and thawed cranberries

1 grapefruit, juiced

4 tablespoons sugar

2 tablespoons water

salt

Pour the cranberries into the slow cooker. Roll your grapefruit along the worktop to loosen it up – it won't juice well otherwise. Cut in half and then squeeze the grapefruit juice over the cranberries.

Sprinkle in the sugar and the salt. Add the water if your grapefruit wasn't very juicy.

Cook the cranberry sauce on low for 6 hours. It will darken and the berries will crack and pop, but still look whole. I gave mine a little squish with a potato masher to turn it into a more sauce-like consistency and then served it with everything I ate for the next week because it was amazing.

Lovely and jammy, it is tart and tasty and I can't wait to make it for my mum...

LEMON CURD

When I was a kid I remember eating home-made lemon curd out of a jar with a spoon when no one was looking, but my ardour for it was dampened by the commercial stuff, which was teeth-itchingly sweet in a way that subdues the lemon. I didn't bother for years and then a few summers ago I bought a mountain of lemons to make limoncello and got sidetracked into trying curd again. It tasted sensational, but I found it nerve wracking to get the texture right. Turns out it's foolproof in the slow cooker. Even I, the person who scrambled microwave custard once, make perfect lemon curd every time in the slow cooker.

MAKES 4 X 300ML
JARS

125g butter
400g sugar
4 lemons
4 eggs, beaten

Start by melting the butter and sugar together in a small saucepan on the hob. Zest 2 of the lemons and add the juice of all 4. Stir it all together well as the butter and sugar melts. This will take about 3–4 minutes.

Pour the melted butter mixture into a 1.2-litre plastic pudding basin with a lid. You could use any bowl that fits inside your slow cooker that can be covered with foil or a lid.

Allow the butter mixture to cool for about 10–15 minutes, then whisk the beaten eggs through it. Leaving it to cool down prevents the dreaded scramble.

Put the lid on your basin and pop it into the slow-cooker crock. Pour boiling water into the crock until it comes about halfway up the side of the basin and put the lid on the slow cooker. Cook the curd on low for 4 hours.

When you take the lid off the basin, the curd will have thickened, but look a little separated at this stage with a layer of melted butter on the top of it. Don't panic, just give it a good whisk and it will come together beautifully. Your curd will be thick and glossy and ready to bottle.

Pour it while it's still hot into sterilised jars and seal as soon as possible. Allow to cool before storing. It will keep for up to 6 weeks in the fridge unopened. It will last about 30 seconds when opened after you've dolloped it on porridge, slathered it onto toast, drizzled it into ice cream, used it on a cheesecake or, yes, just eaten it off the spoon...

Note: You can also make a great rhubarb version of this using 100g stewed and puréed rhubarb to replace the juice of 2 lemons. Or try a blood orange curd with 3 oranges standing in for the lemons.

APPLE BUTTER

I associate this dish with *Little House on the Prairie* or *Little Women*. I have no idea if that's accurate since I've never actually read either of them, but the idea of slow-cooking apples into a soft, spreadable apple 'butter' full of cinnamon and spice to preserve it for a long, cold winter makes me think of American pioneers. Not quite the same as the cider-based black butter from Jersey, it is, however, delicious and very easy to make in the slow cooker. It is excellent on porridge or toast or used with meats such as pork or dolloped in yoghurt as a dessert. I have also used it to coat granola (see page 108) instead of oil and honey.

I've used cooking apples such as Bramleys because I like their tart taste, but you could use anything flavoursome. Avoid things like Golden Delicious that are watery, but a mix of Granny Smiths and Cox's Orange Pippins would work well if you are buying apples rather than using home grown. It can be stored in the fridge in sterilised jars or frozen until needed and it is a great way to give new life to those that look a bit wrinkly.

MAKES 4 X 300ML JARS

- 1kg apples, preferably Bramleys
- 50g brown sugar
- 1 heaped teaspoon ground cinnamon or 1 cinnamon stick
- 1 heaped teaspoon ground allspice
- 1 heaped teaspoon ground ginger
- ¼ teaspoon sea salt
- 250ml water or apple juice
- 4 cloves
- 2 star anise
- 1 tablespoon vanilla extract (optional)

Peel, core and slice the apples. The thinner the slices, the better, but don't worry too much if a few are thicker. Put about half the slices into a large bowl and the rest of them into the slow-cooker crock. Toss the ones in the crock with half the sugar and the ground spices and salt. Do the same with the ones in the bowl and then add them to the crock. (This is the easiest way to mix the sugar and spices without making a mess.)

Add the liquid to the apples. Put the cloves and the star anise into the crock too. Put the lid on the slow cooker and cook for 10 hours on low. The apples will collapse, bubble furiously and turn a deep amber colour while infusing your whole house with a wonderful spiced fragrance.

If your apples still seem a bit watery rather than becoming a thick butter, simply cook for up to another 4 hours. Stir once an hour and when it is all thickened from the apples breaking down with very little liquid on the surface, it is cooked.

Allow it all to cool slightly. Fish out the cinnamon stick, if using, and the star anise. Blend the butter using a hand blender until it is smooth and thickened. Add the vanilla extract, if using. It will be a beautiful deep orangey colour. Ladle into sterilised jars and store in a darkened place for up to 6 months. Keep in the fridge when opened.

Note: You can also make a wonderful version with pumpkin or squash. Simply replace the apple with the same amount of pumpkin. Peel and chop it into 2-3cm cubes and follow the recipe above. Pumpkin is a sweeter taste than apple, so you may want to reduce the sugar. It also lacks the acidity of apple so will not keep as long. It must be kept refrigerated the whole time and will keep for up to 2 months unopened.

SOFT FRUIT JAM

When I was a child, summer was all about the soft fruit. My granny's farmhouse had a huge patch of raspberry canes and any Sunday afternoon there involved wandering through it picking fruit for tea. My capacity for eating raspberries was unrivalled whether straight off the bush or drizzled with sugar and cream. They tasted of sunshine and love. But no matter how many you ate, there were always mountains to bring home too since soft fruit in the summer is literally fruitful in its abundance.

If you have currants, raspberries or strawberries in the garden or allotment or know someone who does, you too will get to a stage when you just can't eat them fast enough. This means the time for jam has come. Not only that, but with a slow cooker you've just discovered you can make jam without getting hot and bothered and allow yourself more time to enjoy the good weather.

People are always surprised when they see how simple jam is. It's basically 50 per cent fruit and 50 per cent sugar cooked to the magic temperature of 104°C, whereupon it all comes together and sets into jam. Long slow cooking can reach this temperature easily without burning the fruit and you will get a jam that sets nicely as it cools.

I've made jam in the slow cooker using both fresh and frozen fruit and I find it's a little bit easier to get a good set if you use jam sugar with added pectin. Pectin is a natural thickening agent found naturally in certain fruits such apples and oranges. It can be found in jam sugar or sold in liquid form, so it can be added to low pectin fruits such as soft fruits.

MAKES 4 SMALL JARS

1kg soft fruit, such as raspberries, strawberries, currants or a mix (see below)

1kg sugar (use jam sugar with pectin if possible)

Note: You can also use frozen and thawed berries if you don't have access to large amounts of fresh fruit.

If you are using fresh fruit, remove any stalks and any bruised fruit. Wash it well and dry it by putting it on a tea towel for 5–10 minutes.

Tip it into the slow-cooker crock and add the sugar. You can scale the amount of fruit up as long as you use equal amounts of sugar and fruit. Put the lid on the slow cooker and cook the sugar and fruit on high for 5 hours.

At 5 hours, I put two saucers in the freezer and then vent the slow-cooker lid for 30 minutes by putting a chopstick under it. This allows any excess liquid in the jam to cook down. You need to think about preparing sterilised jars at this stage (see page 185). Don't forget to do any lids too.

After 30 minutes, take one saucer out of the freezer and put a teaspoon of the jam on it. Allow it to cool slightly and then run your finger through it. If it wrinkles, then you have reached 104°C and you now have jam.

Without touching the inside of your sterilised jars, fill them right to the top with the still hot jam using a wide spoon or a jam funnel. Cover while still warm with cellophane jam jar covers or the sterilised lids. Theoretically the jam lasts 6 months this way, but you'll have eaten it all before then.

DULCE DE LECHE

If you don't know what I mean by dulce de leche, think of that sticky layer on banoffee pie. It's made by slowly simmering condensed milk until it forms a dark caramel (although it doesn't just have to be paired with bananas).

I always keep a Tupperware of it in the fridge as it will keep for up to 6 months. I drizzle it over stewed fruit for a quick pudding, stir through porridge instead of syrup for a treat and add to chai tea on a cold day. It can be used as a tart filling or stuffed into baked apples. It's also excellent on toast.

You may have been put off making dulce de leche because you've heard the tales of tins exploding in hot water, but the slow cooker makes it very safe and simple. I do a couple of tins at a time and then decant them into sterilised jars as gifts since the shop-bought stuff is so expensive for a small can. All you need is a 397g tin of sweetened condensed milk and a slow cooker.

Remove the label from the tin, put it on its side and cover with cold water. There should be at least 2–3cm of water above the tin.

Put the lid on the slow cooker, turn it on and cook on high for 8 hours. At the end of 8 hours, use tongs to remove the tin safely or allow the water to cool down first. Open the cooled tin and marvel at the gorgeous caramel inside.

You can't really overcook this in the slow cooker. I have forgotten about it and left it for up to 14 hours and it's totally fine, looking darker, but not tasting burned. Nor is there any danger of you burning yourself or the tin boiling dry. The only issue is being able to wait patiently for it to cool down enough to be able to dip a spoon into it...

CANDIED PEEL

Remember those little pots of diced-up candied peel that looked like twinkly little jewels, but barely tasted of citrus? I still loved it. When my mum's back was turned, I'd dive into the baking cupboard and cram fistfuls of it into my mouth. It was my favourite bit of the Christmas cake as well. Discovering I can make it easily and economically in the slow cooker makes me almost giddy with excitement.

I squirrel away lemon rinds when I make Preserved Lemons, like on page 186, and hoard my orange peels when the winter citrus season starts, slipping them into a plastic container in the fridge. I love the addition of grapefruit, but omit limes as they overpower everything for me.

This peel is packed with citrus flavour and will last up to 2 years in an airtight jar – if you can keep it away from me when I visit.

**FILLS A 500ML
KILNER JAR**

4 lemons

2 grapefruit

**2 large oranges (not
satsumas)**

1 tangerine

600g sugar

450ml boiling water

100g icing sugar

This recipe takes several days to be ready to eat. Most of it involves allowing it to dry out after cooking though, so don't be put off by that.

You need to cut your peels to roughly the same size. Having cut the fruit in half, I quarter each half so I end up with 8 pieces per fruit. You don't have to be just as precise, but do keep things the same size so they cook evenly.

I usually snip the peel out of the juiced lemons with a pair of kitchen scissors, but find the grapefruit and oranges are easier to peel with your hands. I don't use small satsumas as the peel is very thin and tends to shrivel up when simmered.

Now, prepare the peels by removing any remaining flesh or pith from them.

Layer the pieces into the slow-cooker crock evenly and then sprinkle the sugar over the peels. Add the boiling water and put the lid on. Simmer the peel on high for 7 hours or until it is softly translucent, but not falling apart.

Allow to cool in the crock for about 30 minutes and then, using tongs, carefully lay each piece flat on a wire rack or mesh tray. It mustn't overlap. It's best to line underneath the rack as the peel will drip a bit. Leave it to dry out for between 3 and 5 days. I leave mine in the switched-off oven (with a massive note to remind myself) or an airing cupboard is perfect. The surface should be slightly crunchy with sugar, but still sticky.

Put it all in a freezer bag or large bowl and toss with the icing sugar. If it looks a little damp, add more. This stops it sticking together while you store it. Keep the candied peel in an airtight container like a glass jar and it will last for up to 2 years. I use mine in my Stout-soaked Christmas Pudding on page 248 and the Boiled Cake on page 209.

Note: You can also make candied ginger the same way. Peel about 600g of fresh ginger and slice into pieces 2–3cm thick. Place in the slow-cooker crock in layers and cover with about 600ml cold water and 800g sugar.

Put the lid on the slow cooker and cook on high for 8–10 hours. The ginger will become a dark orange colour and be beautifully softened. Scoop it out with a slotted spoon and allow about two-thirds of it to dry on a lined tray. After 48 hours, sprinkle with brown sugar and keep in a jar until needed.

Put the rest in sterilised glass jars with the hot ginger syrup poured over it and you have both stem and crystallised ginger for baking and cooking.

YOGHURT

I am, not entirely irrationally, irritated by the fact it's almost impossible to buy full-fat yoghurt in the UK anymore. Ninety-nine per cent of yoghurt seems to be fat-free or virtually so and thus is full of sugar and in some cases gelatine to thicken it. I really don't understand it. Full-fat yoghurt is naturally about 4 per cent fat and requires no additives or adverts suggesting it is the most exciting thing to happen to women that week.

In my book, yoghurt is only exciting when you learn to make it yourself in a slow cooker and luckily you can all share in this skill because it's also very easy. In fact, you can basically do it while you're asleep. It's a great way either to make full-fat yoghurt since you can't buy it or simply to save money by making a big batch of yoghurt if you eat it a lot. It's the most fun I've had with yoghurt on any occasion.

This is very low maintenance, but you'll definitely need a thermometer for it. I got a digital one with a curved probe you can hang over the edge of the crock on a well-known auction site for around a fiver.

You make the yoghurt by scalding the milk, cooling to 43°C and adding a small amount of live yoghurt to 'inoculate' it. The milk is then allowed to cool slowly by insulating the crock and leaving it for 8–10 hours to turn into yoghurt. I remember my mum making yoghurt when I was kid by using a thermos flask, but this is much easier and very smooth in flavour.

MAKES 1 LITRE (SIMPLY DOUBLE OR HALVE IT AS NEEDED)

- **1 litre full-fat milk (I used 2 pints, but let's not be pedantic)**
- **2 tablespoons live plain yoghurt**

Start by setting the whole slow cooker on top of a thick bath towel. You'll use this to insulate it all and it's easier to do it now rather than lift a crock of hot milk later.

Pour the milk into the slow-cooker crock. You can use any dairy-based milk, including powdered milk, and you could use semi-skimmed or skimmed if you prefer. I haven't tested it with non-dairy milk.

Put the lid on the slow cooker and heat the milk on high for around 2 hours until it reaches 88°C. I leave the thermometer probe in while it heats so I can keep an eye on it. Mine takes almost exactly 2 hours, but different models will vary, so check frequently.

It is imperative to reach this temperature as it 'scalds' the milk, making it perfectly safe and triggering the necessary reactions for yoghurt or cheese making. Once it reaches 88°C, turn the heat off and take the lid off the slow cooker.

Leave the milk to cool naturally without being disturbed. You want it to reach 43°C exactly, which will take about 2½ to 3 hours to be reached as things cool slowly in a crock. I leave the thermometer in and check every 40 or so minutes. Don't stir the milk.

When it reaches 43°C, skim off any skin that has formed on the top of the milk and put a ladle or cupful of the warm milk into a bowl. Add the 2 tablespoons of live yoghurt to 'inoculate' the milk and stir in well.

Return the inoculated milk to the slow-cooker crock, stirring it in from side to side a few times rather than in circles. Put the lid back on the slow cooker and wrap the whole thing up in your big bath towel.

Leave it undisturbed for at least 8 hours and preferably 10. Unwrap it and lift the lid. It will look like nothing has happened until you stir it and you'll see that it has become a shiny and quite loose-textured yoghurt.

If you like your yoghurt a bit thicker, simply strain it through a muslin cloth in a sieve for about 15–20 minutes to allow the whey to drain out and the yoghurt to thicken. I use this whey for marinating meat or making bread, so don't throw it out.

Pour the yoghurt into a sterilised glass jar or bottle and store in the fridge until needed. It will last up to 10 days chilled. Mix with fruit or granola or add to smoothies for breakfast or snacks. It can be added to soups and curries or used to top dishes. I add vanilla or chopped nuts or lemon curd to make a tastier version of some of the luxury single-serve pots on the market.

Note: Simply reserve a bit of each batch to start the next one and you won't need to buy sugary, shop-bought versions again. Plus you can make jokes about weaving your own yoghurt to people. Can't do that with a celebrity-endorsed pot of yoghurt!

CAKES AND BREADS

I think my favourite discovery was that you can bake extraordinarily good cakes, breads, buns and brownies in the slow cooker. Baked directly into the crock they will all be the shape of your slow cooker, but this is no problem when you see how good they taste. They also save on having to have exactly the right-sized cake tins if you don't bake very often.

I am a fairly relaxed baker. I do weigh everything, but I tend to use granulated sugar for most things because it's much cheaper. I've mentioned caster sugar or brown sugar specifically in the places I think they are best. All my eggs are large because my local shop only stocks large eggs and, for the same reason, I use salted butter too. I've always had good results with the basics brands of flours, but you may find the leavened breads easier with strong bread flour as the higher protein levels give a good rise.

All spoonfuls are level unless otherwise indicated and I do use specific measuring spoons for baking as I find them much easier to work with. Butter is room temperature unless otherwise specified.

My one speciality item is my beloved reusuable baking liner. Bought in the best known of the pound shops in their own kitchen range, it is like indestructible-strength greaseproof paper. The more you use it, the softer and more malleable it becomes, but it lasts ages. When it is newer and stiffer, I tape it onto the crock with paper washi tape or Sellotape before I pour the batter into it or you end up needing a third arm trying to hold it down and balance the batter bowl. Just peel the tape off before you turn the slow cooker on. Simply lift the liner out when your baking is complete. Much easier than greasing the crock and cuts down on the washing up!

All the baking was tested in a 3.5-litre crock and timings may vary in a 6.5-litre crock.

THE PERFECT BANANA BREAD

I have been making this banana bread for the last twenty years. I doubt a month has gone by without at least one batch being whipped up in my house. It is simple and foolproof and I've never met anyone who hasn't loved it. The only thing I've done as often as bake it is write the recipe out for people. It was the first thing I baked in the slow cooker and honestly, I think it's even better than the oven version as it gives a better crust to cake ratio. I'm very excited to have improved on a recipe I grew up on.

This is so simple to make I learned to do it while looking after three kids under ten. And yes, I was bribing them with banana bread since you ask.

SERVES 6–8

350g plain flour

½ teaspoon baking powder

1 teaspoon bicarbonate of soda

½ teaspoon salt

200g sugar

180ml vegetable oil

2 eggs

3 large bananas

2 teaspoons vanilla extract

Line the cold slow-cooker crock with reusable baking liner or greaseproof paper, making sure it comes about 5–7cm up the side of the crock.

Sift the flour into a large bowl. Add the baking powder, bicarbonate of soda and salt.

Put the sugar, oil and eggs into another bowl and mix well until the sugar looks like it is melting and the eggs are beaten. Mash the bananas and the vanilla extract into it.

Pour the oil and banana mixture into the flour and mix until just combined. It will be a slightly puffed up and thick batter.

Pour the batter into the lined crock. Put 4–5 sheets of kitchen roll, double thickness, across the top of the crock and put the lid on top.

Turn the slow cooker to high and cook for around 2 hours. The banana bread is ready when a skewer comes out clean. Remove the now damp kitchen roll and allow the crock to cool just enough to lift the banana bread out onto a rack.

Serve still slightly warm with some ice cream as a dessert or with a cup of tea. It keeps for 2–3 days in an airtight container and it can be toasted too for a fabulous breakfast.

CHOCOLATE BLACK BEAN CAKE

Admit it. You think I'm just having a laugh now, don't you? Chocolate black bean cake in a slow cooker? Is this a real recipe, you ask?

Oh yes, it's a very real and very good recipe. A light, moist, gluten- and wheat-free cake that tastes like bourbon biscuits would if you made them into a cake. It's also dairy-free and incredibly easy to make. I love this cake and often make it when I need a simple cake that impresses everyone. It also makes a great talking point as no one has ever guessed the secret ingredient as they tuck into a second slice. You'll be glad you took me seriously and tried it.

Not only is this a delicious cake that pleases everyone, it's astoundingly easy to make.

SERVES 6–8

150g dark chocolate, chopped

1 x 400g tin black beans, drained, or 250g cooked black beans

3 eggs

100g sugar

1 teaspoon vanilla extract

1 teaspoon baking powder

pinch of salt

100g frozen and thawed black cherries (optional)

Line the slow-cooker crock with greaseproof paper or a reusable baking liner.

Melt 100g of the dark chocolate in a bowl over a pan of warm water, making sure none of the water gets into the chocolate. Supermarket own-brand or basic ranges include excellent chocolate at very reasonable prices, which I use for baking all the time.

Put the beans into a large bowl and pour the melted chocolate over them all. Add the eggs, sugar, vanilla, baking powder and salt and use a hand blender to blitz it all to a thin batter that looks like chocolate milkshake in consistency.

Stir the remaining chocolate chunks through the batter along with the cherries, if you are using them. It doesn't matter if the cherries sink a bit, you want them to go soft and jammy and that happens best if they are low down in the cake.

Pour the batter into the lined crock. Cover the crock with a few sheets of kitchen roll folded over and put the lid on the slow cooker.

Bake the cake on high for 2–2½ hours, testing it with a skewer after 2 hours. The cake is ready when the skewer comes out clean. Allow it to sit in the slow cooker with the heat off for a further 15 minutes.

Lift the cake out and allow to cool completely on a rack before you peel the liner back or try to cut the cake. Flourless cakes are quite fragile and can crumble if not handled carefully. Cut into slices and eat along with a cuppa or serve with crème fraîche as a dessert.

BOILED CAKE

People always look at me strangely when I mention boiled cake, thinking I've taken a cake and dropped it into hot water. Instead, it is an incredibly soft fruit cake where the fruit is literally boiled in liquid to make it dark, sticky and moist. Traditional in Northern Ireland, this cake is quick to make, but lasts well so you always have some when people drop in.

This is my granny's recipe adapted for the slow cooker. You can boil the fruit in the slow cooker during the day if you like or do it on the hob, but baking the cake in the slow cooker creates a chewy crust that made even fruit cake-sceptics adore it at a recent book group. I'm not sure how well it lasts as we ate the whole thing in one go.

SERVES 6–8

175g sugar

350g raisins or a mixture of raisins, sultanas, currants, peel and cherries

115g butter

250ml black tea or water

350g plain flour

1¼ teaspoon bicarbonate of soda

1 teaspoon mixed spice or 1 each of ground cinnamon and allspice

1 egg

Put the sugar, dried fruit, butter and tea or water in a saucepan and boil for 20 minutes. This plumps up the fruit and infuses it with flavour. I have also made this a serious celebration cake by using some stout here. Not that my granny would ever have had stout in the house...

It will take about 5 hours to boil the fruit in the slow cooker and it will smell amazing. You don't need to do this if you've boiled the fruit in a saucepan, but it can be a handy alternative.

Sift the flour into a large bowl and add the bicarbonate of soda and mixed spice. Stir in the boiled fruit and any remaining liquid. Add in a beaten egg and stir until just combined. It will come together like a dough rather than a batter, coming together as one large blob.

Line the slow-cooker crock with greaseproof paper or a reusable baking liner. Pour the cake mix into it the lined crock,put the lid on the slow cooker and bake for 2 hours on high. The cake will rise beautifully, develop a sticky, chewy crust and is ready when a skewer comes out clean.

Lift the cake out and cool on a rack. serve in slices (I like it well buttered) with a strong cuppa. The cake will keep in a tin for several weeks and actually improves with age as it gets softer and stickier.

DULCE DE LECHE COFFEE CAKE

Because dulce de leche is just so easy to make in the slow cooker, I always have some in the house and it adds a gorgeous flavour to anything with little effort, which is how this cake came about when I needed something really good that I could make with ease. It's simple and easy and went down very well with my editor, Laura, who shares my dulce de leche love.

SERVES 6–8

225g butter, softened

180g caster sugar

4 eggs

2 tablespoons instant coffee

1 tablespoon boiling water

3 tablespoons Dulce de Leche (see note)

½ teaspoon vanilla extract

½ teaspoon ground ginger

½ teaspoon ground allspice

½ teaspoon ground cinnamon

225g self-raising flour

2 teaspoons Dulce de Leche, to serve

Line the slow-cooker crock with greaseproof paper or a reusable baking liner.

Put the butter and sugar in a large bowl and cream together until light and fluffy. An electric whisk makes this much easier. Add the eggs one at a time, beating them in well. If the mixture looks a little bit curdled, don't worry.

Mix the instant coffee with the boiling water and allow to cool slightly. Add the dulce de leche to the egg and butter mixture and beat it in. Add the coffee, vanilla extract and the spices and mix well.

Add the self-raising flour and fold it in to prevent the air from getting knocked out of the cake. Stop as soon as the flour is combined and pour the batter into the lined crock. Smooth the top down and put the lid on the slow cooker.

Cook on high for 2 hours. After 2 hours, check with a skewer and if it doesn't come out clean, cover the top of the crock with kitchen roll and put the lid back on. Bake for another 30 minutes.

Lift the cake out of the crock and allow it to cool on a rack. Poke about ten holes all over the cake with a skewer and drizzle 2 teaspoons of dulce de leche over the top of the cake. It will soak in and moisten the cake further and add a beautiful sheen to the top.

Note: You'll find a recipe for Dulce de Leche on page 199, but if you don't have any, replace it in the cake with condensed milk or double cream. Brush the top of the cake with a little sugar syrup instead, made from 25g brown sugar mixed with 25ml water and boiled until a sticky syrup.

LEMON POLENTA CAKE

This cake was created with my friend Adriana in mind. A truly unconditional friend, the only time I've shocked her was when I told her I didn't like lemon drizzle cake. She rallied to hide her disappointment in me, but her devotion to the cake made me wonder what I was missing by shunning it. I find lemon cakes to be too sweet and a bit too dry and wondered if I could create something that was moist and tangy to convert me.

Using whole puréed lemons I've boiled makes the cake very sticky and moist and it keeps brilliantly. I'm team lemon cake all the way now. Adriana need not worry any more.

SERVES 6–8

3 lemons, approximately 450g (if waxed, give them a vigorous scrub under the hot tap)

225g coarse cornmeal or polenta

75g plain flour

1 teaspoon baking powder

125g sugar

50ml plain yoghurt (see home-made Yoghurt page 202)

2 eggs, beaten

1 grapefruit, juiced, or 2 tablespoons lemon juice

Start by preparing your lemons. I usually cook my lemons in the slow cooker. Simply cover them with boiling water, put on the lid and cook on high for 4 hours or until they are soft when poked with a skewer. You could also do it on the hob where they will need to be boiled for about 1½ hours, checking that they don't boil dry.

Take them out of the water and using a hand blender or potato masher, blend them until they are a thick purée. They smell incredible when you do this. Set aside.

Line the slow-cooker crock with greaseproof paper or reusable baking liner. Make sure the paper comes at least halfway up the side of the crock as this cake rises a lot.

Combine the cornmeal, flour, baking powder and sugar in a large bowl. Pour in the yoghurt and beaten eggs. Add the lemon purée and the grapefruit juice and mix until just combined. The acid in the yoghurt and the fruit activates the baking powder so the batter puffs up and becomes very light.

Quickly pour the batter into the lined crock and cover the crock with 4 sheets of kitchen roll, doubled over. Put the lid on the slow cooker and bake for 2 hours. Check with a skewer to see if it comes out clean. The cake will be very moist to the touch, so pressing it with your finger makes it hard to tell if the centre is cooked.

Lift the cake out of the crock and allow to cool completely on a rack. Cut into slices and enjoy. The cake will keep for up to 5 days in a tin.

LANCASTER LEMON TART

Mister North lived in Lancaster for several years and I used to get the boat and train over to visit him, but neither of us ever came across this tart at the time. Think of it as a detour from the branch line of Bakewell with its similar pastry base and frangipane topping, but with the diversion of a tangy lemon curd filling instead of jam. Well worth a return journey to Lancaster, I've adapted it to the slow cooker and given it a biscuit base instead. It's very simple to make and I can't understand why it's not better known as a dessert.

SERVES 6–8

100g digestive biscuits
 or ginger nuts

100g butter, melted

5 dessertspoonfuls
 Lemon Curd (see
 page 196 to make
 your own)

125g butter, softened

125g sugar

2 eggs

125g ground almonds

1 tablespoon plain flour

1 lemon, juiced and
 zested

50g flaked or whole
 almonds (optional)

crème fraîche, to serve

I use a 20cm springform tin in a 6.5-litre slow cooker to bake my tart. A 15cm tin should fit in the 3.5-litre slow cooker, but I don't have one. You could also use individual tart tins or ramekins to make it. Just test how well things fit and lift out of your crock before you start.

Begin by lining your tin with greaseproof paper. Then pop your biscuits into a freezer bag and bash them up until they are small crumbs. Combine well with the melted butter and press them into the lined tin. Allow the crumbs to set into a crust by leaving it to chill for at least 4 hours in the fridge.

Once the crust is set, wrap the base of the tin in two layers of tin foil. This will protect the crust while the tart steams. Spread the lemon curd over the crust with the back of a spoon. Don't make the layer too thick by adding more curd. Less is more.

Now make your frangipane topping. Beat the softened butter and sugar together until light and fluffy. This is easiest with an electric whisk since I'm a bit of a wimp. Add the eggs and beat until the mix is almost like a batter.

Add the ground almonds and the flour and fold in gently with a spoon to keep the air in. Then fold the lemon zest and juice in to loosen it all slightly. Don't over mix the topping.

Spread the frangipane over the lemon curd layer of the tart. It is quite stiff and as you dollop it out with a spoon, it looks as if there won't be enough to cover the whole tart, but don't worry. The amount is just right. Make sure you spread it out to the very edges of the tart so you can't see biscuit or curd.

Press the flaked or whole almonds into the topping to add crunch and decoration (or scatter the tart with a little brown sugar if you don't have any almonds).

Set the uncovered tart tin into your slow-cooker crock and carefully pour boiling water into the crock until it touches the base of the tin. Put the lid on the slow cooker and cook the tart on high for 2 hours and 15 minutes.

Turn off the heat at this stage and lift off the lid. Allow the tart to sit for about 15 minutes until everything is cool enough to handle more easily and then lift the tart out and allow to cool on a rack.

Once completely cool, the tart will shrink away from the edges of the tin. Undo the springform tin and lift the tart out of the tin. Remove the greaseproof paper and serve the tart in slices with a little crème fraîche on the side. The tangy lemon curd keeps the tart sharply pleasing and the steamed frangipane is soft and moist compared to the crunchy base. It's a truly fantastic dessert that lemon lovers won't be able to get enough of.

BAKED CHEESECAKE

My mum didn't make a lot of desserts when we were kids as our pudding lust was easily fulfilled by fruit and ice cream, but when she did make them, they were fantastic and none was better than her baked cheesecake. Light, airy and buttery, it was like a sweet cloud. The one she made for a murder mystery party years ago is still just as talked about for its texture as its helping hand in unmasking the murderer!

Any cream cheese works for this recipe as long as it's the full-fat version. I use two-thirds basic cream cheese and one third mascarpone if I'm feeling extravagant.

If you have a 6.5-litre slow cooker, you can use a 20cm springform tin and bake this as a whole cake. Otherwise, use a smaller springform for a 3.5-litre crock or bake the cake in ramekins.

SERVES 6–8

200g biscuits (either digestive or bourbon are best)

100g butter

100g sugar

3 egg yolks

3 whole eggs

1 tablespoon vanilla extract

600g full-fat cream cheese

1 lemon, juiced

Start by lining the base of your springform tin with greaseproof paper. Crush the biscuits to a fine even crumb. Melt the butter in a pan over a low heat or in the microwave and mix well with the biscuits. Spread the mixture into the base of the springform tin and flatten it down. Chill overnight or for at least 4 hours in the fridge.

Make the filling by beating the sugar with the 3 egg yolks until they are thickened slightly. Beat in the 3 whole eggs until well combined. Add the vanilla extract. Set aside.

Whip the cream cheese until it is starting to become loose and soft. Beat the whisked egg mixture into it until it has become soft and fluffy. It will be a loose enough texture to pour. Add the lemon juice and stir until combined.

Wrap the outside of the springform tin in two layers of tin foil and place into the slow-cooker crock. Pour the cream cheese mixture over the biscuit base. Fill the crock with enough boiling water to reach the base of the tin.

Put the lid on the slow cooker and bake on low for 3½ hours. The filling will expand while cooking to look like it's about to spill over the side, but this will shrink back down as the cake cools. It also means you can't lift the cake out of the slow cooker until this happens. I leave mine for another 30–40 minutes in the slow cooker to settle down.

Remove the cake from the slow cooker and chill overnight before serving in generous slices. If you use ramekins, simply serve directly from them.

Note: This cheesecake can be customised to whatever flavour you want. I sometimes add the Candied Ginger and its syrup from page 201 if I'm using bourbon biscuits or Lemon Curd from page 196 swirled through the cream cheese if I'm using digestives.

CREAM CHEESE BROWNIES

I remember the first time I ever had a brownie. It was from a Sara Lee packet, which was the absolute height of swank for this nine-year old. I had never tasted anything so chocolatey and fudgey and I was bewitched. I never quite recaptured that excitement until I got the slow cooker because no matter what I do with the oven, I always seem to overcook my brownies past fudge point. The slow cooker gets them squishy and squidgy every time.

These brownies are inspired by the lovely Deb at *Smitten Kitchen*. I love cooking her recipes and it was a real honour to bake one of them for her at an event on her UK book tour.

MAKES ABOUT 24 SQUARES

90g dark chocolate (eat the remains of the 100g bar as a cook's perk)

115g butter, cubed

275g sugar

2 eggs

1 teaspoon vanilla extract

90g plain flour

75g cream cheese

1 heaped dessertspoon condensed milk or Dulce de Leche (see page 199)

These are a really simple brownie recipe to make and if you have a heatproof bowl that fits over a saucepan, you can make them in one bowl to minimise the washing up.

Line the slow-cooker crock with greaseproof paper or reusable baking liner. Melt the chocolate in a bowl over a pan of simmering water on the hob. Make sure no water gets into the chocolate or it will become grainy. Add the cubed butter and melt it in too.

Remove carefully from the heat and add the sugar, beating it in well. It will look slightly lumpy, but don't worry. Beat in each egg, one at a time. Add the vanilla extract. Fold in the flour to make a light batter and pour it into the lined crock.

Mix the cream cheese with the condensed milk until it is light and almost runny. It might look almost curdled, but don't worry, that's fine. Take a teaspoonful of the cream cheese mix and drop it onto the top of the batter. Use a skewer to swirl it slightly through the brownie mix. Repeat until you have evenly placed swirls throughout the batter. Don't mix the cream cheese completely into the batter.

Put the lid on the slow cooker and bake the brownies on high for 2–2½ hours. Test with a skewer after 2 hours. The brownies are ready when the skewer comes out of the middle cleanly. (The top needs to look cooked before you lift them out and they may need 30 minutes more than you think to allow the temperature of the slow cooker to return to full heat. Each batch I made varied, but never overcooked.)

Lift the brownies out of the slow cooker and cool them on a rack. Do not try to peel off the liner until the brownies are completely cool or it may stick to the liner and be wasted. Cut the brownies into about 24 small squares. The centres will be sticky and fudgey and the edges are crisp and chewy.

CINNAMON-SPICED BUNS

No matter how you feel about getting up in the morning, wouldn't you enjoy it more if it involved freshly baked buttery buns greeting you as you stumble into the kitchen? With this recipe and a timer on your slow cooker, that fantasy is a reality with very little effort. Just boil the kettle for your hot beverage of choice and you have the breakfast of champions to hand. These are especially good on Christmas morning if you need energy to deal with little people who wake you early.

These are very simple to make the night before you need them. The hefty dose of yeast makes them robust and easy to handle. The buns get two rises in the course of making them even if you don't leave them overnight because the gradual heating of the slow cooker rises them as they bake. How's that for multi-tasking?

MAKES ABOUT
10 (THE DOUGH
FREEZES NICELY)

450g plain flour

75g sugar

¼ teaspoon salt

3 sachets of fast-action dried yeast (honestly, it's a tip from Nigella and it works)

75g butter

200ml milk

1 egg

100g softened butter

100g soft brown sugar

1½ teaspoons ground cinnamon

1 teaspoon ground allspice

½ teaspoon ground ginger

1 tablespoon honey, warmed gently

Sift the flour into a large bowl and add the sugar, salt and yeast. Melt the butter in a small pan and then remove from the heat before combining it with the milk and egg in a jug or bowl.

Add the butter and milk mix to the flour and bring together to form a dough. It should be just the right side of sticky. Use your hand to combine it. When it comes together it will look slightly ragged.

Tip it out onto a floured surface and knead gently until the surface becomes smoother and the dough is a little bit drier. Pat it into a ball and put it back in a clean, oiled bowl. Cover with a clean tea towel and allow to rise in a warmish place for at least 30 minutes. If you end up leaving it longer, that's fine.

While the dough is proving, mix the soft butter with the brown sugar and add in the spices. Set aside while you lift the dough out onto a floured surface and roll into a large rectangle. It should be 1cm thick and about 45cm long and 20cm wide. As you roll, try and keep it as evenly shaped as possible.

Once rolled out, use the back of a spoon to spread the spiced butter onto it. Make sure you don't miss the edges. Then carefully tease up one of the longer sides of the dough and start to roll it as tightly as possible to make a giant sausage. Fold the remaining edge of the dough over on top of the sausage and stick it down well. Use a little bit of butter or water to make sure it is well sealed.

Line the base of your slow-cooker crock with a piece of reusable baking liner or some greaseproof paper. Brush the sides with a little bit of oil. Start cutting the cinnamon sausage into rounds 2–3cm thick. If the rounds droop slightly when you lift them, don't worry. As you set them into the slow-cooker crock, simply tuck the ends together so they are tighter. Leave about 1cm of space between the buns to allow them room to rise again as they cook. I can get about half of the dough into a 3.5-litre crock and I freeze the rest uncut.

Put 4 sheets of kitchen roll, double thickness, over the top of the crock and put the lid on top of it. Cook the buns on high for 1½ hours. They work equally well if you set the timer or do them straight away. The kitchen roll absorbs the majority of the moisture and allows the buns to develop a lovely crust.

About 30 minutes before the buns have finished baking, brush the tops with the honey to allow them to develop a lovely sticky, shiny glaze.

These are best served still warm, but will keep for up to a day in a sealed container. You can brush them with more honey before you serve them.

I received an email from a friend the day after I last cooked these, which was headed, 'Your buns are lovely.' What more could you want from breakfast?

WHITE BREAD

Of all the things I've made in the slow cooker, few have had the response of slow-cooker bread. Most people are highly sceptical that such a thing is possible, including my mum when I suggested making some over Christmas. She makes fabulous sourdough loaves and mine needed to be good to win her over. And won over she was. We devoured the loaf in next to no time and she was suitably impressed by the light, open crumb and soft, chewy crust. She also deciphered the instruction manual to the timer plug and allowed me to wake up to freshly baked bread in the morning. Had Santa brought me a Teasmade too, my mornings would be complete…

MAKES 1 X 500G LOAF

500g plain flour (or 150g strong white and 350g plain flour)

14g fast-action dried yeast (equivalent to 2 sachets)

1 teaspoon salt

25g soft butter, cubed

320ml warm water

Sift the flour into a large bowl and make two little wells on opposite sides in it. One is for your yeast and one is for your salt. If you add them together, the salt can stop the yeast from working and you end up with a sad, flat loaf.

Put the yeast and the salt in these wells and then scatter the chopped butter across the flour and add about half of the warm water. Bring the flour together with your hand and it will start to form a sticky, ragged dough. Bring it together as much as you can and then add about another 100ml of the water. Add the rest if the dough is stubbornly dry.

Strangely, adding more water makes the dough less sticky and easier to work with and you should be able to pick up the loose bits of flour and dough in the bowl at this stage and allow the dough to form a ball.

Turn this ball out on an oiled surface and start kneading. This activates the gluten, channels any life tensions and gives a sense of achievement. It's useful to lift and slap the dough and give it some welly. The dough will soften and smooth after about 10 minutes of kneading.

Pop it into a clean oiled bowl, cover with clingfilm and leave to rise for an hour in a warm place. After an hour, it will have doubled in size. Take it out of the bowl, punch the dough down, knead for about 10 seconds and shape into a tight ball.

Line the slow-cooker crock with a sheet of reusable baking liner or double-thickness greaseproof paper. Don't use foil as this will make the bottom of the bread burn. Place the dough into the slow cooker and then cover the top of the crock with 4 sheets of kitchen roll, doubled over. Put the lid on the slow cooker.

Either set the slow cooker on a timer to come on in the morning or switch to high and begin cooking the bread. Both ways allow the bread to rise a second time, which gives it a lovely texture. The bread will take about 2–2½ hours to cook. If you can, turn the loaf 30 minutes before the end to brown the top slightly, but if you can't, don't worry. It tastes just as good, only slightly paler.

Lift the bread out of the slow cooker and allow it to cool for as long as you can, then slice. It should keep for about 3 days, but honestly I've never managed to hold myself back long enough to test this theory. This is seriously delicious bread with the minimum of effort. Perfect, especially if you don't want to heat the oven in warm weather or need it free over Christmas.

BOSTON BROWN BREAD

This bread was traditional in Boston when wheat flour was scarce and cornmeal was more common. Rather than baked, it was steamed in round cans over the fire. I first had it twenty years ago when I au paired out in Boston, but never knew it as anything more than 'bread'.

While I haven't quite got over some of the events of that trip, such as crashing a bike in the bush, falling off rollerblades and a small child standing on a baby stingray, I have continued to pine for the dark, molasses-rich rounds ever since.

I've tweaked the basic recipe for the slow cooker and so you don't need to find a metal coffee tin to cook it in, but the moist treacle taste is the same. This bread uses cornmeal, which may well be labelled as polenta in supermarkets. It's simply the uncooked meal made from grinding dried corn. It keeps beautifully.

MAKES 1 X 450G
LOAF

75g plain or wholemeal flour

50g coarse cornmeal or polenta

½ teaspoon bicarbonate of soda

¼ teaspoon salt

1 tablespoon vegetable oil

60ml black treacle

125ml buttermilk or 75ml yoghurt (see home-made Yoghurt page 202) and 50ml water

1 egg, beaten

By some strange quirk, loaf tins are usually sized in pounds rather than grams. A 1lb one is perfect here. I used a foil-lined loaf tin for the bread, doubling up the foil to make it easier to lift the loaf out. Grease lightly with oil.

Sift the flour into a large bowl and add the cornmeal, bicarbonate of soda and salt. Pour in the oil and the treacle. (I use black treacle as it's easier to come by, but if you have some molasses, use it instead.) Mix just enough for it to start to combine.

Add in the buttermilk. If you can't get buttermilk then dilute some yoghurt with water or use the same amount of milk and add a teaspoon of lemon juice or vinegar. This sours it and creates a quick version of buttermilk. You need the acidity in buttermilk or yoghurt to activate the bicarbonate of soda in the bread, so don't skip this stage.

Beat in the egg until all the flour and treacle is evenly dispersed. Pour the runny batter into the tin, leaving about 4cm for the bread to rise.

Carefully set the loaf tin into the slow-cooker crock and pour boiling water into the crock, making sure you don't splash the bread. The water should come about halfway up the side of the tin. Put the lid on the slow cooker and steam for 2 hours.

After 2 hours, check the bread with a skewer. If the centre is still liquid, cover the crock with 4 sheets of kitchen roll, doubled over, and put the lid back on. Steam for another 30 minutes. Lift the tin out of the slow cooker when a skewer comes out clean and allow to cool for about 30 minutes in the tin. Upend it and allow to slide out. Serve warm with the Brixton Baked Beans on page 94.

STEAMED CORNBREAD

I love cornbread. It was the kind of thing people made in the books about the American West like *My Friend Flicka*, which I read endlessly as a pony-mad kid with a fascination for America. It made me think of billy cans and jackalopes, despite not knowing exactly what either was. I first ate it in the nineties when I was experimenting with yeast-free breads and I learned three things about it.

Firstly, if you make it with 100 per cent cornmeal, it will be so dense and heavy you could kill any marauding coyotes outside your wagon with it. It needs flour to add lightness. Secondly, it doesn't keep very well — a maximum of 24 hours. And thirdly and most importantly, it makes the most depressing French toast ever.

I worked the third one out after just one bite, but was slower to the first two. It wasn't until I met my friend James and ate squares of his light, buttery, crumbly cornbread that I mastered it. In many ways meeting him was like striking gold, but especially with my cornbread skills!

SERVES 4–6

200g coarse cornmeal or polenta

75g plain flour (or rice flour to be gluten-free)

1 tablespoon sugar

½ teaspoon salt

1 teaspoon bicarbonate of soda

400ml plain yoghurt (see home-made Yoghurt page 202)

2 eggs, beaten

25g butter, melted

This is very easy and quick to make. Start by lining the slow-cooker crock with some reusable baking liner or greaseproof paper.

Put the cornmeal and flour in a large bowl along with the sugar, salt and bicarbonate of soda. Pour in the plain yoghurt and the beaten eggs and mix well. You'll see the mixture puff up like a thick batter. Beat the butter in and pour the batter into the lined slow-cooker crock.

Smooth the top down and put the lid on the slow cooker. Cook the cornbread on high for 2 hours. It is ready when the top is still springy, but a skewer poked into the centre comes out cleanly.

Lift out of the slow cooker and serve in slices on the side of chilli or a rich stew. It is very filling. Don't be tempted to cook it on top of the chilli as it soaks up the moisture from the beans and leaves them dry, while giving the cornbread the dreaded soggy bottom!

CHOCOLATE HAZELNUT FUDGE

This is one of those things you mention making in the slow cooker and people look at you in bewilderment. Surely you can't make fudge in the slow cooker due to those stages of heating sugar? But trust me, you can make this fudge in the slow cooker. It's more like frosting than true butter-based fudge, but it's amazing all the same.

This recipe is popular on the internet, but I've tweaked it to make it easier to cook and much less sweet than the previous versions I tried. It's very rich and grown-up with dark chocolate and keeps for up to a month in the fridge as it's dairy free.

SERVES 6-8

500g dark chocolate

120ml coconut milk

60ml golden syrup

1 teaspoon vanilla extract

50g hazelnuts, chopped (optional)

Break your dark chocolate into the slow-cooker crock, leaving the chunks as they are. I use quite a basic brand here as the chocolate is enhanced as you go, but go for what you prefer. I wouldn't use 100% milk chocolate though as it separates. A mixture of dark and milk works well.

Pour the coconut milk and golden syrup over the chocolate. Put the lid on the slow cooker and heat for 3 hours on low. Don't stir it during this time.

After 3 hours, stir to make sure the chocolate has melted and then leave to cool down for about an hour. I usually lift the crock out of the slow cooker to speed this up.

Once it has cooled enough to be starting to thicken, beat it with a spoon or electric whisk for around 5 minutes. It will change from what looks like just melted chocolate to a fluffy, whipped texture that leaves the sides of the bowl clean. It will look like frosting and would work well as a cake filling at this stage.

Add the vanilla extract and the chopped hazelnuts and beat through well.

Pour into a dish you have lined well with reusable baking liner or greaseproof paper and chill in the fridge overnight. It will set into a firm fudge you can cut into 2cm pieces and tastes like a chocolate hazelnut spread.

FLAPJACKS

The Scottish side of me is powered by oats. They make equally good breakfasts and biscuits and this baked oat treat is no exception to the rule. It's fantastic in that you can add anything you fancy to this, from dried fruit, nuts, seeds, chocolate chips and apples to desiccated coconut. But the best bit is that it's super easy and makes almost no washing up, while keeping well in a tin. I have been known to have it for both breakfast and lunch...

SERVES 6–8

300g porridge or jumbo oats

100g dried fruit

50g brown sugar

50g nuts, chocolate chips or desiccated coconut

2 teaspoons baking powder

1 teaspoon ground cinnamon

1 teaspoon ground ginger

1 medium apple, peeled and grated

50g butter, melted

2 eggs

250ml milk

1 teaspoon vanilla extract

Line your slow-cooker crock with some reusable baking liner or double-thickness greaseproof paper to make it easier to lift the flapjack out when it is cooked.

Put all the dry ingredients, including the apple, in a large bowl. Pour the butter into the bowl. Break in the eggs and add the milk and vanilla extract. Mix well until it all becomes a soft batter.

Pour the batter into the lined slow-cooker crock and then put 4–5 sheets of kitchen roll, folded to double thickness, in between the crock and the lid. This soaks up any condensation in the slow cooker and stops it dripping onto the flapjack and making it damp.

Bake on low for about 5 hours. If your slow cooker runs hot, check after 4½ hours. The edges should have crisped slightly and a skewer in the centre should come out clean.

Lift out with the liner and allow to cool. Serve the flapjacks cut into slices. It is excellent slightly warm with plain yoghurt as a dessert or cold as a snack or if you like your oats more portable than porridge. It will keep for up to 4 days in an airtight container.

PUDDINGS AND STEAMED PUDDINGS

Steamed puddings are one of those things that Britain does really, really well and whenever anyone starts banging on about how terrible the food is in the UK, my mind turns to visions of a spotted dick or Sussex pond pudding or a treacle sponge and I think how wrong they are. Especially when you learn how easy it is to make a steamed pud in the slow cooker.

I use my slow cooker as a steamer quite a lot and, using these tips, I have foolproof puddings every time.

I use plastic basins with a fitted lid instead of a ceramic one. Partly because it's lighter to lift out of the slow cooker and partly it saves on a lot of tin foil, but mainly because I'm absolutely rubbish at pleating tin foil and tying string into handles.

You cannot grease a pudding basin quite enough. Butter is best for this. Smear it round the basin with giddy abandon, not forgetting the rim and the lid itself. Then flour it all down lightly and your pudding will glide out easily.

Many steamed puddings use suet. Suet is a form of animal fat that makes ethereally light pastry and puddings. If you are vegetarian, you can use veggie suet instead, but I find it is a little more dense as it's essentially like grated margarine. I much prefer the real thing if I can.

All steamed puddings need to be steamed immediately after making. They will take about twice as long to steam in the slow cooker as on the hob, but the advantage is that they can't overcook and you don't need to keep topping up the water and worrying that the pan is boiling dry, making them very easy to cook in the slow cooker while you have a nap or a long walk before lunch.

Steamed puddings aren't the only desserts that work brilliantly in the slow cooker. You can use it as a mini oven, steamer or water bath and create simple and stunning custards and chocolate puddings or lovely cooked or stewed fruits. You'll be amazed how many old favourites you can make here with great ease.

BREAD PUDDING

Not to be confused with bread-and-butter pudding, this is more like a cake made from leftover stale bread. Rich and dense, it suits long, slow cooking even when you bake it in an oven. This is very easy to make and keeps very well. I like mine rich with spices and candied peel and served in a hefty chunk with a cup of tea at about four in the afternoon. It's perfect for a packed lunch or taken on a walk to keep you going.

I often use lard instead of butter in my bread pudding as you need very little of it and it's so much cheaper than butter. It gives it a richness like some German fruited breads or traditional British lardy cake. Simply use butter instead if you want it to be vegetarian.

SERVES 6-8

300g stale white bread

600ml milk

300g raisins

100g Candied Peel, chopped (see page 200)

1 teaspoon ground ginger

1 teaspoon ground cinnamon

½ teaspoon ground allspice

½ teaspoon ground cloves

¼ teaspoon ground mace

2 tablespoons poppy seeds (optional)

50g sugar

50g plain flour

25g lard or butter

2 eggs, beaten

Line the slow cooker crock with reusable baking liner or greaseproof paper.

Tear the bread into medium pieces and put in a large bowl. I use white bread here, but you could omit the added poppy seeds and use something more brown and virtuous with seeds in it if you prefer.

Pour the milk over the bread and allow it to soak for about 30 minutes. Mix the bread and milk well with a fork to break it up and combine the crusts.

Add the dried fruit, spices, poppy seeds and the sugar and flour and mix it in. Melt the lard and pour it into the mix along with the beaten eggs. Combine well so it has quite a loose texture.

Pour the mixture into the lined slow-cooker crock. Put the lid on the slow cooker and cook on high for 4 hours. After 4 hours, lift the lid and cover the crock with a couple of sheets of kitchen roll and replace the lid. Cook for another 45 minutes or until a skewer comes out clean.

Lift the bread pudding out of the crock and allow to cool on a rack. It will set and become quite solid. Any melted fat will settle back into the pudding as it cools. Cut into thick chunks and serve with a proper strong cuppa. Store the leftover pudding in an airtight container for up to 3–4 days.

SPICED TAPIOCA PUDDING

This recipe came from an old cookbook of my grandmother's. She was a farmer's wife and along with her own family to feed, she would have cooked lunches for farm workers too. Food was simple, economical and utterly delicious. I loved the milk puddings she made and retain a soft spot for semolina, rice, sago or tapioca puddings. I am firmly team frogspawn. If you only had school-dinner versions, try this much lighter, spiced steamed version and be converted.

SERVES 4–6 AND
KEEPS WELL

50g tapioca or sago

250ml milk

150g breadcrumbs

1 medium apple, grated

50g Candied Peel
(optional) (see
page 200)

50g sugar

150g raisins

25g butter, melted

1 teaspoon cornflour

¼ teaspoon
bicarbonate of soda

1 teaspoon vanilla
extract

1 teaspoon ground
ginger

1 teaspoon ground
cinnamon

½ teaspoon grated
nutmeg

Wash the tapioca under cold running water to remove any excess starch. Soak it for at least an hour, or overnight, in the milk.

When you are ready to make the pudding, mix the soaked tapioca and the milk with the breadcrumbs, apple, candied peel, sugar, raisins and the melted butter. Stir well and add the cornflour and bicarbonate of soda, vanilla and the spices.

Pour it all into a 1.2-litre lidded pudding basin. Snap the lid on tightly and slip the basin into a cotton string bag and place in the slow-cooker crock. Pour boiling water halfway up the side of the basin and put the lid on the slow cooker. Steam the tapioca for 4 hours.

It will firm up and thicken. Remove the bowl using the handles of the bag and turn the pudding out onto a plate. Serve slices of it, but be amazed by how filling it is. It makes a lovely soft, sticky dessert or can be eaten as a great alternative to porridge.

STEWED EARL GREY PRUNES

Much as I love a cup of builder's tea, I have a real soft spot for those seen as more refined and genteel. Take me to a tea room and I'm giddy with choice. A malty Assam, a floral rose-infused number or the smoky tones of Lapsang Souchong, I love them all of an afternoon. But my favourite is the bergamot flavour of Earl Grey.

A light, citrus flavour, bergamot is one of my favourite smells. My mum used Bergasol tanning oil on our childhood holidays, so I associate it with hot sunshine, jumping into an ice-cold swimming pool and lots of laughter. Earl Grey brightens and lifts my mood any time I smell or taste it, taking me back to childhood.

This is clever since it is a long-running family joke that I am like a little old lady. You'd think it comes from my sedate lifestyle, pottering to the library and being fixated by slippers, or maybe my fascination with blouses and slacks in my teens. But I suspect it's because I am obsessed by stewed prunes.

I am that person who sees them at hotel buffets and gets excited by them. I heap them onto porridge and would have seconds and thirds if they didn't have *that* reputation. I adore their soft stickiness and their ability to absorb flavours. You'll love these.

SERVES 2–4

250g dried prunes
2 Earl Grey teabags
250ml freshly boiled water
½ teaspoon vanilla extract

You can use any dried or unsoaked prunes for this as the slow cooking will plump them up into something special.

Make the tea by infusing both Earl Grey bags in the freshly boiled water for about 5 minutes. Remove the teabags and add the vanilla extract.

Put the prunes into the slow-cooker crock and pour the infused tea over them. Put the lid on and cook on low for 4–5 hours. The prunes will become fat and sticky and flavoursome. They are lovely with the Granola on page 108 or Porridge on page 109 or can be used in the Sticky Toffee Pudding on page 245.

SPICED ROAST PLUMS

I much prefer roasting fruit in the oven rather than stewing it. Roasting without added liquid intensifies the flavours, while stewing often mutes them, relying on lots of sugar instead. But it seems a shame to turn the oven on for small amounts of fruit. The slow cooker allows to you to cook the fruit overnight so you wake up to a beautiful aroma and piping-hot fruit for your porridge.

I particularly love cooked plums. Often the punnets you buy lack flavour and the texture is a little bit woolly. A low heat softens the fibres of the fruit and enhances the flavour. Doing a batch with cinnamon and allspice makes them something special.

SERVES 2-4

1 punnet of plums,
    approximately 400g
1 heaped tablespoon
    dark brown sugar
5 allspice berries
1 star anise
½ cinnamon stick

Halve and stone the plums. Lay them flat on the base of the slow-cooker crock. It doesn't matter if you have several layers. Scatter with the brown sugar. Tuck the spices in around the plums evenly.

Put the lid on the slow cooker and cook on low for 6–7 hours or high for 3–4. The fruit will collapse slightly, but hold its shape. There will be quite a lot of liquid, so don't be tempted to add any during the cooking. Remove the spices before eating. Dry the cinnamon stick for reuse.

Serve with Dulce de Leche (see page 199) or custard as a dessert or pile on the Granola from page 108 or Porridge on page 109. They are also beautiful with yoghurt, like the home-made version on page 202.

POACHED SPICED PEARS IN VERMOUTH

My idea of living on the edge these days is to buy pears and see whether they become over ripe almost instantly, stay stubbornly rock hard forever or occasionally end up perfect and juicy with a sliver of Parmesan on the side as a dessert.

More often than not, they stay firm and I use them up by poaching them. This recipe adds just enough spice to warm up the flavour and takes advantage of the herbal and lemon hints in white vermouth. This fortified wine works out much cheaper than a bottle of wine as it doesn't go off as quickly and it comes in much bigger bottles. It is a kitchen essential for me.

SERVES 2-4

250ml boiling water

125g sugar

4 pears (Conference or Williams are best)

125ml vermouth

1 teaspoon vanilla extract

1 star anise

2-3cm piece of fresh ginger, peeled

½ cinnamon stick

Put the boiling water and the sugar into the slow-cooker crock and turn to high while you peel the pears, but leave the base and stalk in place. If you remove these, the pears will disintegrate while cooking and be impossible to lift out again.

Once the sugar has almost completely dissolved, turn the slow cooker down to low and add the vermouth, vanilla and the spices. You could switch these around, also using cloves, allspice, nutmeg or mace if you have them.

Lower the pears into the poaching syrup and set them on their side so they are completely submerged. Depending on the size of your pears, you may need to add a bit more water. If it's more than 100ml, add another 50g of sugar.

Poach the pears on low for 5-6 hours. They will soften and darken slightly as they infuse with flavour.

Serve warm with a tiny drizzle of the poaching syrup and a dash of cream or serve cold on top of Porridge from page 109 or Granola from page 108.

BAKED APPLES

On an autumn night as the temperature dips and the nights start to draw in earlier, the perfect dessert is a baked apple. These work beautifully in the slow cooker, the heat diffusing through them gently until the flesh goes soft and frothy, collapsing when you pour a drizzle of dulce de leche onto them. I tend to do them two ways, either stuffed with candied peel and raisins, maybe with a few leftover nuts if I have them, or filled with syrup and oats for a take on granola. I've given both recipes here.

I use Bramleys for their tart taste and fluffy texture, but anything fairly crisp and thin-skinned will work well. Avoid apples like Golden Delicious as they just get mushy.

MAKES 1 (SCALE UP
AS NEEDED)

**2 tablespoons porridge
oats**

**1 heaped teaspoon
golden syrup**

pinch of salt

**½ teaspoon ground
ginger**

1 apple

**scattering of dried fruit
(optional)**

**cream or plain yoghurt
(see home-made
Yoghurt page 202),
to serve**

OR

1 apple

**1 tablespoon Candied
Peel (see page 200)**

**1 tablespoon raisins or
mixed dried fruit**

**½ teaspoon caraway
seeds (optional)**

**¼ teaspoon ground
cinnamon**

**scattering of pecans,
flaked almonds or
pistachios (optional)**

**drizzle of Dulce de
Leche, to serve (see
page 199)**

Line your slow-cooker crock with some reusable baking liner or greaseproof paper. This simply makes it easier to get the fragile cooked apples out again by lifting the sides of the liner rather than trying to scoop the fruit out.

Put the oats, golden syrup, salt, and ginger in a bowl and heat for about 20 seconds in the microwave. Alternatively, use a spoon you've heated in boiling water to pour the syrup into a bowl and melt it enough to mix in with the oats.

Core the apple, either with a corer or by hollowing the core out with a teaspoon. Place it on the liner or greaseproof paper and then pack the oats into the empty core. Or if using the fruit, seeds and nuts, do the same with them.

Put the lid on the slow cooker and cook the apple on low for 2½–3 hours, depending on the size of the apple. Lift the liner out and then serve the apple.

I like the granola version with some cream or plain yoghurt, but the fruit-and-nut version is amazing with some home-made dulce de leche. I prefer the apple to be tart and to add sweetness to taste rather than pack the apple with added sugar.

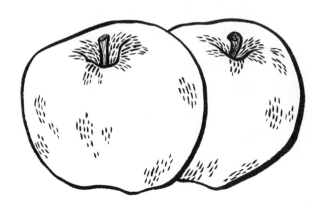

FRUITS OF THE FOREST VANILLA COMPOTE

Do you remember how fruits of the forest used to be the thing in yoghurts and desserts? Then they just went out of fashion and I miss them. So when I saw that you can buy a frozen fruits-of-the-forest berry mix in some supermarkets, I had to do something with them. Drizzle in a little bit of vanilla, cook it all down and you'll have no trouble getting your five a day with these beauties. I like to serve with yoghurt or granola for breakfast, but it also makes a stunning dessert served with the Poached Meringues on page 234.

SERVES 4

400g fruits of the forest or cherries

1 teaspoon cornflour

100g sugar

1 tablespoon vanilla extract

If you are using fresh cherries, you should definitely remove the stalks, but leaving the stones in will add extra flavour if you don't have time to pit them.

Put the fruits of the forest or cherries in the slow-cooker crock, adding any juice they give out. Sprinkle the cornflour over them along with the sugar and the vanilla extract. Put the lid on the slow cooker and cook on low for 5–6 hours until they are almost jammy round the edges.

Eat with porridge, yoghurt, over vanilla ice cream or make a pie with this compote. The little bit of cornflour thickens them just enough to make sure you don't lose a drop of the fabulous juice the fruits give out.

POACHED MERINGUES

These meringues are usually seen served on custard as the classic French dessert *île flottante* and they are light and delicious at the end of a meal. They are also incredibly easy to make in the slow cooker and can be cooked in advance to really impress people with your culinary skills.

SERVES 4

2 egg whites

100g caster sugar

**1 teaspoon white wine
or cider vinegar**

About 45 minutes before you want the meringues to be ready, half fill your slow-cooker crock with hot tap water and put the lid on. Turn it to high and leave it to come to approximately 80°C, which is the perfect poaching temperature. If you have a thermometer, don't miss the chance to play with it here to test the waters. Otherwise, just trust me. It works.

Separate your eggs and put your egg whites in a clean and grease-free bowl. Using an electric whisk, beat them for 1–2 minutes until they are quite frothy looking.

Start adding the sugar a spoonful at a time, beating as you go. This gradual addition of the sugar helps make the meringue glossy and gorgeous and allows lots of air to get in there. Whisk for 5–6 minutes until the egg whites are in stiff peaks and you can hold the bowl upside down for a second or two without them sliding onto the floor. Add the vinegar.

Take the lid off the slow cooker and add dessert spoonfuls of the meringue. You should be able to get four in there at a time. Replace the lid and cook the meringues on high for 15 minutes. Because of the steaming action of the slow cooker, you don't need to turn them like you do when you poach them on the hob.

After 15 minutes they will be firm to the touch and puffed up. Remove them from the crock with a slotted spoon and dry them off on a clean tea towel or muslin cloth. Keep going until you have as many as you need.

The meringues can be kept chilled for up to 24 hours and are served cold. The sweetness is perfect with the Fruits of the Forest Vanilla Compote (see page 233) or other berry compotes, but if you'd like to try the *île flottante*, then use the custard recipe for the Crème Brûlée on page 239. Chill and serve the meringues on top. Simple and stunning-looking.

CARAMELISED BANANAS

While you can't beat a banana as the ultimate quick snack food, sometimes they deserve a little more attention to turn them into a delicious dessert. Everyone loves these and they are incredibly easy to make. Serve them just as they are or, if you are feeling especially extravagant, drizzle a little bit of chocolate sauce over them too.

SERVES 4

4 bananas

25g butter

4 teaspoons brown sugar

Peel the bananas and lay each one on a rectangle of tin foil. Put a quarter of the butter and a teaspoon of sugar on top of each one. Wrap each banana up so it is completely enclosed.

Put the bananas into the slow-cooker crock. If you are doing more than four, you can do two layers.

Put the lid on the slow cooker and cook the bananas on low for 4 hours. Remove the bananas from the crock and carefully open each one. The butter and sugar will have cooked down into a simple and delicious toffee sauce.

Serve the bananas with the sauce over the top. Some ice cream doesn't go amiss here either.

CRÈME CARAMEL

There really are no words for how much I love crème caramel. I was always fascinated by those little pots of it when I was a kid, which you were supposed to upend and then pull the little silver tab off to allow the caramel to pour out over the wobbly crème. I could never wait and just dug straight into the pot with my spoon, pouring the caramel out onto it when I'd eaten the custard. As I got more grown-up, I occasionally treated myself to the posh ones in glass ramekins and ate them more slowly. Then I learned how to make them myself and life became a million times better.

Do not think about making this with skimmed or semi-skimmed milk or it won't set properly and will collapse on itself if you try to turn them out of the ramekins.

SERVES 4

120g sugar
60ml water
generous pinch of salt
400ml full-fat milk
3 eggs
25g caster sugar
1 teaspoon vanilla
    extract

Start by making the caramel. Put the sugar and the water in a stainless-steel pan (non-stick pans can make the caramel crystallise and become granulated). Melt the sugar over a medium heat, stirring constantly.

When the sugar is completely melted, stop stirring and allow the caramel to boil to a dark, rich colour. Keep a close eye on it to make sure it doesn't burn. It should take about 10 minutes. Remove from the heat immediately. Add the salt and stir in.

Pour an equal amount of caramel into 4 ramekins and set aside to cool and harden. Don't put them in the fridge or the caramel becomes soft and tacky. It will take about an hour for the caramel to set.

When the caramel is set, brush the inside of the ramekins with a little bit of flavourless vegetable oil to allow the custard to slide out more easily. Set aside until needed.

To make the custard, warm the milk in a pan over a low heat. While it is coming to a simmer, beat the eggs in a bowl with the caster sugar until they are thickened. When the milk is warm, pour a little bit of it into the eggs and whisk. This tempers the eggs to stop the custard splitting.

Pour the tempered eggs into the remaining milk and whisk together. Heat gently until the custard coats the back of a spoon. Remove from the heat immediately, add the vanilla extract and pour the cooked custard into the ramekins, leaving a few centimetres for expansion.

Set the filled ramekins into the slow-cooker crock and pour enough boiling water into the crock to come about two-thirds of the way up them. Put the lid on the slow cooker and cook the crème caramel on high for 1 hour.

Lift the crème caramels out of the slow cooker. There should be no bubbles round the edges. Allow the crème caramels to cool for an hour or so and then put them into the fridge overnight. This means the caramel will absorb into the crème.

When you are ready to serve, simply turn the crème caramels out onto small plates and eat. These are so much better than the milky, jellied versions you can buy in a supermarket and you'll want to make them time and time again.

BROWN BUTTER RHUBARB COBBLER

While I do love a good crumble, my American Studies degree made up for repeated readings of *Moby Dick* by introducing me to the all-American dessert of cobbler. Best described as a sweet scone dough combined with fruit, cobblers are warm and comforting. They also work surprisingly well for breakfast, which you can't say about the humble crumble.

This cobbler is inspired by a recipe from American blogger Joy the Baker. She used brown butter and plums, but it was all a bit sweet for me, so I've used sharp rhubarb, tweaked the sugar levels and added creamy evaporated milk before part baking, part steaming it all in the slow cooker. It's very easy. Don't skip the browned butter though. Joy was right about its nutty goodness making life itself better.

SERVES 4–6

- 125g salted butter
- 125g plain flour
- 75g sugar
- 250ml evaporated milk
- 1½ teaspoons baking powder
- 4 stalks of rhubarb, cut into 4cm chunks
- ½ teaspoon vanilla extract

Set the slow-cooker crock on a sheet of greaseproof paper and trace round it. Cut the shape of the base out and then cut two long strips of greaseproof paper about 10–12cm deep that will go round the walls of the crock. Brush the inside of the crock with a little bit of oil and then press the paper inside so it sticks to it. Or if the *Blue Peter* feel doesn't appeal, use a sheet of reusable baking liner.

The butter is the star of the show here. Cube it, put it in a small pan and, watching carefully the whole time, heat it over a medium heat. It will crackle and snap as the water evaporates and the butter turns brown. As soon as the noise stops and the colour changes, take it off the heat. There is a fine line between brown and burnt. Leave aside.

Mix the flour, sugar, evaporated milk and baking powder together in a large bowl. Bring together with a spoon, add the cooled brown butter and mix until you have a thick, puffy batter. Drop the chunks of rhubarb and vanilla into it and mix well.

Pour the batter into the slow-cooker and cook on high for 3 hours or low for 5 hours. It will form a lovely crust on the base and become softly puffed up on top. Lining the crock allows you to lift the cobbler out if you want to and cut it into slices to serve or you can simply scoop it out and not have to soak the crock for ages.

Note: You can use apples or plums or a mix of fruit for this if you don't want to use rhubarb. Halve the plums or quarter the apples and follow the instructions as above.

CRÈME BRÛLÉE

I am the least musical person on earth, as anyone who has heard my attempts at violin playing will know. Yet crème brûlée makes me want to burst into song. I could wax lyrical about the contrast between smooth, creamy custard and the crunchy sugar topping, but I'm not going to. I'm just going to order you to make it in the slow cooker immediately. Not only is the slow cooker the perfect water bath, it makes custard so luxurious you'll actually want to bathe in it.

The day I learned how easy crème brûlée is to make was actually quite dangerous because I'm tempted to make it any time I have cream in the house. Luckily everyone else thinks it's quite tricky, so you can really impress them by making it any time. Scale it up or down using one egg yolk to 100ml cream and you can make one large dish instead of individual ramekins if you prefer.

SERVES 4

400ml double cream

1 tablespoon vanilla extract

4 egg yolks

15g sugar

pinch of salt

4 teaspoons demerara sugar

Heat the cream and the vanilla extract in a small saucepan, but don't let the cream boil. It should be just warm enough to dip your finger in without burning it.

As the cream heats, beat the egg yolks with the sugar in a large bowl. Add the pinch of salt and then carefully pour a splash of the warmed cream into the egg yolks. This tempers the eggs and stops them scrambling when you make the custard over the heat.

Pour the tempered egg yolks into the remaining cream and heat gently over a low heat, stirring all the time. The custard is ready when it coats the back of a spoon or spatula. Don't let it boil.

Remove the custard from the heat and pour it into your ramekins, making sure it doesn't fill them past any lip or rim the ramekins have. You could also use a ceramic serving dish if you are making one large crème brûlée.

Set the ramekins into the slow-cooker crock. Carefully pour in enough boiling water to come halfway up the sides of the ramekins. Put the lid on the slow cooker and bake the custards for 1 hour. Lift the ramekins out carefully as soon as they are cooked; allow to cool completely. They will keep for 2 days in the fridge like this.

To serve, scatter the top of each ramekin with a teaspoon of demerara sugar and put them under a hot grill for 4–5 minutes until the sugar blisters and melts. Remove from the heat and allow the sugar to cool and harden for 5 minutes.

Serve and enjoy plunging your spoon through the crisp crackling layer of sugar into the custard for a simple and perfect dessert.

BLACK FOREST CHOCOLATE POTS

Sometimes only chocolate will do and you need a dessert rich with its decadent feel. This is just the one for that occasion, whether it's chasing the blues away, showing someone you love them or simply indulging yourself because you can.

These little chocolate pots remind you just how good the combination of cherries and chocolate is. Best combined in the wonderful Black Forest gateau, the nation collectively overdosed on this dessert in the seventies and eighties and needs to be shown its great ways again. I never have kirsch in the house, so I've used a little spiced dark rum instead since I always keep some for medicinal purposes. You could use any tipple you like.

SERVES 4

150ml double cream

150ml full-fat or semi-skimmed milk

100g chocolate, broken into small pieces

2 tablespoons sugar

1 egg

2 egg yolks

50g dark cherries, frozen and thawed

35ml rum or alcohol of your choice

100ml whipped double cream, to serve

Even though I really like milk chocolate, this dessert should be slightly bitter and grown-up rather than soft and milky. I use half milk and half and dark chocolate, but all dark chocolate works well too.

Heat the double cream and the milk slowly in a pan over a low heat and warm it gradually so that it doesn't blip or bubble. Add the chocolate pieces and stir until they are all melted and smooth. Remove from the heat and set aside for 5 minutes.

Beat the sugar, whole egg and the egg yolks together in a bowl until slightly thickened. Add a splash of the chocolate mixture into the eggs to temper them and then pour all the eggs into the chocolate cream and stir well.

Mix the cherries with the rum and divide them evenly into 4 ramekins, reserving 4 for the top of the pots when serving. Pour the chocolate custard over them, leaving a little room at the top.

Set the filled ramekins into the slow-cooker crock and carefully pour boiling water into it so it comes about halfway up the sides of the ramekins. Put the lid on the slow cooker and bake the chocolate pots for 3 hours on low.

Allow the ramekins to cool enough to handle, lift them out of the crock and chill the chocolate pots completely, leaving in the fridge overnight. They will set firmly and develop a lovely deep crust on top for added decadence.

Heap some whipped double cream onto the pots along with a cherry on the top. Serve immediately.

GOOEY RED VELVET PUDDING

Red velvet cake with its mix of cocoa powder, buttermilk and cream cheese frosting has had a new lease of popularity thanks to the cupcake trend. I love the rich red colour and slightly tangy crumb and I can wolf the cream cheese frosting straight out of the bowl, barely even pausing to use a spoon. I've tweaked the basic recipe to turn it into two-layer chocolate pudding made in the slow cooker. Enjoy moist, light cake with rich chocolate sauce and a whipped cream cheese frosting on the side for a wonderful slow-cooker dessert.

This is very easy to make so don't be discouraged by the seemingly long list of ingredients. I used unsweetened cocoa powder for this recipe. If yours is sweetened, I'd reduce the sugar in the cake by a third. Leave the sauce as it is.

SERVES 4–6

For the cake:

175g plain flour

100g sugar

75g cocoa powder

2 teaspoons red food colour powder or liquid

1 heaped teaspoon baking powder

25g butter, melted

115ml plain yoghurt (see home-made Yoghurt page 202) or buttermilk

60ml water (if using yoghurt)

1 tablespoon cider or white wine vinegar

1 teaspoon vanilla extract

For the sauce:

60g cocoa powder

150g brown sugar

300ml boiling water

For the frosting:

150g cream cheese

½ teaspoon vanilla extract

25g icing sugar

Line your slow cooker with reusable baking liner or greaseproof paper. Mix the flour, sugar, cocoa powder, food colouring and baking powder in a large bowl. Combine the melted butter with the yoghurt and water or buttermilk, vinegar and the vanilla extract and mix this into the dry ingredients. (You need yoghurt or buttermilk here to activate the baking powder.)

The batter will be quite stiff, but if you are struggling to mix it, add about 50ml more water or buttermilk, a little at a time, until it stirs easily. Stop mixing as soon as the batter is mixed and pour it into the lined slow cooker.

To make the gooey chocolate sauce, mix the cocoa powder and the brown sugar together and sprinkle it evenly over the batter. Pour the boiling water over it all. Do not stir and allow the water to sit on top of the cake batter.

Put the lid on the slow cooker and cook on high for 2 hours. After 2 hours, check the pudding. The sauce will have sunk to the base of the crock and the batter will look like cake. Push a skewer 2–3cm into the pudding and if it is still sticky, cover the crock with a layer of kitchen roll and cook for another 30 minutes. Once the pudding is cooked, turn off the heat and allow it to sit in the crock, uncovered, for 20 minutes.

Make the cream cheese frosting by beating the cream cheese with the vanilla extract and icing sugar until it is light and fluffy. It should be slightly sharp and tangy so don't keep adding sugar.

Serve the pudding directly from the crock, scooping a layer of both steamed pudding and chocolate sauce into deep bowls. The sauce will be like dark chocolate and the pudding will be a deep, rich red. Add a spoonful of the cream cheese frosting to the top of each bowl and enjoy.

CHAI BREAD-AND-BUTTER PUDDING

Is there a better way to end a meal than bread-and-butter pudding? Well, what if I offered you chai-spiced bread-and-butter pudding without the serving dish to scrub out? You'd find it hard to say no, which is just as well because that's what this recipe is for. It's warm and comforting and when I've made it for people, their faces have lit up. In fact, they couldn't even wait for the meal to finish and got stuck in then and there!

SERVES 4–6

6–8 slices of white bread

1 teaspoon ground cinnamon

½ teaspoon ground ginger

½ teaspoon ground allspice

¼ teaspoon ground cloves

¼ teaspoon ground nutmeg

1 cardamom pod, seeds lightly crushed

100g butter, softened

250ml milk

150ml condensed milk

3 eggs

50g brown sugar

75g dried fruit (optional)

Everyone has different preferences for the bread, but I like mine to be white and quite thick. It should be slightly stale to soak up the custard without becoming too soggy. Remove the crusts and cut the slices into triangles to fit the crock better. Line the crock with a sheet of reusable baking liner.

Beat the spices into the butter until they are all well combined and the butter is quite fluffy and dark. Butter each side of the bread well and then arrange it into the slow-cooker crock so that the tips sit up nicely.

Warm the milk and the condensed milk together in a pan over a medium heat, making sure it doesn't boil. Beat the eggs in a bowl and pour a splash of the hot milk into them, stirring well. This tempers the eggs so they won't curdle.

Pour the tempered eggs into the saucepan of milk and stir until it creates a custard that coats the back of a spoon. Carefully pour the custard over the buttered bread. The very tips of the bread should be poking out of the pool of custard. Sprinkle the sugar and dried fruit, if using, over the top of it all.

Put the lid on the slow cooker and bake the bread-and-butter pudding on high for 2 hours. The custard will become light and pillowy and the tips of the bread will crisp on top where they poke out. Serve generous portions and enjoy.

APPLE DUMPLING

I could tell you here about the rich culinary tradition of the 'clootie dumpling' or puddings steamed in a cloth as I introduce this apple dumpling. But I never knew that as a kid. For me and my brother, this dish is simply the essence of Hallowe'en.

While the turnip lantern spluttered and sent out its unique odour, our mum would make a huge apple dumpling. Swaddled in a large cloth, it steamed in a massive pot while we turned our attention to indoor fireworks or the terror of holding sparklers out in the garden if the weather was good. We'd troop back in, rosy-cheeked with cold, and devour a plate of soft, sticky dumpling and see who found the charms and coins hidden inside. I still make it every Hallowe'en from the recipe my granny handed to my mother. I skip the sparklers though. They still petrify me.

SERVES 4–6

150g cold butter, cubed

280g plain flour

100g sugar, plus 3 tablespoons

2 teaspoons baking powder

125ml milk

175g apples, sliced

1 heaped teaspoon ground cinnamon

1 heaped teaspoon ground ginger

You will need a large muslin cloth for this recipe. I usually use one of the muslin squares you can buy in the baby section. Make sure it is scrupulously clean. I iron mine to sterilise it. Soak the cloth in cold water while you make the dumpling.

Rub the cubed butter into the flour until it resembles fine breadcrumbs. Add the 100g of sugar and the baking powder and mix. Add half the milk to begin to turn it into a firm dough. Add a little at a time as you may not need it all.

Lift the cloth out of the water and wring it out. Spread the cloth out and flour it liberally. Then add a little bit more for luck. Roll the dough out to about 2–3cm thick, keeping it as rectangular in shape as possible. Set on the floured cloth.

Toss the sliced apples in the ground cinnamon, ginger and the remaining 3 tablespoons of sugar and then place in the middle of the dough. Gather the whole thing up so the apples are completely enclosed and it looks like a purse. Tuck the ends in and make sure the dough is sealed underneath with your fingers.

Wrap it up in the cloth, making sure there is room for the dumpling to expand considerably. Secure the ends with some string. Set a small dish or saucer in the base of the slow cooker. I use an enamel dish. Place the dumpling on top and carefully pour boiling water into the slow-cooker crock, making sure the dumpling doesn't get wet. Put the lid on the slow cooker and steam for 6 hours on high.

Remove from the crock and allow to cool for 5 minutes. Unwrap and serve in slices. Custard is perfect with this, as is vanilla ice cream.

CHERRY BAKEWELL PUDDING

I am never quite sure which is a Bakewell tart and which is a Bakewell pudding, but this has all the fabulous cherry and almond flavour of either. This is so good I made it for my mum a while back and next thing I knew, she had cleaned all my windows and hoovered the whole house to say thanks.

Use frozen cherries as they have much more juice to make the pudding stickier and moist. The ground almonds make it incredibly light and moreish, so try not to skip them if you can.

SERVES 4–6

- 150g cherries, frozen and thawed
- 115g sugar, plus 3 tablespoons
- 110g butter, softened
- 2 eggs
- ½ teaspoon almond essence
- 75g self-raising flour
- 75g ground almonds
- 2 tablespoons milk

Start by buttering and flouring a 1.2-litre pudding basin, including the lid if it has one.

Heat the cherries and the 3 tablespoons of sugar in a small saucepan until the sugar dissolves and the fruit starts to burst and the juice is released. Take off the heat before the fruit collapses and set aside.

Cream the butter and the remaining sugar together until light and fluffy. Beat in the eggs one at a time until the mixture is loose and airy. Add the almond essence and combine.

Fold in the flour and ground almonds. Add in the milk and combine gently. The batter should be a light texture.

Put 100g of the cherries in the bottom of the basin and then pour the batter over the top of them. It won't fill the basin, but don't worry as this will give it space to expand as it cooks. Reserve the remaining cherries until later.

Cover the basin with the lid; set it into the slow-cooker crock. Pour boiling water into the crock to come halfway up the side of the basin. Put the lid on the slow cooker and steam on high for 4 hours. It will rise, becoming a light, fluffy sponge.

Turn the pudding out onto a plate, piling the reserved cherries on top, and allow the cherry juice to drizzle down the sides of the pudding before cutting into slices. Serve with plain yoghurt or custard.

STICKY TOFFEE PUDDING

Usually baked in the oven, I find sticky toffee pudding can be a little dense for my desire to eat second helpings. I steam mine in the slow cooker to make it much lighter. I also use prunes instead of dates since prunes are much easier to get and much cheaper. It is then drizzled with toffee sauce and this delicious dessert always leads to contented silence and clean plates at the table. Can't say better than that!

SERVES 4–6 WITH LEFTOVERS

2 tablespoons demerara sugar

200g prunes (see page 229 for the Stewed Earl Grey Prunes, which are perfect here)

3 tablespoons boiling water

1 teaspoon vanilla extract

50g butter, cubed

175g demerara sugar

2 eggs

2 tablespoons black treacle

1 teaspoon bicarbonate of soda

200g self-raising flour

For the toffee sauce:

115g demerara sugar

115g butter

140ml double cream

pinch of salt

Grease a 1.2-litre pudding basin well with butter, not forgetting the lid, and add the 2 tablespoons of demerara sugar. Put the lid on and shake well to help scatter the sugar evenly. Set aside.

Using a hand blender, purée 150g of the prunes with the 3 tablespoons of boiling water until you have a thick consistency. Reserve the remaining 50g prunes and add the vanilla extract to the prune purée.

Cream the butter and sugar together until they are light and fluffy. Add the puréed prunes, both eggs, treacle, bicarbonate of soda and the flour and mix until just combined. Chop the remaining prunes very roughly and stir through.

Pour the batter into the greased pudding basin, leaving about 5cm for the pudding to expand. Put the lid on the basin and place it in the slow-cooker crock. Fill the crock about halfway with boiling water.

Put the lid on the slow cooker. Steam on high for 4 hours. About 10 minutes before you are ready to serve, make the toffee sauce by combining the sugar, butter and cream together in a saucepan with a generous pinch of salt. Melt together over a medium heat for about 10 minutes. Allow to thicken slightly.

Turn out and serve the pudding in slices with a hefty drizzle of toffee sauce. Some ice cream doesn't go amiss either.

SUSSEX POND PUDDING

When I first moved to England, I lived near Brighton and was knocked out by the beauty of the South Downs and the surrounding area, even if I desperately missed the regular buses and taxi companies of city life for getting around them. Occasionally I had a weekend off work and my flatmates and I would go to Lewes for a pub lunch. That is where I first encountered the majesty of the Sussex Pond Pudding. When you cut into the light, fluffy suet pastry you find a whole lemon in a little pond of lemon juice, butter and sugar and you will know true joy. I love London, but it's never offered up dessert like this!

SERVES 4–6
(BEST EATEN PIPING
HOT AND FRESH
FROM THE DISH)

**1 lemon (if waxed, give
it a vigorous scrub
under the hot tap)**

200g self-raising flour

100g suet

75ml cold milk

**100g cold butter,
cubed**

**100g brown sugar,
preferably demerara**

You'd expect such a show-stopping pudding to be tricky to make, but it's incredibly simple. Impress people with barely any effort.

Grease and flour a 1.2-litre pudding basin. I use a lidded plastic one and if you do too, don't forget to grease and flour the lid as well. If you couldn't get an unwaxed lemon, make sure it is dry after scrubbing under the tap.

Mix the flour and suet in a large bowl and add the milk gradually to mix it into a ball. You may not need all the milk so go carefully; you don't want the dough to be sticky.

Dust your work surface with a little flour and roll out two-thirds of the suet pastry. You want it to be about 2cm thick. Line the basin with it, making sure there are absolutely no gaps.

Put half the cubed butter and sugar into the pastry-lined basin. Prick the lemon all over with a fork and place on top of the butter and sugar. Add the remaining butter and sugar so the lemon is as well covered as possible.

Roll out the remaining pastry so that it makes a lid for the pudding and put it on top of the filled pudding, crimping the edges together with your thumb and forefinger. Cut two holes in the centre to allow the steam out. Put the lid on the pudding basin.

Set the pudding basin into the slow-cooker crock and carefully pour boiling water into the crock until it comes about halfway up the side of the basin.

Put the lid on the slow cooker and steam the pudding for 4–5 hours on high. Carefully lift the basin out and invert the pudding onto a wide plate or platter. Cut into it and watch the lemon pond spread. Serve in bowls and enjoy.

MARMALADE ROLY-POLY

A steamed roly-poly oozing hot, sticky marmalade is the ultimate vehicle for custard. I love a pudding steamed in a basin, but there's just something about the way you can slice a roly-poly and smother it in custard that's unbeatable. I bet if I tried hard enough, I could construct an actual custard sandwich out of two slices of this steamy, sticky roly-poly and a tin of Bird's. Be right back…

SERVES 4–6
DEPENDING HOW
POLITELY ONE SLICES
THE PUDDING

225g self-raising flour

100g suet

pinch of salt

120ml lukewarm water

200g marmalade or jam

This is very easy to make. Lay out two large sheets of greaseproof paper and foil before you start. I make one long roly-poly and then cut it in half, setting them across the slow-cooker crock as it's tricky to fit the longer one in a 3.5-litre slow cooker. The roly-poly needs to be wrapped to allow it to steam without getting wet.

Combine the flour, suet and salt in a large bowl. Add about half the water and start to bring the pastry together, adding more water gradually. It should be a firm dough that isn't too sticky. You may not need all the water.

Turn out the pastry onto a floured work surface and roll it out to about 1cm thick. Don't knead or overwork the dough as you create a rectangle that's about 25cm long by 20cm wide.

Spread the marmalade over the pastry, leaving a border of 2–3cm all the way round. Brush the edges with a little bit of warm water and starting rolling the long side of the pastry away from you. Fold the end underneath the roly-poly and stick down. Don't fold the sides in, but leave them as they are.

Cut the roly-poly in half with a sharp knife and then wrap each one loosely in greaseproof paper, tucking the ends in, but leaving room for the roly-poly to expand. Wrap the greaseproof paper parcels in a further layer of foil, also allowing room to expand. Twist the ends to make sure no water can get in.

Set two shallow ramekins on the base of the slow-cooker crock. The ones that come with posh desserts are the perfect height, I find. Set the roly-poly parcels on them and pour boiling water into the crock until it comes about two-thirds of the way up the ramekins.

Put the lid on the slow cooker and cook on high for 2 hours. The pastry will rise and become light and pillowy, while the marmalade caramelises. I love that the pudding isn't too sweet, but is still sticky and moreish. Serve slices of the roly-poly in deep bowls with a lake of custard and enjoy!

STOUT-SOAKED CHRISTMAS PUDDING

Christmas is a time for a little luxury but, as this pudding proves, the festive season doesn't have to break the bank. This is a light Christmas pudding, both in texture and colour. I've used breadcrumbs and suet and combined them with apple so the pudding is really moist and doesn't need lashings of expensive booze to feed it. I've also used stout here instead of spirits – a lot more affordable and it gives a great flavour. I usually make my own Candied Peel (see page 200) too. Supermarkets do mixed dried fruit in their basics range and once you've soaked it in stout and treacle for a couple of weeks, you'd be hard pushed to know it wasn't top of the range.

This pudding can be made the day before Christmas, as long as the fruit has soaked for at least 3 days beforehand, or up to 6 weeks before. Leave the cooked pudding sealed in its pudding basin and the flavours will develop over time. As long as you don't open the basin once it's cooked, it will keep until Christmas in a cool, dry place. The amounts I've given make two 1.2-litre puddings, so halve if you only need one. If you have a 6.5-litre slow cooker, you could do a 2.4-litre pud instead.

Rope in everyone in the house on the day to help you stir the pudding – friends or family. This is the tradition on Stir-Up Sunday – the last Sunday of November – and everyone who stirs gets a wish for the forthcoming year.

MAKES TWO PUDDINGS

- 500g mixed dried fruit
- 2 heaped tablespoons black treacle
- 500ml bottle of stout (or plain black tea)
- 2 cooking apples
- 100g Candied Peel (see page 200)
- 75g glacé cherries
- 75g almonds, pistachios or pecans (optional)
- 200g plain flour
- 115g brown sugar
- 100g breadcrumbs
- 100g suet (use vegetarian if you prefer or 100g melted butter instead)
- 1 tablespoon vanilla extract

Before you start making the pudding, you need to soak your mixed dried fruit. Put it all into a Kilner jar or airtight container. Don't add the candied peel or the cherries though. Drizzle the fruit with 1 tablespoon of treacle. Then pour the stout over it all. Leave for at least 3 days or up to a month in the sealed jar. It won't go off.

I'm using lidded plastic pudding basins here. (I prefer to keep my paper and string antics for the presents at Christmas.) Grease them well with butter and dust well with flour. Don't forget to do the lids too.

Peel and grate your apples. It doesn't matter if they oxidise a bit and go brown when you set them aside in this recipe. Place them in a large bowl. Drain the soaked dried fruit, reserving the lovely treacley stout. Place the soaked dried fruit in the same large bowl as the apples. Start adding all the other ingredients, including the extra tablespoon of treacle.

Once you have all the ingredients in the bowl, start stirring. Stirring the pudding will take some effort and it will go from a dark brown to a chestnut brown and look like a loose, puffy batter. Add the reserved treacle-infused stout to loosen it all. When the batter is ready, pour it into the basins, leaving about 6cm of space for the pudding to rise.

- 1 teaspoon baking powder
- 1 teaspoon bicarbonate of soda
- 1 teaspoon ground ginger
- 1 teaspoon ground cloves
- 1 teaspoon ground cinnamon
- 1 teaspoon ground allspice
- ½ teaspoon ground nutmeg
- ½ teaspoon black pepper
- 2 eggs

Clip the lid on tightly and then place in the slow-cooker crock. Pour boiling water into the crock until it comes halfway up the basin and then steam for 14 hours on high.

Remove the basin from the water and store, without opening, until you need the pudding. Keep it in a cupboard. (If you open the lid, it will allow bacteria in, which is why I like the lidded basins rather than the traditional foil and string arrangement. I also think they work out cheaper than buying lots of foil.)

On the day, repeat the steaming for 6 hours, on low this time, or until needed. This heats the pudding through, but in the slow cooker you just can't overcook the pudding or have it boil dry. You can also keep the pudding warm if serving at different times.

Carefully remove the pudding from the slow cooker, invert onto a serving plate and serve. If you are more daring, you can douse it in booze and flambé it or simply enjoy with a dollop of brandy butter or cream.

Note: My spare Christmas pudding kept for 6 months unopened until we devoured it at the photoshoot for the book.

ACKNOWLEDGEMENTS

Thank you to all the people who helped and supported me with the book. I have converted many of you to my cult of the slow cooker in the process…

Thank you, in no particular order, to Mike Ward, Lindsay Roberts, Nayan Gowda, Emma Flinn, Lindsay Faller, Rebecca Schaeffer, Alex Lemon, Lyndsay Houlette, Ashley Lewis, Lauren Sudsworth, Eleanor Lawton, Kirsty Marshall, Hannah Kaye, Liza Miller, Ali Hines, Catriona Redmond, Mike Catto, Paddy Brown, everyone at Dombey's Meats and the Nour Cash and Carry, Brixton, Nicholas Balfe, Sherri Dymond, Brian Danclair, Tony Feenan, Cathy Sloan, the Brixton Blog team, Zoe Jewell, Tim Dickens, Valerie Catto, Adriana Hightower and family, Laura Higginson, Caroline Hardman, Allan Jenkins, Gareth Grundy, Sarah Chamberlain, Donna Corley, Olia Hercules, Catherine Phipps, Nigel Slater, Diana Henry, the endless encouragement of people on Twitter and, of course, my brother Mister North and the rest of my family.

Apologies to anyone I have forgotten or am no longer bringing portions of food to on a regular basis!

INDEX

*Note: page numbers in **bold** refer to information contained in picture captions.*

INDEX OF RECURRING INGREDIENTS

I find it really annoying when I have to buy an ingredient to make a recipe then have loads left over just sitting there in the cupboard, so here's a list of the recipes that use these store cupboard ingredients time and time again.

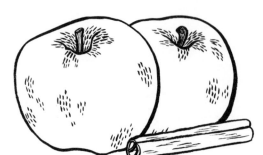